MODERN — COMBAT UNIFORMS

MARK LLOYD

Brian Trodd Publishing House

First published in 1988 by
Brian Trodd Publishing House Limited
27 Swinton Street, London WC1X 9NW

© 1988 Brian Trodd Publishing House Ltd

Typeset by The Word Shop, Haslingden

ISBN 1 85361 019 4

Printed in Hong Kong

Contents

Introduction

Uniforms, especially military uniforms, have been a source of fascination for people of all ages for centuries. In ancient times uniforms were first used as a method of distinguishing friend from foe, bright colours being used for coats and facings so that groups of men could be identified in the heat and smoke of battle. Individual pride, and pride in the regiment, also played an important part in the selection and wearing of a uniform, *élite* units often being issued with a more distinctive, and often more colourful, uniform. Armies with troops not wearing identifiable uniform were often considered rabble or guerrillas and as such, not being afforded protection under the presiding rules of war, were sometimes killed on capture. Uniform not only offered recognition, but in many cases protection.

The introduction of khaki by the British forces in South Africa as a standard colour for military clothing in the field introduced the practical concept of camouflage for the first time. Prior to the Boer War, few units had made any real attempt to blend into their surroundings. Some of the few exceptions to this rule were America's Rogers' Rangers and Britain's Royal Greenjackets, both of which wore green uniforms as early as the seventeen and eighteen hundreds.

As the uniforms of each army and indeed each country became less distinctive, various unit insignia were introduced to identify the wearer. Each country adopted a variety of badges and headgear to distinguish between one type of fighting soldier and another. In many cases clothing and headgear were not only used to identify different arms and services but were practical as well. Some changes were universal. During the First World War the British adopted the steel helmet as a measure to protect their servicemen from shell fragments and rifle fire; the Americans followed suit when they entered the war in 1917 although they were obliged to borrow Allied helmets as they had none of their own.

It was the Second World War that proved to be the turning point with regard to the introduction of camouflage clothing and totally functional headgear, footwear and personal equipment on a wide scale. The Waffen SS were among the first to adopt camouflage, followed by the Luftwaffe's paratroops and the German Army itself. Indeed camouflage became an almost German preserve. When parts of the US Army adopted a camouflage uniform after D-Day, a number were mistaken for Germans and shot at by Allied troops. Camouflage uniforms were used in limited quantities by UN troops during the Korean War and by the French paras and legionnaires during their campaign in Indo-China.

Although camouflage clothing has now been almost universally adopted as part of the fighting soldier's combat gear, types of camouflage still vary greatly. Among most NATO forces disruptive pattern (DP) has been adopted as the best all-round camouflage. Although the pattern and shade vary from country to country, the colours basically consist of a mix of sand, green, brown and black. However, both the camouflage print and the type of cloth used also depend on the theatre of operations. 'Tiger Stripes', a type of camouflage favoured by US Special Forces in Vietnam, consisted of similar colours to DP but with black as the predominant colour, with the print itself being markedly horizontal – hence the 'stripes'. However this type of camouflage is special to purpose and rarely effective outside its particular theatre.

Personal equipment or webbing also differs from country to country. Although most types consist of a fighting order (with canvas pouches to accommodate ammunition, rations, and other necessities), and marching order (with a pack for spare clothing and other equipment), styles and materials vary. Essentially there are three styles: the traditional belt, pouches, harness and rucksack arrangement – worn by most NATO, Warsaw Pact and Third World Armies; chest webbing, with pouches suspended around the chest from the shoulders – worn by many communist armies; and 'waistcoat webbing', the newest concept in personal load-carrying equipment. Already adopted by the Israeli Armed Forces and being trialed by a number of western nations, this type of equipment consists basically of an integral harness/waistcoat with attachment points for a variety of pouches. These systems work on the add-on concept, with various equipment pouches being added onto a main harness which can be adjusted to fit the body closely for maximum comfort and freedom of movement.

Helmet design has also changed in recent years. The British have been experimenting with lightweight plastics while the US Armed Forces have adopted a Kevlar helmet with excellent ballistic protection. Although made of highly advanced material, the Kevlar helmet owes its style to the old Wehrmacht helmet of the Second World War – and is consequently known as the 'Fritz'.

In an age of modern materials and manufacturing methods, it is still the soldier's boot that causes many of the problems encountered by the troops on the ground. Leather, or leather and canvas, high leg combat boots are *'de rigeur'*. However, due to the heavier weights that must be carried by today's infantryman, with his superior firepower and subsequent ammunition load, the boot must be manufactured to a high standard. It must be able to withstand a variety of terrain and climatic conditions, and be able to fit well after a minimal wearing-in period. Not all do.

Finally, as the world moves towards the ominous prospect of chemical, if not nuclear, confrontations, the soldiers of NATO and the Warsaw Pact have to be capable of operating in protective clothing. These impersonal suits, complete with respirators (gas masks), rubber gloves and boots, have again changed the style of combat clothing, and made it more difficult to distinguish friend from foe.

THE 101st AIRBORNE DIVISION (AIR ASSAULT)

The new issue helmet, nicknamed the 'Fritz-Hat' for obvious reasons, is nevertheless comfortable and effective

The new nylon load-carrying system incorporates quick-release buckle, pouches and water-bottle

The combination of the M16 A1 rifle and the M203 40 mm grenade launcher places considerable firepower in the hands of the individual soldier

The 101st Airborne Division (Air Assault) is the only unit of its kind in the world. Formed on 15th August 1942 at Camp Clairborne, Louisiana, the Division saw active service in Normandy, Bastogne, Holland and Berchtesgaden. The 'Screaming Eagles', as they were known, were deactivated in November 1945 but not before they had twice been awarded the Distinguished Unit Citation, plus the French Croix de Guerre with Palms, the Belgian Croix de Guerre and Dutch Orange Lanyard. Reactivated in 1956, the 1st Brigade was deployed to Vietnam in July 1965 to be followed by the remainder of the Division in 1967. As the dependence on helicopter operations grew, the Division was redesignated 'Air Mobile' and shared with the 1st Cavalry the task of offensive support. In October 1974, over two years after its withdrawal from Vietnam, the Unit was formally designated the 101st Airborne Division (Air Assault) and took upon itself new and varied responsibilities.

Today, although the 'Screaming Eagles' possess neither the firepower of conventional armour nor the durability of mechanized infantry, their unique integration of organic helicopters and ground forces into a highly manoeuvrable combined-arms team renders them excellently suited to 'out of area' operations in mountainous terrain, urban areas, the jungle or the Arctic.

The Division consists of three brigades, each with a headquarters and three air assault infantry battalions; an aviation group of two assault helicopter, one medium and one attack helicopter squadrons; an air cavalry squadron and divisional artillery headquarters with three integral 105mm howitzer battalions, a target acquisition battery and 155mm howitzer battalion assigned in general support. It has its own signals, engineering and intelligence battalions together with totally dedicated medical and maintenance support and can thus operate as a completely independent entity anywhere in the world. The vast majority of the 800 members of each air assault battalion are airborne trained, as are many of the support troops including the helicopter pilots.

A wide assortment of some of the finest helicopters in the world provides mobility. The UH–60 Blackhawk, of which there are over 100 in the two assault helicopter squadrons, provides lifting power for the troops and their equipment, the venerable twin-rotor CH–47 Chinook constitutes the backbone of logistical support whilst the new and deadly AH–1S Cobra, belonging to the air attack and air cavalry squadrons, provides the anti-tank capability. Airborne control and reconnaissance are undertaken by OH–58 Kiowas attached to each brigade headquarters.

For a large-scale air assault to work effectively, numerous skills must be brought together. Helicopter pilots must learn 'nap of the earth' (NOE) flying under day or night conditions whatever the weather, hugging the contours and never climbing above 200 feet however rough the terrain. The Division conducts its own small Air Assault School at which its own techniques are taught and specialist skills such as flying and reconnaissance honed to perfection by constant practice. All troops are taught emplaning and deplaning drills so as to reduce to a minimum the helicopter's hovering time, the loading and unloading of heavy equipment, helicopter marshalling and the use of underslung nets. Extremely high obstacle courses are utilized both as a means of gaining fitness and a way of conquering fear of height. The course finishes with a repelling section, in which the various methods of descent are taught to such a degree that descents from 90 feet with full kit become second nature.

Selected officers and NCOs attend the Strategic Deployability School, where air and rail movements duties are taught. The Division has 30 integral rail boxcars and undertakes training at least bi-annually in the movement of its personnel and equipment.

The mobility, firepower and versatility of the 'Screaming Eagles' make them a highly potent combat force. Normally assigned to a Corps, the Division can as easily reinforce defences as it can exploit weaknesses and as such gives the US Army an excellent fighting concept envied throughout the world.

The amphibious Bradley Infantry Fighting Vehicle, armed with the Hughes Chain Gun and TOW anti-tank missile is the heaviest armour support available to the 101st.

11

US 75th RANGER REGIMENT

The standard flak jacket with front-mounted ammunition pouches is often issued operationally and during training

Rangers are equipped with the latest automatic weapons which may be selected for particular operational requirements

Standard woodland pattern DPMs are worn during training but may be replaced operationally depending on conditions

Most Rangers choose footwear for comfort. In this case trainers are being worn

The 75th Ranger regiment draws its inspiration from two excellent if individualistic Units of World War Two. The 75th Infantry Regiment was activated as 5307th Composite Unit (Provisional) on 3rd October 1943 specifically for service in Indo-China, in which theatre it earned itself the nickname of 'Merrill's Marauders' in honour of its far-sighted and dashing commander, Major General Frank D. Merrill. Throughout the spring and summer of 1944, the 5307th operated behind Japanese lines in support of the Chinese 22nd and 38th Divisions, harrying supply lines and disrupting communications. The 'Marauders' were reorganized and redesignated the 475th Infantry Regiment on 10th August 1944, deactivated on 1st July 1945 and reformed as the 75th Infantry Regiment on 21st June 1954. It was subsequently deactivated in March 1976.

The original Rangers, who adopted the name of a team of pre-Independence Indian fighters, were formed in 1942 at Carrickfergus, Northern Ireland, under the command of Major William Derby. Trained by, and closely emulating, the British Commandos, the Rangers took part in Operation Torch, the invasion of North Africa, and subsequently in the battles for Sicily and Italy, during which they sustained terrible losses. The 2nd and 5th Ranger Battalions played a crucial role in securing the D-Day beaches. Small groups of Rangers fought in the Korean War but were deactivated soon afterwards, although unusually the Ranger School at Fort Benning, Georgia, remained to teach Ranger skills to the Army at large.

The outbreak of the Middle East War in 1973 re-emphasized the need for a highly mobile light infantry unit able to operate in any part of the world at minimum notice. As a direct result the 75th Infantry Regiment, reformed yet again in January 1969, was redesignated the 1st Battalion (Ranger) 75th Regiment and immediately began recruiting and training. The 2nd Battalion was formed at Fort Lewis, Washington, on 1st October 1974 and the 3rd Battalion at Fort Benning on 1st October 1975.

Redesignated the 75th Ranger Regiment in 1986, its three battalions currently form a component of the US Army's 1st Special Operations Command together with the Special Forces groups, a Psychological Operations and a Civilian Affairs Battalion. Each battalion, which constitutes a headquarters, headquarters company, three rifle companies each of three platoons, and a support platoon equipped with 60mm mortars and 90mm anti-tank launchers, has a complement of 38 officers, two warrant officers and 571 men. Equipment specifications scales are necessarily low and light so as not to hamper mobility, although at times these will have to be augmented.

All officers are highly experienced. Battalion and company commanders will have held a similar appointment elsewhere and all platoon commanders are at least full lieutenants with leadership experience.

The Ranger School at Fort Benning offers a general eight-week course open to anyone who

considers himself fit enough, during which all aspects of Ranger techniques including mountaineering, survival, navigation, patrolling, weapons handling, long-range reconnaissance and unarmed combat are covered. The course is designed primarily to enhance the individual soldier's self-confidence and leadership and as such is utilized as an advanced training cadre for officers and NCOs who will subsequently return to their units rather than transfer to the regiment.

Volunteers for the 75th Ranger Regiment must all be parachute trained and will usually have attended the Ranger School. All attend a three-week Ranger Indoctrination Programme (RIP) to assess their suitability. Each programme has a maximum of 30 students and a very favourable student-instructor ratio. Individuals are monitored and assessed carefully and only about 55 per cent are eventually accepted for Ranger training.

Training within the battalions is severe and unremitting, consisting of two 24-week cycles separated by two 14-day block leaves at Christmas and mid-summer. Exercises are carried out throughout the United States and abroad, whenever possible in hostile climates.

Ranger battalions are the most lightly armed in the US Army. Until recently each squad had a 7.62mm M 60 machine-gun, but this has recently been replaced by the new 5.56mm Squad Automatic Weapon compatible with the M 16 A1 rifle carried by the rest of the squad. Each squad has a 40mm M 203 grenade launcher and all ranks are fully trained in the use of foreign weapons to enable them to utilize enemy equipment when captured.

All ranks wear standard US Army uniform. Trainees wear jungle fatigues and patrol hats, but once qualified wear camouflage uniforms and the famous black beret and Ranger badge. The 'Ranger' flash on the right sleeve is worn by all who have successfully attended the Ranger School and is not an indication of membership of a Ranger Battalion.

The lessons of Ranger training are practised under a wide range of arduous conditions.

Unarmed combat is just one of the basic skills a would-be Ranger must master.

PARATROOPER, 82nd AIRBORNE DIVISION

The airborne version of the Kevlar 'Fritz-hat' is worn operationally but at other times is discarded in favour of the Divisional beret

The divisional patch incorporating the letters 'AA' (for 'All American') is worn on the left shoulder

The Colt M16 A2 is the current standard personal weapon of the 82nd Airborne Division

In this instance, temperate and European camouflage uniform is being worn. However, special patterns are available for desert or jungle operations

14

The US Army's 82nd (All American) Airborne Division is one of the largest airborne formations in the world and the major ground force element of America's strategic combat forces. The Division, which consists of 18,000 troops, is combat-ready and capable of deploying anywhere in the world at very short notice – and it is prepared to go into combat immediately on landing. Almost all divisional personnel are airborne trained and all the Division's combat equipment – motor transport, mortars, artillery, tanks, etc. – can be parachuted or air-landed into the battle zone. With its support weaponry, the 82nd Airborne Division has more firepower and mobility than the seven Allied World War Two airborne divisions combined.

Formed as an infantry division in August 1917, the 82nd was deployed to France in 1918 where it spent more consecutive days in the front line than any other American unit. Deactivated in 1919, the 82nd Division was reformed as an airborne formation in 1942 and distinguished itself in action throughout the Second World War. By the war's end the Division had spent nearly two years overseas, including 442 days in combat. Since then the 82nd Airborne Division has been in combat a further three times. In 1965 it was deployed on Operation 'Power Pack' to Santo Domingo in the Dominican Republic to rescue US nationals trapped during a revolution. Between 1968 and 1969 the Division served for nearly 22 months in Vietnam, where it was instrumental in countering the Tet offensive. More recently two brigade-sized divisional infantry units played a major role in Operation 'Urgent Fury', the invasion of Grenada in October 1983 by US armed forces to protect the lives of US nationals on the island and restore law and order.

The 82nd Airborne Division proved its rapid deployment capability during Operation 'Urgent Fury'. The 'All American' Force, consisting of the two brigade groups plus an army aviation task force and a large contingent of the Divisional Support Command (DISCOM), was in combat in Grenada within eighteen hours of being notified at their base at Fort Bragg, North Carolina. This ability to deploy at 'no notice', together with its combat readiness and intensive training programme, has made the 82nd Airborne Division the US Army's primary rapid reaction force.

Prior to joining the Division all personnel, regardless of military occupation speciality (MOS), must complete the US Army's jump school at Fort Benning, Georgia. The idea that a paratrooper is just an infantryman who uses a parachute as a way of getting into battle is quickly dispelled by the instructors of the 4th Airborne Training Battalion. Training is hard and aggressive, and one of the aims of the course is to instil the proper 'airborne spirit'. The Basic Airborne Course (BAC) is undertaken by both officers and soldiers, and lasts for three weeks. Five jumps are needed to qualify for the wings which, when awarded, are worn on the left breast above the pocket. Over 21,000 personnel qualify from the 4th ATB each year and a number of these are sent to serve with units of 82nd Airborne.

Two major factors affecting the ability of the Division to deploy overseas are climate and terrain, and because of this there is an extensive off-post training programme. Each year battalions within the Division train in the Alaskan tundra, Mojave Desert or Panamanian jungle. Personal clothing and equipment varies according to the area in which a battalion is operating, but is usually standard US Army issue. In temperate climates high-leg jump boots are favoured and these distinguish the airborne from the non-airborne soldier. Other distinguishing features include the airborne tab and the 82nd's divisional patch, the letters AA in a circle within a square, both of which are worn by all divisional personnel on the left shoulder of their combat uniforms. In addition, the maroon beret has been officially adopted by 82nd Airborne Division and is worn when in barracks with all uniforms. The beret is discarded in favour of the airborne version of the Kevlar helmet when parachuting or when deployed in the field. However, the beret is the paratrooper's traditional headgear and is worn whenever possible.

A paratrooper hurries to collapse his parachute canopy before moving off the drop zone.

Below: Paras of the 82nd relax or make last-minute adjustments to their kit, aboard a C-130 *en route* to the drop zone.

US ARMY SPECIAL FORCES

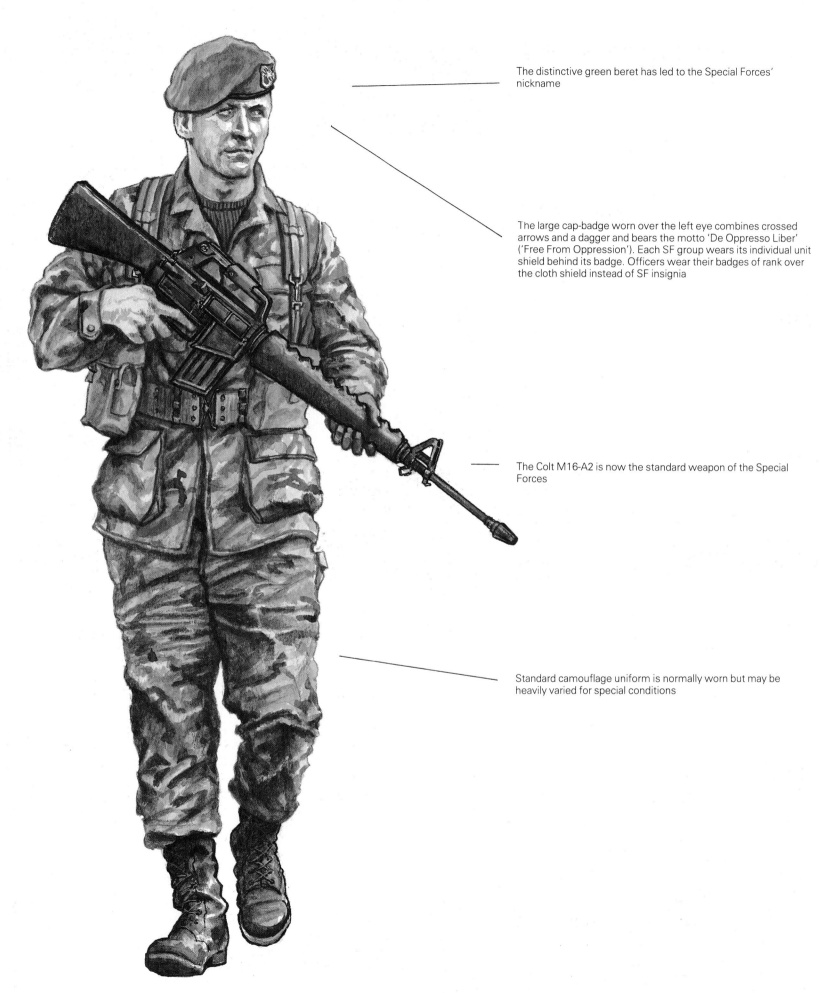

The distinctive green beret has led to the Special Forces' nickname

The large cap-badge worn over the left eye combines crossed arrows and a dagger and bears the motto 'De Oppresso Liber' ('Free From Oppression'). Each SF group wears its individual unit shield behind its badge. Officers wear their badges of rank over the cloth shield instead of SF insignia

The Colt M16-A2 is now the standard weapon of the Special Forces

Standard camouflage uniform is normally worn but may be heavily varied for special conditions

The original Special Forces group, raised during World War Two as a joint US-Canadian unit to execute sorties behind enemy lines, was disbanded with the coming of peace. During the early 1950s it was realised that, should the Cold War lead to armed conflict, the West would have difficulty in withstanding the might of the Soviet Union (which had still not fully demobilized) and that consequently large areas of territory would be overrun. Accordingly it was decided to create a force, skilled in guerrilla warfare, which would harass the invader, aid the resistance groups which it was assumed would spring up and pave the way for ultimate liberation. The 10th Special Forces Group (Airborne), commanded by Colonel Aaron Bank, was activated at Fort Bragg, North Carolina, on 20th June 1952 to fulfil this role. Despite its paper complement of 2,500 men, the initial group numbered no more than one officer, one warrant officer and eight enlisted men. However, within nine months Colonel Bank had gathered around him over 1,000 men, many of them ex-Rangers and OSS, who were to form the nucleus of the United States' latest elite fighting group. 77th Special Forces Group was formed in September 1953 and 1st Special Forces Group in 1957. 5th Special Forces Group, formed in 1961, served throughout most of the conflict in Vietnam. It was soon found that its guerrilla training was of little use against an enemy themselves operating as guerrillas. Emphasis was immediately changed to the raising of Civilian Irregular Defence Groups (CIDGs) among the semi-nomadic Montagnards of central Vietnam.

Today Special Forces groups operate throughout the US sphere of influence, providing advisers and technicians to friendly Third World countries, particularly in Asia and Central and South America. There are currently eight Special Forces Groups (Airborne) under the control of the 1st Special Operations Command (Airborne), four of them – the 1st, 5th, 7th and 10th – active, each with a battalion deployed outside of the United States, two in the Reserve and two in the National Guard.

Special Forces Groups contain 1,500 men organized into 'A', 'B' and 'C' detachments or teams. The 'A' detachment, the basic operational unit, consists of two officers and eight NCOs. Four or five 'A' teams are controlled by a 'B' team, itself commanded by a major with his own staff of five officers and 18 soldiers. Nine 'B' teams, each capable of operating as an independent entity, constitute a 'C' team.

All ranks are airborne-trained and many are free-fall experts. Every member of an operational detachment is trained in irregular warfare and must hold additional primary and secondary specialist qualifications in weapons handling, demolition, communications, engineering or intelligence. Most are fully conversant in at least one foreign language.

Training is rigorous and tough, although some would say less so than in the days immediately prior to Vietnam. All applicants are High School graduates and must pass a detailed security vetting before selection. Although training in irregular warfare, weapons handling and escape and evasion are common to all students, the majority of time is dedicated to the acquisition of specialist skills.

US Special Forces are currently being issued with the new much-improved M 16A2 rifle with its burst capability and effective range of 800 metres (875 yards), but all ranks have a working knowledge of most of the world's major small arms systems.

Special Forces wear camouflage uniform but are immediately recognizable by their striking green beret, from which they derive their nickname. The large distinctive Special Forces crest, which combines crossed arrows, a dagger and the motto 'De Oppresso Liber' ('Freedom from Oppresion'), is worn over the Group flash as a beret badge.

A typical 'Green Beret' NCO.

A brief respite during training allows feet and socks to be dried over a camp fire.

When on operations far from one's own lines, it is essential to be skilled in advanced first-aid techniques.

17

U.S. ARMOURED FORCES

The AFV crewman's helmet incorporates radio/intercom connections. Goggles protect the eyes in dusty conditions

A variety of undergarments, including micro-climate and ballistic protection clothing, can be worn underneath the coveralls

Standard-issue webbing is worn, including pouches capable of holding fragmentation grenades

Although modern tanks can provide collective NBC protection, soldiers will always carry their own personal respirator

During the last decade the US Army has greatly increased the size and strength of its armoured forces in an attempt to keep pace with the massive growth in Soviet landpower. Over 3,600 M2/M3 Bradley Infantry Fighting Vehicles (IFVs), armed with the potent 25mm Hughes Chain Gun, had entered service by the autumn of 1987, as had 4,500 M1/M1–A1 Abrams Main Battle Tanks.

Although the M1 Abrams proved immensely popular with its crews from the moment of its acceptance into troop service in 1981, due to the immense power generated by its massive 1,500 hp turbine engine coupled with its accuracy, enhanced by new thermal sights and laser rangefinder, it lacked the firepower of such potential adversaries as the Soviet T–64B and T–80 series with their 125mm guns and AT–8 anti-tank missiles. This problem has recently been rectified by the introduction of the M1–A1 Abrams, a variant retrofitted with the world-beating West German 120mm Rheinmetall smooth-bore gun, increased armour protection and integral NBC over-pressure system.

The bulk of US armour is at present stationed with the four armoured divisions, each with six tank, five mechanized infantry, four support artillery, one air defence, one cavalry and one aviation brigades and with the six mechanized divisions, all identical save that each has five tank and six mechanized infantry brigades.

The three armoured cavalry regiments are peculiar to the US Army. Whilst most European regiments are in reality little more than the size of a battalion, a United States armoured cavalry regiment (ACR) is as large as many brigades. The 2nd and 11th ACRs are stationed in West Germany and the 3rd ACR, the first to receive the new M1–A1 Abrams, in Fort Bliss.

Each regiment has three squadrons consisting of a headquarters, headquarters troop, three cavalry troops, a tank company and 155mm self-propelled howitzer battery. Each cavalry troop has two tank and two reconnaissance platoons and the tank company three tank platoons. A fourth aviation squadron with three helicopter-equipped air cavalry troops and two anti-tank attack helicopter troops, together with a support squadron with its combat engineer and intelligence companies, completes the inventory.

Each ACR is an independent corps, asset-controlled directly by the corps commander who uses it as a spearhead or screen in an offensive and covering force in a defensive. The ACRs are the only true regiments in the United States Army, having their own regimental structure.

The 3rd Armoured Cavalry Regiment, formed in 1846 as the Regiment of Mounted Riflemen, is one of the oldest in the United States. It served in the Mexican-American War, where it earned the regimental motto 'Blood and Steel', fought in the Civil War, extensively in the Indian Wars and in both World Wars. It served in Korea, in Berlin during the 1961 crisis and is now co-located with the Air Defense School at Fort Bliss, Texas.

3 ACR began maintenance training for the new M1–A1 in July 1986, before actual delivery of the

tank which was subsequently issued to 'H', or Heavy Troop, 2nd Squadron in September 1986. Gunnery training was completed in January of the following year and in February the Squadron successfully completed its evaluation.

New uniforms have been introduced to complement the new generation of tanks. Crews are now issued with specially designed combat vehicle crewmen's (CVC) coveralls made of flame-retarding Nomex fabric into which can be introduced a removable liner in cold weather. A ballistic undergarment may be worn under the overalls to afford limited protection against shrapnel should an enemy round penetrate the armour. A special microclimate conditioning vest, which circulates a cooling liquid to carry off excess body-heat, can be worn under an NBC suit or in hot conditions. In cold weather a winter-weight Nomex jacket, which includes an opening at the back to the casualty evacuation strap, is worn. Nomex gloves, face mask and balaclava are also issued.

The M1 Abrams Main Battle Tank combines high manoeuvrability with good armour protection and a low silhouette. These M1s will be up-gunned to M1A standard in the near future with a 120mm smooth-bore gun.

The ability to generate smoke has been a standard feature of Soviet tanks for many years but is a novelty in the West. This platoon of M1s shows how effective the system is.

DELTA

Informal headgear, suitable for the environment, is the norm

The M 60 machine gun is among the weapons available to Delta Forces

Standard US Army webbing is adjusted for personal comfort. A grenade will often be carried attached to the ammunition pouch

Comfortable trousers, sometimes civilianized, are worn operationally, often in place of regular issue

Upon his return from service with the British SAS in 1963, Colonel Charlie A. Beckworth sought to create a United States unit with the same motivations, organization and functions. At that time all Special Forces groups were heavily committed to the Vietnam War, making change virtually impossible, and in the immediate post-war period there was a series of cutbacks among the smaller elite units. By the mid-1970s, however, it was apparent that international terrorism would become the major problem of the future and it was precisely to combat this that Beckworth was given clearance on 19th November 1977 to form the 1st Special Forces Operational detachment-Delta, known locally simply as Delta.

Beckworth, who adopted the motto 'Surprise, Speed and Success' for his new unit, gathered around him a nucleus of hand-picked specialists in covert reconnaissance, counter-terrorism, barricade operations and hostage rescue and began the difficult task of selection and training.

Under Beckworth's command, selection and training processes were virtually identical to those of his British SAS members, although it is possible that since he relinquished command these have been refined to take into account Delta's more specialist role. All potential transferees must attend a lengthy and very searching initial interview with a number of serving officers and NCOs of the Group and must undergo psychological assessment before they are even accepted for selection. This is to ensure that they are self-possessed and mature enough to endure the hours, perhaps days, of extensive monotony invariably preceding the few minutes of sheer naked aggression which mark the final stages of most operations. 'Gung-ho' adventurers are not accepted.

Fitness is of the essence. As well as completing timed speed and endurance marches, candidates for the first selection have to perform an inverted crawl over 36.6 metres (40 yards) in 25 seconds, swim 100 metres (110 yards) fully clothed and in boots, and complete 37 sit-ups and 33 press-ups each in less than one minute.

Fast yet deadly accurate marksmanship is demanded. Snipers must attain 100 per cent accuracy at 545 metres (600 yards) and 90 per cent accuracy at 915 metres (1,000 yards), whilst all members must be able to discharge their weapons safely in the close confines of a terrorist situation involving a building or aircraft cabin.

Training covers all aspects of conventional soldiering, with particular regard paid to the handling of foreign weapons and deep reconnaissance, together with the more esoteric skills of vehicle theft, aircraft refuelling and hostage reassurance.

The size and organization of Delta is secret, although the entire Force is considered to number no more than 100 'operators'. In line with traditional SAS thought, the standard operational group is the four-man squad, each member of which has a primary and secondary specialization which may include communications, demolition or a very high degree of field medicine. Four squads form a troop and two or more troops a squadron, terms again borrowed from the SAS.

Delta's most famous and tragic action was Operation Eagle Claw, the ill-fated attempt in 1980 to rescue the US hostages from Iranian hands. As a direct result, a top-level re-evaluation of all counter-terrorist resources was made. Delta was retained virtually intact and now forms one of the four wings of the multi-service Joint Special Operations Control (JSOC) based at Fort Bragg, North Carolina, and responsible for all anti-terrorist and hostage operations.

Once again, Delta's weapons and equipment are secret, although clearly these must include the best available from the arsenals of the western world. Snipers are known to use the Remington 40XB rifle with 12x Redfield telescopic sights, whilst machine-gunners are issued with a variety of M-60 and Heckler & Koch HK 21 systems. Shotguns and grenade launchers, notably the 40mm M 203, are used to support more conventional automatic rifle fire.

The concept of 'surprise, speed and success' is currently implemented by rehearsal of airborne and heliborne insertion techniques.

UNITED STATES MARINE CORPS

The traditional US steel helmet shown here is now being replaced by the 'Fritz Hat', which offers more protection to the wearer

The M60 machine gun is still a first-class support weapon despite intensive trials to find an alternative system

This obviously experienced marine has elected to carry three water bottles, additional first aid equipment and extra ammunition in his 'free-style' webbing arrangement

Standard camouflage trousers are the only conventional part of this marine's outfit

The United States Marine Corps is the largest and one of the oldest of its kind in the world. Formed by Act of Congress in 1798, the Marines fought with distinction throughout both World Wars, in Korea – during which they attained equal status with the other armed services – and in Vietnam where they sustained 12,936 dead and 88,594 wounded in some of the bloodiest operations of the War.

Although not regarded officially by the US Government as part of its Special Operations Forces, the Marines nevertheless undergo rigorous selection and training.

The present active strength of the US Marine Corps is stated by the international Institute for Strategic Studies as 199,600 including 9,700 women, the whole divided into three Marine Divisions, two Marine Corps Security Force battalions and three Active Air wings consisting of over 40 squadrons of fixed and 30 squadrons of rotary wing aircraft. The 472 combat aircraft, together with the 84 armoured and approximately 450 support helicopters, themselves a frequent bone of contention with the rival US forces, provide the marines with a unique versatility which it is unlikely they will ever be asked to surrender.

The cream of the US Marine Corps volunteer for the Force Reconnaissance Units responsible for intelligence gathering prior to an amphibious landing. Known as 'Recons', the unit receive training similar to, but otherwise independent of, the US Army Special Forces or US Navy's SEALS. Recon units are divided into Force Recon Company and Battalion Recon Company groups. Force Recon operates covertly in four-man teams reminiscent of the British SAS. Each member has his own speciality but is cross-trained in a second skill in case of emergency. All members are trained paratroopers, strong swimmers and skilled divers capable of using open and closed breathing apparatus. Battalion Recon is larger, each Division having a battalion of around 500 men, and less specialist. Divided into platoons and companies, its members are subordinated to specific battalions and, utilizing SCUBA diving techniques, helicopters and light vehicles, obtain general intelligence regarding beaches to be used for landing by the parent battalion.

The basic structure of the 17,000-strong Marine Division is triangular with three infantry regiments each divided into three battalions, the whole supported by a reconnaissance battalion, tank, engineering and amphibious battalions, an artillery regiment and air defence battalion. Although Marine Divisions are some 20 per cent larger than their Army equivalents, due to financial constraints their battalions are smaller.

US Marine Corps training and equipment are geared heavily to the concept of the aggressive assault, which has been at the forefront of the Corps' ideology since its inception. All members are volunteers and must successfully undergo 11 weeks of basic training at either San Diego, California, or Parris Island, South Carolina, before being accepted into an active unit. Although a small percentage of officers are accepted from the Annapolis Naval Academy, most are re-

cruited via Officer Candidates Schools or from among the best Platoon Leader candidates.

Each battalion consists of a headquarters company, three rifle companies divided into 13-man squads, and a weapons company. The standard squad weapon is the improved M 16A2 rifle supported by a 5.56mm Squad Automatic Weapon (SAW) issued one per fire team. The Weapons Companies are presently acquiring a new heavy machine-gun platoon with eight firing teams each allotted a vehicle armed with a 0.5in and a Mk 19 40mm heavy machine-gun, although in essence the latter is effectively a small grenade launcher. Artillery firepower and target acquisition are also being improved, with the result that today the US Marine Corps, although smaller than in recent times, can boast an aggressive capability greater than ever before.

This USMC M48 only just gets its tracks wet as it comes ashore from an LCT.

Marines dismount rapidly from their LVTP7 amphibious assault vehicle.

US NAVY SEALS

A camouflaged sweatband or floppy hat is usually worn in preference to a steel helmet

A conventional camouflage uniform will often be festooned with additional ammunition belts

Webbing is based on standard US issue but may be adapted to personal preference

'Seals' may draw upon a variety of weapons, in this instance the Stoner M63A1 MG used exclusively by US Naval SOF teams

The selection of footwear is largely a matter of personal preferences, dependent upon operational requirements and conditions

The US Navy SEALS were created, with a high degree of Presidential patronage, on 1st January 1962. A re-evaluation study commissioned in 1960 had reported the need for an independent group capable of conducting counter-insurgency operations, conventional and clandestine, on land and at sea. Existing Underwater Demolition Teams (UDTs) were carrying out their duties of reconnaissance, beach and mine clearance excellently, but theirs was a passive rather than offensive role and it was not considered appropriate to extend their field of operation.

The word SEAL, derived from an acronym for Sea, Air and Land, captures at once the sheer breadth of ability of the Unit. All members are para-trained and if required can reach their areas of operation from carrier- or land-based aircraft. More usually they will be carried close to the shore by submarine, which they will leave either on the surface or submerged to continue their journey by inflatable boat which, depending on circumstances, may have a 7.5hp silent outboard engine or be powered by human muscle and paddle-power. Once ashore, the SEALS can be regarded as a match for any conventional land-based enemy, particularly as prior to the completion of their mission their presence will almost certainly be unexpected.

Currently there are six SEAL Teams in commission, divided into approximately 50 platoons, although it is hoped that by 1990 this number will be increased to 70. SEAL Teams 1, 3 and 5 are stationed at the Naval Amphibious Base, Coronado, San Diego, and 2 and 4 at Little Creek, Norfolk, Virgina. SEAL Team 6, formed in 1980, is specially trained for counter-terrorist operations and, unlike the others, which are under the command of two Naval Special Warfare Groups (known rather unpronounceably as NAVSPEC-WARGRU 1 and 2), it is controlled directly by the US Navy's Atlantic Command in Norfolk, Virginia.

Officers and men undergo identical base training, save that officers are expected to bear the added responsibility of team leadership. Trainees undergo a vigorous 23-week course at the Basic SEAL Training Department of the Naval Amphibious School, Coronado, from which approximately 55 per cent emerge unsuccessful. An initial four-week period spent on runs, physical training, team games and water sports is followed by a fifth so-called 'motivation' week in which the physical and mental strengths and weaknesses of each student are tested. It is at this stage that the majority of failures occur. The residue of the course is conducted under simulated combat conditions with sleep, regarded as a necessary evil, kept to a minimum. Towards the end of the course, students transfer to San Clemente Island where they practise heavy underwater and land demolitions and complete a series of long swims, culminating in a five-mile marathon. Upon completion of basic training, swimmers are assigned to a SEAL Team with which they may expect to spend 70 per cent of their time attached to an operational platoon. Opportunities exist for the individual to undertake specialist advanced training in bomb dispos-

al, deep reconnaissance and the mastering of various swimmer delivery vehicles (SDVs) or midget submarines essential for long range incursions.

SEAL Teams use a wide variety of weapons and equipment, the majority of which is common to all US special units. Many swimmers carry the stainless steel, and therefore rustproof, Smith & Wesson Navy Model 22 9mm silenced pistol for close-quarter work, relying on the M63 A1 light machine-gun, with its 150-round drum magazine, for firepower support.

Personnel wear a standard naval dress with unit insignia in barracks but, when operational, wear a scuba or combat suit appropriate to the environment. This will often take the form of conventional camouflage uniform with the addition of extra ammunition belts. Floppy jungle hats are invariably worn in preference to the heavy and cumbersome steel helmet.

Clandestine infiltration via waterways is just one technique regularly practised by members of the US Navy SEALS.

US HELICOPTER PILOT

The helicopter pilot's helmet differs from that issued to the fast-jet pilot in that it has a boom mike rather than a face-piece

The major's badge of rank shows clearly on both shoulders

This badge denotes that the pilot is serving in a unit integral to the 82nd [All American] Airborne Division

A zip jacket with pouches and knife is issued to increase his combat and survival capability

The 45 M1911 A1 Colt is being replaced the 9mm Beretta within the US armed forces

The helicopter was first used in the air assault role during the Korean War in the 1950s. Helicopters were later used during the Suez operation and during the French campaign in Algeria, but it was not until the US involvement in SE Asia that the helicopter really came into its own. The deployment of helicopters onto the battlefield was an imaginative move on the part of the United States armed forces. Helicopters allowed troops to be moved rapidly from one location to another at short notice on a scale not previously imagined.

Throughout the conflict in Vietnam there was continued improvement in both helicopter design and development, and in the tactics used in their employment. Aside from the air assault aspect, helicopters evolved to take on the responsibility for other types of mission such as recovery of both men and material and observation for both artillery and air strikes. Most importantly, perhaps, for combat troops on the ground, it was used for casualty evacuation. Known in military parlance as 'medevac', a system of employing helicopters to conduct airmobile casualty evacuation from the battlefield itself quickly evolved, and was to save the lives of thousands of wounded troops who would otherwise have died. Most battlefield casualties were heli-lifted to rear areas for treatment during the war, either to be treated at base hospitals or flown out to major medical centres in SE Asia or the United States. During the eight years between 1965 and 1973, the US Air Force's Military Airlift Command evacuated a total of 168,832 battlefield casualties.

Such was the success of casualty evacuation by helicopter that it considerably increased the morale of the troops on the ground and, although modified Bell UH–1D helicopters fitted with special litters for stretchers were used specifically for the tast of recovering casualties, any helicopter would do – including those tasked with taking the troops into action.

During the conflict in SE Asia the basic tactics for airmobile operations were established, and these have remained essentially the same to date. Once a mission had been planned, the first troops, the landing zone (LZ) control party, would be taken in by helicopter (usually a UH–1D). These men would secure the LZ and advise the airmobile force commander of the situation on the ground. The force commander, himself airborne in a helicopter command post, would then decide how to deploy his force. The initial assault force would then arrive in UH–1Ds (carrying up to 14 men each), followed by the larger CH–47 helicopters (each capable of carrying 44 troops) dependent on the particular mission requirement. The enemy could then be engaged using either ground troops, offensive air support (including helicopter gunships) or artillery tasked by observers flying overhead. Two types of helicopter, the OH–6 Cayuse and the OH–58 Kiowa, were used for visual observation and target acquisition, although the former was more usually employed in a 'Pink Team'. These teams would consist of a Cayuse and a AH–1G

Huey Cobra gunship. The Cayuse would carry out fast, low-level reconnaissance over suspected enemy positions, supported by the Cobra gunship which would engage any targets found. These teams were also useful for defending the UH–1Ds which, because of their relatively slow speed, were particularly vulnerable to ground fire during the landing phase of an airmobile operation.

These tactics are still employed today, although the helicopters themselves have changed. The Bell UH–1D, once the prime mover, is gradually being replaced by the UH–60 Blackhawk – a more sophisticated, purpose-built helicopter. The Cobras are still in use, now equipped with Tow anti-tank missiles rather than rockets and machine-guns, but it is likely that these too will be replaced by the more modern Apache helicopters when the latter come into service.

One thing that remains essentially the same, however, is the aircrew themselves. They are still highly motivated and highly trained, and bear a close resemblance to their forebears of the Vietnam conflict. One- or two-piece olive green flight suits are normally worn over long under-wear. Both the flight suits and underwear are made of flame resistant material. When on tactical operations, a flight/survival vest is worn over the suit. The vest consists of a green nylon mesh body, without arms, on which are sewn a variety of pouches containing items which would be required in an emergency. Most of what a pilot normally needs is carried in his flight suit or flight jacket, or indeed in the aircraft itself. There are various designs of boot worn, depending on the operation, environment and individual, but boots with laced-in zip-fronts are popular with aircrew. Helmets, too, vary depending on the aircraft flown but are usually one-piece with integral headphones and boom microphone, and a push-back sun visor.

A flight of UH-60 Blackhawk helicopters makes a low-level approach on exercises.

US AIR FORCE SPECIAL OPERATIONS WING

The USAF Special Operations Wing's clothing and equipment are based on the standard issue throughout the US Air Force. However, because of their role, a certain latitude of dress is allowed

Various bullet-resistant 'flak jackets' are worn, especially by personnel involved in low-level operations

The type of flying glove worn depends on the individual's specialisation. Pilots wear thin leather gloves while aircrew/winchmen wear thicker all-purpose gauntlets

Flight or combat boots can be worn with or without zips, depending on personal preference

A US Air Force Special Operations force was formed in 1961 and is now based at Hurlburt Field, Florida, from where it operates closely with a number of the US Army's elite forces. The original 1st Air Commando Group was created on 29th March 1944 at Hailakandi, India, specifically to provide air cover, resupply and airlift support for Wingate's Chindits, then operating behind the Japanese lines in Burma. Nicknamed the 'Burma Bridge Bombers' for their unorthodox activities, the Group was awarded the Distinguished Group Citation for consistent valour prior to its disbandment with full military honours in 1948.

The 4400th Combat Crew Training Squadron was reactivated in 1961 and on 8th July 1968 was formally constituted the 1st Special Operations Wing of the US Air Force Special Operations Force. The Wing grew steadily, mushrooming in the late 1960s, until at the height of the Vietnam War it numbered 31 squadrons, 10,000 personnel and 550 aircraft.

With the reappraisal of all special forces activities after the War, the force was reduced considerably and now consists of a civilian and military workforce of 3,000 supporting a fleet of 28 aircraft.

In 1975 the Group was renamed 1st SOW and subordinated to the Second Air Division, itself part of 23rd Air Force. The Special Operations Wing is divided into the 8th, 16th and 20th Special Operations Squadrons, the 834th Combat Support Group and a co-ordinating Special Operations/Combat Control Team.

Operationally 1st SOW supports all unconventional warfare groups including those involved in psychological operations (Psy Ops) and security. Much of the work undertaken is necessarily secret but is known to include the movement of special teams in and out of tactical locations, resupplying them and providing them with close air support if necessary.

Members of 1st SOW are trained to operate three distinctive types of aircraft, two of which are based on the world-famous, tried and tested C–130 Hercules. The MC–130E 'Combat Talon' is capable of flying low level terrain-hopping tactics day or night and in all weather conditions. It is sophisticated enough to make extremely accurate, single approach, high or low level resupply parachute drops and carries the latest electronic counter measure (ECM) systems to frustrate enemy radar. A few 'Combat Talons' are fitted with the Fulton Surface to Air Recovery (STAR) system capable of plucking two people, or a load of 500 lbs, from the ground or water, essential in certain covert incursion missions.

Reconnaissance, interdiction and close air support is the prerogative of the AC–130H Spectre, often referred to as 'Puff the Magic Dragon'. Fitted with two 20mm Vulcan cannon, a 40mm Bofors cannon and a modified 105mm howitzer, all fired through the side of the hull, the aircraft relies on optical, infra-red and electrical sensors to direct its considerable firepower against its selected target.

The HH–53H PAVELOW III, a highly modified

The Special Operations Wing, which trains regularly with elite Special Forces units has the ability to drop infiltration teams deep into enemy territory.

version of the HH–53 Super Jolly long range helicopter, is ideally suited to special operations. Fitted with forward-looking infra-red radar mounted behind the refuelling boom, an inertial navigation system borrowed from the B–52 bomber, a Doppler navigation system, terrain-following radar and an on-board computer, the helicopter can be navigated precisely to a landing zone via a pre-destined course to avoid enemy concentrations.

The US Air Force, through the 1st SOW, is fully committed to Special Force operations and is without doubt the finest Group of its kind in the world.

The AC-130 H Spectre, often known as "Puff the Magic Dragon", is fitted with an amazing array of two 20mm Vulcan cannon, a 40mm Bofors cannon and a modified 105mm howitzer. The devastating effect of this firepower concentrated on a single target can only be imagined.

SAS TROOPER (UK)

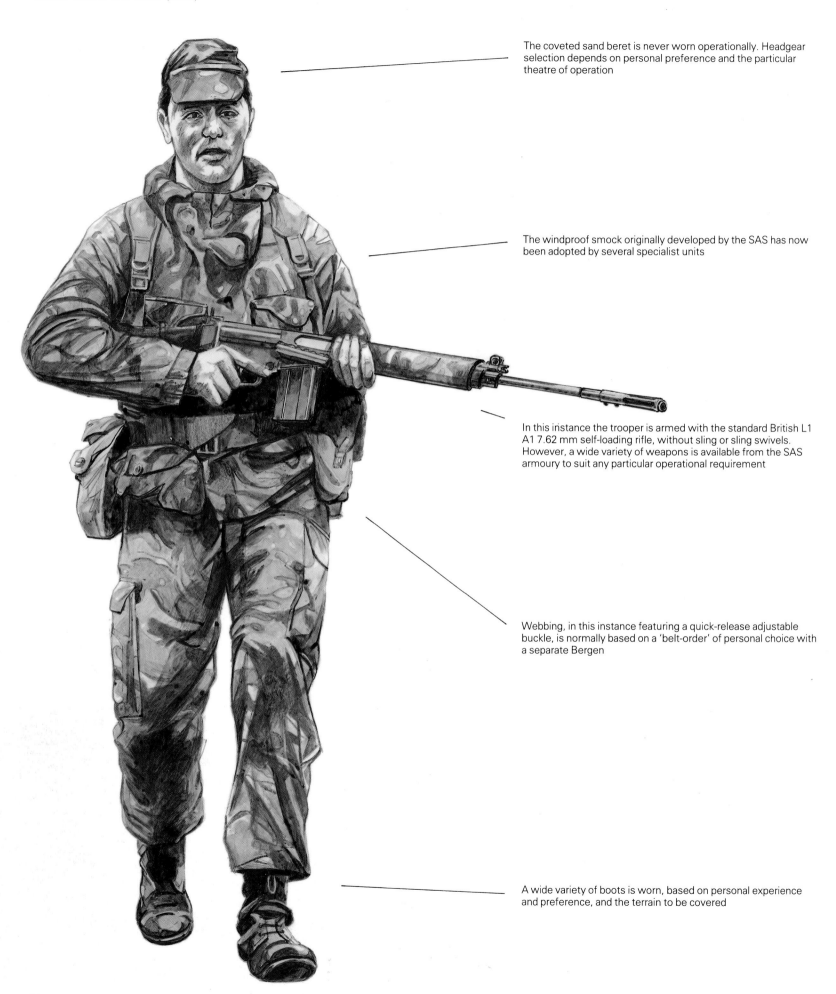

The coveted sand beret is never worn operationally. Headgear selection depends on personal preference and the particular theatre of operation

The windproof smock originally developed by the SAS has now been adopted by several specialist units

In this instance the trooper is armed with the standard British L1 A1 7.62 mm self-loading rifle, without sling or sling swivels. However, a wide variety of weapons is available from the SAS armoury to suit any particular operational requirement

Webbing, in this instance featuring a quick-release adjustable buckle, is normally based on a 'belt-order' of personal choice with a separate Bergen

A wide variety of boots is worn, based on personal experience and preference, and the terrain to be covered

Britain's Special Air Service Regiment, the SAS, is one of the best-known special operations force units in the world. Formed in the Western Desert during the Second World War, it earned its reputation by carrying out daring operations behind enemy lines, and by the war's end consisted of 1st and 2nd SAS (British), 3rd and 4th SAS (Free French), and the 1st Belgian SAS. These units formed the 1st SAS Brigade and came under the direction of HQ Airborne. Disbanded after the war, the British SAS was reformed in the early 1950s as 22nd SAS Regiment and tasked with seeking out Communist terrorist (CT) units in the jungles of Malaya.

Since the 'Malayan Emergency', as the campaign was known, 22 SAS have fought in every British theatre of operations including the jungles of Borneo, the mountains and deserts of Oman, and the 'bandit country' border areas of Northern Ireland. Capable of operating in a wide range of terrain and under varied climatic conditions, the SAS trooper is likely to wear a number of different styles of combat uniform. What the SAS soldier wears and the equipment he carries depends not only on his operational area but the particular mission he is undertaking.

Much of the SAS Regiment's operational work is clandestine in nature and, because of this, no identifying insignia are worn. The sand-coloured SAS beret is usually only worn when in barracks or in headquarters. The same goes for the distinctive 'sabre' or SAS parachute wings which, when worn, are pinned to the upper right sleeve rather than sewn on. Badges of rank, worn on epaulette slides by both officers and men are never worn in the field. Indeed the most common mode of SAS combat wear is the windproof smock, which has no epaulettes on which to fix the slides. This garment, manufactured in DPM cloth made from tightly woven Egyptian cotton, is one of the few 'giveaways' to the identity of the wearer (it is warm, light and dries out exceptionally quickly). Even then, the windproof smock, with its hood and large pockets, is also a favourite of Britain's airborne and amphibious forces.

The windproof smock is usually worn with either olive green (OG) trousers or 'denims', or DPM windproof trousers. The former trousers are both green in colour and are useful for camouflage in that they break up an individual's overall shape, while the windproof trousers have the same qualities as the smock and similar large cargo pockets. Headgear varies greatly and is dependent on personal preference as much as anything else. The peaked DPM combat cap or a woollen balaclava are among the most common choices. The hood of the windproof smock is worn only in severe climatic conditions as it restricts a man's hearing. Footwear also varies greatly, from mountain or para boots to suede boots or sandals, dependent on the individual's preference and the job he is doing.

Personal webbing is one of the most obvious indications of whether or not a man belongs to the SAS. The webbing, worn around the waist and known as 'belt kit', carries the individual's ammunition, water, rations and survival gear.

A candidate 'on selection' pauses for a quick drink of water somewhere in the mountains of South Wales. He is competing against the clock and cannot afford to stop for long.

The pouches containing this equipment are generally British in origin, either '44 or '58 pattern webbing. However, it is not unusual to find US, West German or other foreign equipment hanging from an SAS soldier's belt.

A variety of individual weapons is carried by the SAS trooper on operations. In the past these have included shotguns (especially useful for close-quarters work in the jungle), and small calibre, high-velocity rifles such as the 5.56mm M-16 and the Colt Commando. The standard battle rifle, the 7.62mm SLR with its heavier round, has also been widely employed. Occasionally snipers' rifles or silenced sub-machine-guns are issued. However, everything – all equipment and clothing – relates directly to the individual SAS soldier and the specific mission being undertaken. Indeed, it could be said that there is no 'uniform' combat kit for Britain's Special Air Service Regiment.

A well-camouflaged hide is essential for surveillance operations. SAS troopers might stay in their OP for days or even weeks.

PARATROOPER (UK)

Before being accepted for parachute training, every candidate must undergo a rigorous selection course including the notorious P Company, in which their nerves and aptitude are tested to the full

The large Bergen rucksack weighs between 50-70lb

The standard-issue PT vest is invariable sweat-soaked after the first mile

A standard SLR with magazine weighing 11lb

No allowance is made for the fact that the combat high boot is far from an ideal running shoe

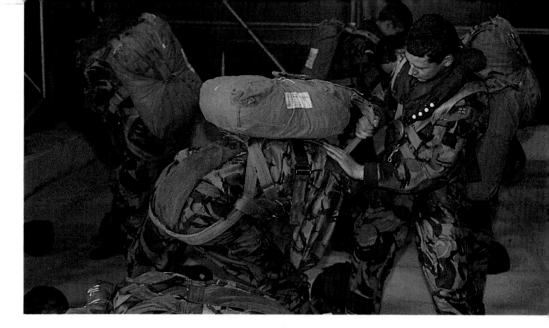

The 'Paras', as Britain's paratroops are known, were officialy formed in September 1941 when the 1st Parachute Brigade, consisting of the 1st, 2nd and 3rd Battalions of The Parachute Regiment, was raised. Specially selected and trained, this all-volunteer force grew until it comprised two complete Airborne Divisions. In the immediate post-war period the Paras, like all Allied wartime airborne formations, were drastically reduced in strength, a trend which was to continue until the disbandment of 16 Parachute Brigade in 1974. However, throughout the period leading up to dispersal of Britain's sole surviving airborne formation, the Paras were constantly active in overseas campaigns. These included operations in Palestine, Malaya, Cyprus, Suez, the Middle East, Aden, and Borneo.

With the disbandment of 16 Parachute Brigade, Britain lost its capability to mount large-scale airborne operations and the three remaining regular parachute battalions were reduced to filling one 'para-role' battalion slot by rotation. This unhappy state of affairs continued until after the Falklands Campaign, in which the 2nd and 3rd Para Battalions were developed. During the campaign the Paras proved yet again the need for highly-trained and motivated special operations troops and this, coupled with the need to create a rapidly deployable out-of-area (OOA) operations brigade, led to the formation of 5 Airborne Brigade in 1983.

Today, 5 Airborne Brigade consists of two of the three Parachute Battalions plus various para- and airmobile-trained supporting arms and services. As with all airborne forces, there are a number of items of personal equipment which distinguish them from other units, most notably the red (maroon) beret. The red beret, initially introduced by Britain's airborne troops and since copied by many of the world's parachute forces, is worn by all members of the Brigade. Men of the Parachute Regiment can be distinguished by their cap badge, a stylised set of wings and parachute surmounted by a crown and lion, while members of the various supporting arms wear their respective corps or regimental cap badges. In addition each regular (1st, 2nd and 3rd) and each TA (4th, 10th and 15th) battalion wears its own DZ (drop zone) flash. These insignia are worn on the upper right arm below the 'wings' worn by all para-qualified personnel. These, together with badges of rank, are all the insignia usually worn on the paras' combat uniform, although men who have gained foreign parachute wings on courses overseas sometimes wear these over the right breast pocket of their smock. The parachute smock itself has changed little in design since the original 'Dennison' airborne smock of 1942, the main exceptions being the disruptive pattern material (DPM), the standard camouflage throughout Britain's armed forces, the full-length zip and the woollen cuffs. The smock is worn with either standard DPM combat or DPM jungle trousers, the latter being lighter and having the additional advantage of larger cargo pockets. Considerable concern has been caused over the last five years by the standard-issue high-leg combat boots. Found to cause blisters on many a hardened foot during long marches, many men have acquired more suitable alternatives such as the lined West German airborne boot or the Scandinavian Lundhags.

One item of personal equipment peculiar to the paratrooper and the special forces soldier is the Bergen, a large capacity rucksack with a strong tubular external frame. In this the Para carries much of his personal and specific-to-task equipment, a load that can weigh between 50 to 80 lbs or more. Personal webbing is also an important part of the airborne soldier's equipment, and usually consists of a belt, various canvas pouches and a yoke-brace attachment. The paratrooper, who, because of his role, has to carry everything he needs with him, must be able to get to certain essential items quickly. These items, such as ammunition, rations, cooking and survival equipment, are worn in the webbing around the waist. One advantage of this is that in situations which require rapid movement, the Bergen can be quickly discarded and the individual can fight on with what he is wearing.

The standard infantry personal weapon is carried by both officers and men alike. At present the 7.62mm self-loading rifle (SLR) is being replaced by the new SA-80 weapon system. The latter is 5.56mm in calibre and the smaller, lighter round means that more ammunition can be carried by each man.

Everything the individual paratrooper needs to sustain him in combat during the early stages of an operation can be carried with him when he parachutes from the aircraft. The standard PX 1 Mk 4 main and PR 7 reserve parachutes are currently in service with Britain's airborne forces. When jumping, the Bergen and webbing are secured under the reserve 'chute which is fitted on the front. The rifle can either be secured with the Bergen or fitted down the man's side beneath the parachute harness. To top him off, the modern British paratrooper wears a lightweight ballistic helmet which was introduced in the late 1970s and replaced the earlier, heavier helmet of World War Two vintage. Both types of protective headgear have one thing in common however – once on the ground, they are usually replaced by the distinctive red beret, considered by many to be an offensive weapon of a psychological nature.

A jumpmaster adjusts a paratrooper's PX1 main parachute prior to emplaning for a water jump.

SPECIAL BOAT SQUADRON

Squadron members train regularly in dry suits to enable them to operate in cold conditions. Oil rig protection exercises are regularly carried out in the hostile environment of the North Sea

The US M16 Armalite is standard issue. However, under certain circumstances the silenced L43 A1 Sterling will be preferred

To enable the SBS to fight once ashore, waterproof holdalls are provided to carry specialist equipment such as demolition charges, beach-marking equipment or burst-transmission radios

Members of the Special Boat Squadron comprise the special forces element of the Royal Marines and as such justifiably consider themselves the elite of the elite.

During World War Two, a number of specialist units were raised to undertake beach reconnaissance and raiding duties along the European and Far Eastern coastlines. The value of these groups was so self-evident that, whereas the SAS was disbanded, they survived the inevitable post-war cutbacks and amalgamations to form the nucleus of the 'Small Raids Wing' attached to the Royal Marines Amphibious School. During the next 20 years Special Boat Sections found themselves involved in reconnaissance missions against Chinese coastal emplacements during the Korean War, undertaking counter insurgency operations in the Malayan peninsula, supporting the Army in Borneo and working closely with 45 Commando in Aden. In 1977, in recognition of the consistently high standards attained by them throughout, they were renamed the Special Boat Squadron.

Royal Marines wishing to transfer to the SBS undergo three days of intensive selection during which their stamina, individual skills and leadership are tested to the full. Successful aspirants then undertake 12 months of specialist training before joining an operational Special Boat Section. Physical fitness is stressed throughout the course, at the end of which individuals must be able to swim long distances both on the surface and underwater. Much emphasis is given to the use of SCUBA equipment, the handling of canvas and inflatable boats, and navigation and demolition techniques. As the Marine must be equally at home on the land as at sea, long distance cross-country navigation, survival, escape and evasion are also taught. Towards the end of training all entrants undertake a four-week parachute course, during which they are taught to operate both standard and steerable parachutes.

It is indicative of the standard of the course that, despite the obvious high quality of all applicants, only 30 per cent are successful. Once accepted into the SBS, most candidates remain for the rest of their career, although inevitably some will return to one of the Commandos to obtain faster promotion.

Once qualified as a 'swimmer-canoeist', the Marine takes his place in one of the Sections where training continues relentlessly. Although based at Poole in Dorset, the SBS operates worldwide. In recent years SB Sections have been deployed to Northern Ireland on border and coastal surveillance and have exercised extensively with US Navy Seals and the Royal Netherlands Marine Corps. Much of their role involves the defence of NATO's Northern Flank in Norway and it is almost certain that they liaise closely with Commanchio Company tasked with the protection of off-shore oil installations.

The SBS played a crucial role in the Falklands campaign. They were the first ashore on South Georgia, having initially flown from the United Kingdom and parachuted to a submarine in the freezing waters of the South Atlantic. They worked closely with 'B' and 'G' Squadrons of the SAS, providing OPs and reconnaissance patrols for the beach landings, and may have been involved in intelligence gathering on the Argentine mainland itself, although this must always remain a matter of conjecture.

Unlike the SAS, who have a very distinctive beret and cap badge, the SBS wear standard Royal Marine uniform and the Commando green beret. Royal Marine parachuting wings and a 'Swimmer-Canoeist' badge, in the form of a crown surmounted by the letters SC flanked by laurel leaves, are worn on the right shoulder and forearm and provide the only indication of SBS service.

SBS four-man patrols are normally equipped with US M16 Armalite rifles or specially-silenced versions of the British Sterling sub-machine-gun but are also taught to use any weapon which may fall into their hands. Although Gemini power boats and 'Rigid Raiders' are used for long-distance journeys, the SBS usually rely on custom-built Klepper Mk 13 collapsible boats for inshore work.

Two swimmers carry out a beach reconnaissance prior to an amphibious assault.

SBS members are closely involved in regular defensive patrols on the North Sea oil rigs.

MOUNTAIN LEADER, M & AW CADRE RM

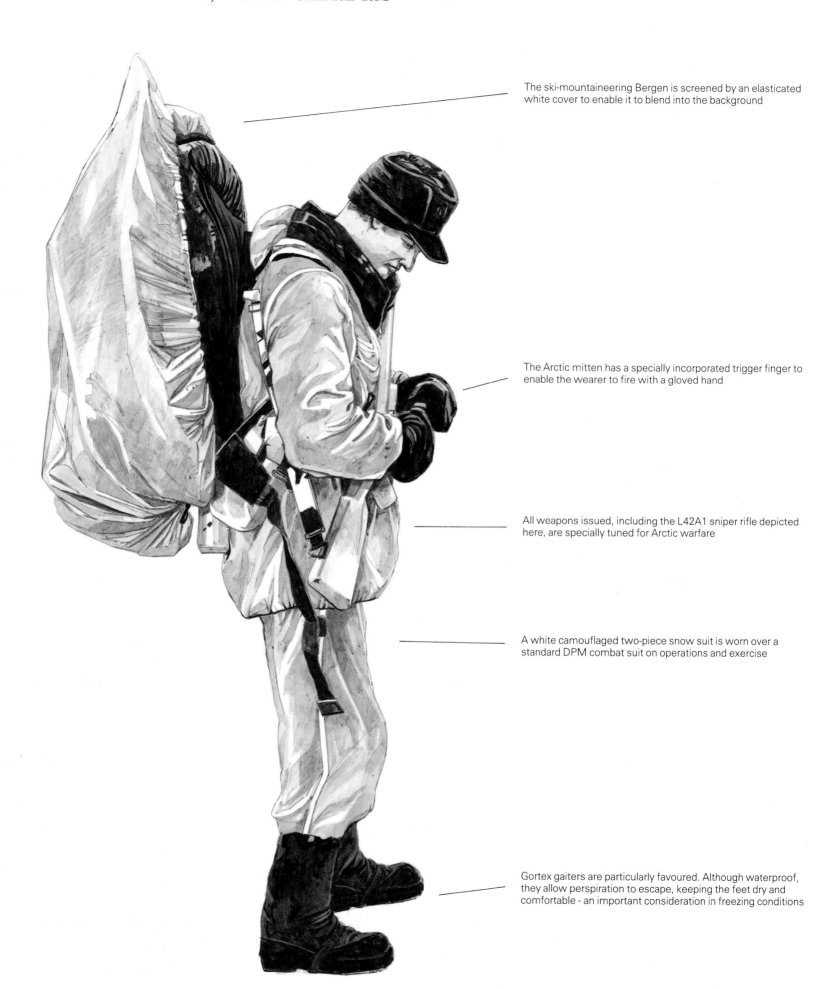

The ski-mountaineering Bergen is screened by an elasticated white cover to enable it to blend into the background

The Arctic mitten has a specially incorporated trigger finger to enable the wearer to fire with a gloved hand

All weapons issued, including the L42A1 sniper rifle depicted here, are specially tuned for Arctic warfare

A white camouflaged two-piece snow suit is worn over a standard DPM combat suit on operations and exercise

Gortex gaiters are particularly favoured. Although waterproof, they allow perspiration to escape, keeping the feet dry and comfortable - an important consideration in freezing conditions

The Mountain and Arctic Warfare (M & AW) Cadre of Britain's Royal Marines is one of the most highly-trained special operations forces in the world. Specialising in ski, mountain and winter warfare, the men of the Cadre are all experienced marines who have served with one of the three Royal Marine Commandos (41, 42 or 45).

The M & AW Cadre is an essential part of Britain's 3 Commando Brigade RM which includes both 42 and 45 Commandos RM. The Brigade is responsible for reinforcing NATOs Northern Flank in Norway and specializes in both amphibious and winter warfare. Norway is of vital strategic importance to NATO and is located between two of the largest Soviet maritime concentrations, one to the north and one to the south. The Brigade deploys to Norway every year for three months of winter warfare exercises and one of the tasks of the M & AW Cadre is to train the commandos of the Brigade in the complexities of Arctic Warfare. In addition the Cadre also supplies the Brigade with its primary reconnaissance asset, a role in which the men of the Cadre excelled during the Falklands Campaign.

In order to become a member of the Mountain and Arctic Warfare Cadre, a marine must first qualify as a Mountain Leader (ML) grade 2. To do this the marine, usually a junior NCO, must pass what is one of the most arduous selection courses in the British armed forces. The course, which lasts around eleven months, takes place in England, Wales, Scotland, Norway and the Alps. During the course, volunteers must learn to climb, ski, survive and fight in some of the most inhospitable terrain in the world. They must become skilled snipers, learn to parachute and succeed in passing a series of strenuous tactical exercises, one of which lasts for two weeks in Norway in the middle of winter. One indication of the severity of the ML2 course is the pass rate, which is usually around 20 per cent. Considering the high standard of fitness, and the degree of experience among the applicants, all of whom have served with the Royal Marine commandos for a number of years, the pass rate is low. However, a number of men drop out of the course due to injury, mostly broken limbs, and some who fail the first time go on to pass the second time around.

To survive and fight in the Arctic, the MLs must be both highly trained and properly equipped. During the harsh winter the temperature can change quickly, and the difference of a few degrees can mean the crisp snow being replaced by heavy rain and slush, which soaks through clothing and shelters and makes tracks almost impassable. In flat country, such conditions are bad enough, but when on patrol 2000 metres up the side of one of Norway's many narrow valleys, weather like this can prove disastrous.

The men of the M & AW Cadre are among the best equipped of NATOs forces deployed in Norway. Standard issue Arctic combat clothing, consisting of a windproof smock and trousers, is worn over thermal underclothes. A white camouflaged two-piece snow suit is worn over the standard DPM combat kit. Although not waterproof, the

snow suits help keep the men dry and help them blend into their surroundings. A cover made of the same material is fitted over the large ski mountaineering Bergen carried by the MLs. This large-capacity rucksack, with an external aluminium H-Frame, is capable of carrying a load of up to 100 lb. This load includes dry clothing, tent/shelter, snow shovel, climbing equipment, extra rations, cooking stove, and specific-to-task equipment, such as ammunition, radio, etc. It should be noted that, with experience, it is easier and less tiring to ski with heavy loads than it is to march.

Other equipment, such as magazines, a mess tin and rations, is carried in each man's personal webbing. This is usually of the standard '58 pattern and either painted white or covered with white tape, as is the individual's rifle. In the past the personal weapon of the MLs was the M-16. Its light weight made it better suited to the Cadre's long range reconnaissance patrols and it is easier to operate than the SLR when the firer is wearing mittens or gloves. However it seems likely that the MLs now carry the new British rifle which has been issued to the Royal Marines. Known as the SA-80, this weapon is of the same calibre as the M-16 (5.56mm) but due to its 'bullpup' design is much shorter, making it more convenient to carry and easier to operate when encumbered by all the equipment an ML has to carry.

The M & AW Cadre is responsible for trying out much of the new equipment destined for British troops in the Arctic. This means that the MLs have the best equipment available while it is under evaluation, and are among the first to receive new equipment when it comes into service. With the exception of their quiet confidence, some slight differences in equipment, and their outstanding ability when it comes to operating in the hostile snowy wastelands of the Arctic, there is little to tell the men of the Mountain and Arctic Warfare Cadre apart from other Royal Marines, something the men themselves do not mind in the least.

The BV202 has a very low ground pressure and can cope with most snow conditions. When it is carrying cargo, skiers can be towed behind.

Below: Mountain Leaders must be skilled rock climbers under combat conditions.

COXSWAIN, 539 ASSAULT SQN, RM

A green inflatable life-vest with a strobe light is standard wear for small craft operations

The suit is designed to enable the wearer to fit several layers of clothing underneath in order to combat the coldest of conditions

A one-piece, totally waterproof immersion suit is standard issue for the crews who regularly operate in Arctic waters

Personal weapons are 'winterized' to prevent the oil and grease from freezing in Arctic conditions

The rubberised overboots are an integral part of the suit

539 Assault Squadron Royal Marines is a unique, independent, amphibious unit comprising just over one hundred officers and men. Formed as a direct result of British experience during the Falklands Campaign, the Squadron is one of the youngest units in the British order of battle, but nevertheless has amassed unrivalled experience in the art of amphibious warfare.

Prior to April 1982, the Royal Marines had two distinct types of unit responsible for carrying out amphibious operations, assault squadrons and raiding squadrons. The assault squadrons were comprised of marines from the Royal Marines Landing Craft (LC) Branch, which had been established in 1943, and were responsible for providing crews for the Royal Navy's assault craft. During the early 1970s the LC Branch was expanded as a result of 3 Commando Brigade's commitment to the defence of NATOs northern flank, when the importance of a strong amphibious capability was recognised. The second type of amphibious unit within the Royal Marines, the 1st and 2nd Raiding Squadrons, had been an integral part of the LC Branch until the early 1970s, when the 1st Squadron came under the direct control of the Commando Logistic Regiment and the 2nd Squadron was disbanded. The only other unit of this type, the 3rd Raiding Squadron, was formed in 1980 to provide British Forces in Hong Kong with amphibious support.

During the Falklands conflict a special unit, known as the Task Force Landing Craft Squadron, was established. This Squadron comprised elements of both the LC Branch and the 1st Raiding Squadron which had, over the previous years, been conducting a series of Arctic trials. The experience of the crews contributed greatly to the ultimate British victory.

When the Task Force returned from the South Atlantic, the case for an independent amphibious squadron was put forward and accepted, resulting in the formation of 539 ASRM in April 1984. At present the Squadron consists of four Troops: the Landing Craft Troop, with two Landing Craft Utility (LCUs), four Landing Craft Vehicle Personnel (LCVPs) and an Assault Beach Unit (ABU); the Raiding Troop, with three sections each equipped with five Rigid Raiders; the Headquarters Troop which provides the Squadron with its motor transport, communications and logistical support; and the Support Troop, which provides the Squadron with its mechanical and engineering support.

The entire Squadron, with the exception of Royal Naval personnel serving with the Support Troop, are all fully trained commandos in addition to their amphibious specializations. The lowest specialist grade within the Squadron is Coxswain LC 3. All marines joining the Squadron must achieve this grade, which involves pass-ing a four-week course in seamanship and allows those who qualify to crew a landing craft. Only after serving with the Squadron for over a year will a man be considered for the ten-week LC 2 course which will allow him to cox either an LCVP (capable of carrying up to thirty-six fully equipped troops), a Rigid Raider or a Gemini in-

flatable. Practical experience is considered vital to training, and there is no way to learn seamanship except through going to sea.

One of the most demanding jobs within the Squadron is coxing one of the Rigid Raiders. These 17-foot craft, designed primarily for conducting small scale amphibious commando raids, are powered by 140 hp outboard engines and capable of a top speed of 40 knots. Able to carry up to nine fully-equipped troops (normally five/six in the Arctic), the Raiders are open to the elements, an important consideration when planning operations in the Norwegian winter when temperatures can drop below −70 degrees centigrade. This does not restrict operations, however, as Arctic evaluation trials in Norway proved. During Exercise 'Cold Winter 75', an Arctic Warfare section of Raiders travelled over 250 kms in under 10 hours, carrying out a surprise attack far behind enemy lines.

To operate under such extreme climatic conditions, and in waters where a man, if unprotected, would be expected to survive for less than a minute, requires the correct clothing and equipment. The Raider coxswains wear a one-piece immersion suit similar to that worn by pilots. This totally waterproof suit, with its permanently attached boots, is worn over layers of clothing, both thermal and woollen. In fact just about anything is worn that will keep the man warm. A green inflatable life vest (with a strobe light/beacon attached) is worn on the chest and secured around the neck and between the legs, and a combination of woollen gloves and waterproof mittens is usually worn on the hands. In addition, each coxswain wears a woollen ski mask and skiing goggles over his head and face so that there is no skin exposed to the air, or rather the salt water spray which turns to ice almost immediately. Unlike his human cargo, who wear a similar though less sophisticated one-piece suit, the coxswain has to stand upright while steering the vessel. He must therefore be able to take everything the hostile climate and sea can throw at him, even though he may look like the Creature from the Black Lagoon.

539 Assault Squadron operates wherever the Marine Commandos deploy. Its duties may take it to the heat of the Mediterranean, the inhospitable conditions of the Falklands or the frozen wastes of Arctic Norway. In this instance, a crew clad in cold weather kit are seen exercising in Northern waters.

THE GUARDS DIVISION

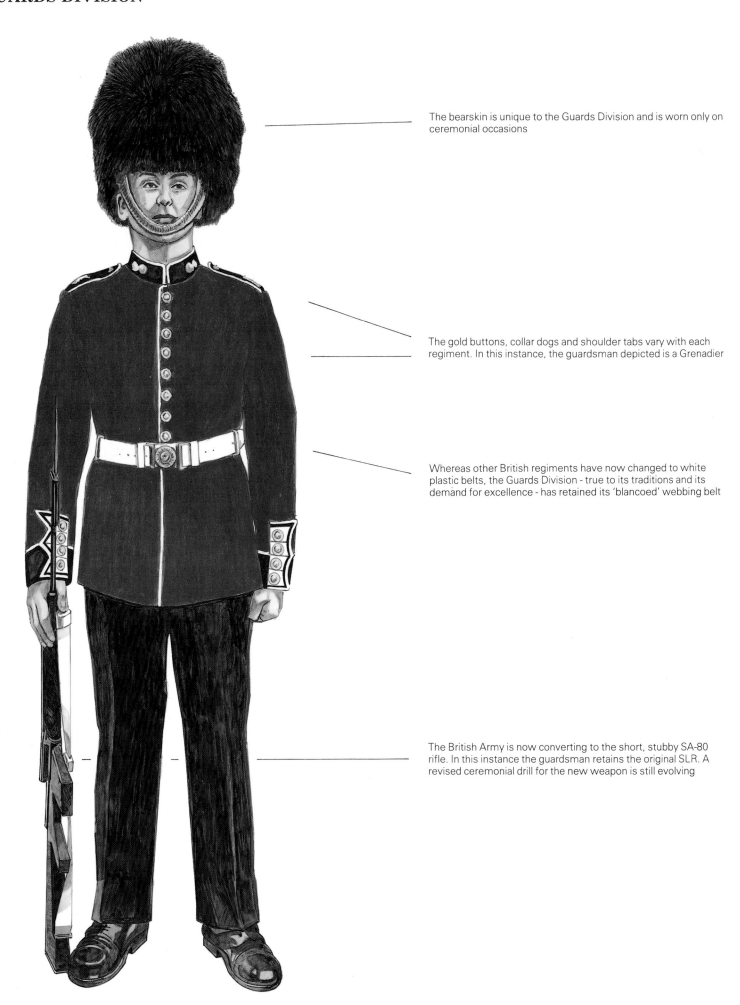

The bearskin is unique to the Guards Division and is worn only on ceremonial occasions

The gold buttons, collar dogs and shoulder tabs vary with each regiment. In this instance, the guardsman depicted is a Grenadier

Whereas other British regiments have now changed to white plastic belts, the Guards Division - true to its traditions and its demand for excellence - has retained its 'blancoed' webbing belt

The British Army is now converting to the short, stubby SA-80 rifle. In this instance the guardsman retains the original SLR. A revised ceremonial drill for the new weapon is still evolving

The Guards Division enjoys one of the oldest and proudest traditions in the British Army. Its battalions defeated the Napoleonic 'Old Guard' at Waterloo, contained the Russian hordes in the Crimea and routed the Boers in South Africa. It fought valiantly through two world wars and has been engaged on active duty on many occasions since. Its battalions regularly serve for short tours in Northern Ireland, where they invariably earn the praise of the local population and the grudging respect of the extremists.

Potential recruits to the Guards Division, or 'family' as many will come to regard it, must satisfy stringent height and fitness requirements before being allocated to a regiment and posted to the Depot at Pirbright, Surrey. Basic training is divided equally between conventional soldiering and drill. Those not attaining the highest standards in both are back-squadded as it is important that soldiers posted to battalion are competent to undertake all duties, whether active or ceremonial.

The Guards Division is justifiably proud of its reputation for providing the finest ceremonial troops in the world. Crowds of tourists gather to watch the ceremony of the Changing of the Guard which takes place on most days in the forecourt of Buckingham Palace. Guards also mount at St James Palace, the home of the Queen Mother and other members of the Royal Family, at Windsor Castle and at the Tower of London. Until recently a Guard also mounted nightly at the Bank of England to protect the nation's wealth against marauding mobs but, due to a lack of manpower and a happier economic situation, this has now been discontinued.

When not mounting guard or on public duties, battalions train for the numerous other events in which they become involved each year. During his first tour in London a guardsman may find himself lining the route for the State Opening of Parliament, forming a guard of honour for a visiting head of state, representing the Army at the Service of Remembrance at the Cenotaph or participating in Trooping the Colour.

Dress uniform for state occasions consists of a bearskin with plume according to regiment, a red tunic with blue facings, white piping and yellow buttons grouped according to regimental precedence, dark blue trousers with a red side piping, white leather belt and gleaming black ammunition boots. Regiments can be differentiated by the colour and position of their plumes and by the number and positions of their buttons. Grenadier Guards wear a white plume on the left side of the bearskin and single buttons; and Coldstream Guards a red plume on the right and buttons in pairs; Scots Guards have no plume and buttons in threes; Irish Guards wear a blue plume on the right and buttons in fours. Finally, the Welsh Guards wear a green and white plume on the left and buttons in fives.

Battalions not involved in ceremonial duties undertake the role of conventional infantry units. The 1st Battalion, Welsh Guards, for example, took part with 2nd Battalion, Scots Guards in the recapture of the Falklands in 1962 and have since

A guardsman of the Grenadier Guards stands at ease, having changed his rifle from the right to the left hand. This occasional movement is necessary due to the weight of the SA80, which cannot be rested on the ground as it is so much shorter than the old SLR.

Below: The guardsman on duty outside St James Palace salutes two passing officers. Note that the officers' uniforms differ in having a broad trouser stripe, red sash belt and gold epaulettes.

As well as appearing on ceremonial parades, the various Guards Bands give regular public performances. When on active service, the bandsmen provide first aid teams and man the Regimental Aid Post.

been based at Hohne in North Germany as part of 1 (Armoured) Division.

The Guards owe their unique junior NCO rank structure to a complaint by Queen Victoria that it was unbecoming for the Royal Family to be guarded by detachments commanded by corporals. As a consequence, the rank of corporal became known as lance sergeant. The only distinguishing feature between sergeants' and lance sergeants' insignia is seen on parade uniform. The lance sergeant does not have the red sash which is worn over the right shoulder by sergeants and above in Guards and line infantry regiments. When peaked caps are worn in lieu of bearskins, the number of rings on the edge of the peak vary according to rank and act as a further distinguishing factor.

Although Guards officers no longer require a private income to survive the sheer expense of Mess life, it is fair to say that the vast majority are still affluent. Many young officers limit themselves to a short service commission before taking up a City appointment, but others regard the Guards Division as a career and an important part of their lives and go on to achieve great military success in their later years.

TROOPER, THE LIFE GUARDS

Unlike the foot guards, who wear a distinctive olive brown beret, the Household Cavalry wear the original navy blue

The combat jacket has a woollen sleeve built in for added comfort

The Sterling 9mm sub machine-gun is favoured because of its small size. Its hitting potential is, however, severely limited

The lightweight trousers are often tapered for warmth and comfort

The Household Cavalry consists of two Regiments, The Life Guards and The Blues and Royals (Royal Horse Guards and the 1st Dragoons). They are the senior Regiments of the British Army and fully integrated into its organisation.

The Life Guards are the most senior, although not the oldest, regiment in the British Army. Formed from Royalist supporters who followed Prince Charles to Holland after the Civil War, the Life Guards have served as a mounted bodyguard to the Sovereign for over three hundred years.

The Regiment has a distinguished fighting record, beginning with their first action at Maastricht in 1673. Since then they have fought in many of the British Army's major campaigns including all the Napoleonic Wars, culminating in the Battle of Waterloo in 1815. In 1882 the Life Guards formed a composite regiment with the Blues and took part in Wolseley's Campaign in Egypt.

During the First World War the Regiment again went into action and by the war's end had earned a total of 28 Battle Honours. During the Second World War the Regiment became a part of the Guards Armoured Division and saw service in north-west Europe, where they earned themselves a further 21 Battle Honours.

In the years since the end of the Second World War the Life Guards have remained active. Between 1946-48 they served in the Canal Zone and Cairo, and conducted internal security operations during the Arab-Jewish conflict. In 1952 the Regiment spent a year patrolling the border between East and West Germany and in 1954 deployed to Egypt, from where it conducted counter-terrorist operations in Aden and Cyprus. 1957 saw a change when the Regiment converted from the Armoured Car role to an airportable one and became part of the Strategic Reserve.

Since the late 1950s the Life Guards have served a number of tours overseas, Aden, Oman, Cyprus, Malaya, Singapore and Borneo among them. Elements have been involved in various campaigns and individual squadrons served in Northern Ireland between 1969-70. In 1971 the Life Guards became a Tank Regiment for the first time in their history, and on conversion from armoured cars to tanks moved to West Germany where they relieved the Blues and Royals. Then in 1972 the Regiment had another 'first' when they served a four-month tour in Northern Ireland in the infantry role, a deployment they repeated in 1974.

In late 1975 the Regiment returned to Windsor, where they took on the new Scorpion and Scimitar tracked armoured reconnaissance vehicles. Between 1976-1980, squadrons were deployed to Norway, Denmark and Cyprus, while the Regiment continued to provide squadrons for tours in Northern Ireland. These squadron tours were continued between 1980-84 while the Life Guards rotated once again with the Blues and Royals in West Germany.

The Life Guards returned from Germany in January 1984 and became part of the newly-formed 5 Airborne Brigade based at Aldershot. The Regiment was well suited to the airmobile role and a number of men became airborne qualified. In addition to the airmobile role the Regiment is tasked with providing part of the security cover to London's airport in the event of a terrorist threat – a role for which their internal security duty in Northern Ireland has made them particularly suited. Additionally, over the same period and to date, the Life Guards have provided three Squadrons for six-month UN 'peacekeeping' tours in Cyprus. In all, very little time is wasted and the Regiment has an extremely full training programme while simultaneously providing detachments for various duties.

As one would expect from a Regiment with as much tradition as the Life Guards, its various uniforms are especially distinctive. Standard combat dress for its personnel consists of combat boots, olive green lightweight trousers, a heavy wool jersey and a combat jacket. As a unit within the Airborne Brigade, the men wear a DZ (drop-zone) flash of red over blue to distinguish them from other members of the formation. Headgear consists of a dark blue beret (which has been retained even though other elements of 5 Airborne Brigade have now adopted the maroon beret) on which is worn the Regimental cap badge made of brass.

Webbing, weapons and personal equipment are similar to those worn by other armoured reconnaissance units. This usually consists of a belt, respirator case, waterbottle and a magazine pouch. The standard issue weapon is the 9mm Sterling sub-machine-gun, which is used because its short length makes it easy to stow away inside an armoured vehicle. Because space is so restricted inside the Regiment's Scorpion recce vehicles and Fox armoured cars each man has, in addition to his webbing, a small rucksack containing his personal and spare equipment. This is strapped to the outside of his vehicle and is immediately at hand should the need arise – for instance if the vehicle is damaged or the men have to urgently adopt the infantry role.

The Life Guards are a highly trained, thoroughly professional, armoured reconnaissance unit. The Regiment's varied experience, acquired operationally around the world over recent years, has allowed it to retain its fighting capabilities while at the same time reaffirming the faith placed in traditional values such as a high standard of training and discipline.

A Scimitar armoured recce vehicle on the range. The green flag signifies that the 30mm cannon is unloaded.

A reconnaissance troop keeps watch during an exercise in Norway.

THE GURKHA RIFLEMAN

Jungle hats are frequently worn with a distinguishing colour band to indicate the individual battalion

The traditional Gurkha fighting knife, the Kukri, is always carried whether in combat or on ceremonial duty

Due to their diminutive stature the Gurkhas have always preferred the lighter M 16 to the 7.62 mm SLR

Rubber-soled boots with canvas uppers are superior to conventional leather boots in a jungle environment

Tragically, with the impending cession of Hong Kong to the Chinese Republic, the role of the Gurkha Brigade within the British Army is now being called into question. Tenacious, loyal and intelligent, the Gurkha has fought at the side of the British Army continuously since 1815, never once disgracing himself in battle. In the last 50 years he has fought from the deserts of Libya to the foothills of Italy, from the jungles of Borneo to the wind-swept plains of the Falklands, always without complaint and constantly in search of glory for his village and country.

Until 1947, the 10 Regiments of Gurkhas were part of the British Indian Army but, with the coming of independence that year, the units were split equally between the new Indian Army, with which some 80,000 still serve, and the British Army. Numbers serving with the British have dwindled steadily to a present figure of no more than 8,100 officers and men, and are likely to continue to decrease. The Brigade itself is far larger than any other in the British Army, consisting of a headquarters in Hong Kong, five infantry battalions (the 1st and 2nd Battalions 2nd King Edward VIIs Own Gurkha Rifles, the 6th Queen Elizabeth's Own Gurkha Rifles, 7th Duke of Edinburgh's Own Gurkha Rifles and 10th Princess Mary's Own Gurkha Rifles), signals, transport and engineering support.

The infantry battalions themselves are organized on standard lines with a few amendments to incorporate local custom and religious beliefs. Officers, who were once exclusively British, are now mostly Nepalese, the majority having worked their way up through the ranks to warrant officer before taking a commission. At present, three of the battalions are stationed in the New Territories of Hong Kong, where they spend much of their time combatting smugglers and illegal immigrants. One battalion is on attachment to Brunei at the express invitation and expense of the Sultan, and one battalion is based in Church Crookham, near Aldershot in England. Service in England is regarded as a mixed blessing. Gurkha basic pay is based by agreement on Indian Army income and as such is considerably below that of the British Army. It is, however, brought up to British standards for the United Kingdom-based battalion by means of a 'Gurkha allowance' which, if anything, leaves the recipients better off than their British equivalents. Furthermore, every soldier is provided with a smart 'walking-out' uniform of civilian flannels and navy blue blazer. As a result, they have little need to spend money and many accumulate considerable savings. On the other hand, few Gurkhas speak more than rudimentary English and despite close links forged with the locals, who regard them as extremely polite and well disciplined, many are lonely.

Selection is fierce and, despite the uncertain future, potential places are always heavily over-subscribed. Aspiring recruits willingly walk for days to attend the selection courses in the full knowledge that up to half will fail. Successful candidates undertake a nine-months training course in Hong Kong before joining their battalions. Gurkhas serve for a minimum of five years, although most serve for 16 years and the best to the age of 50. Home leave is rare because of the sheer distances involved, although when awarded it is for extended periods. Soldiers serving for a minimum of 16 years receive a land grant, enabling them to farm for the rest of their lives in comparative affluence, and a pension is paid every six months in cash.

Gurkhas wear their own distinctive variations of standard British uniform. Parade uniform is rifle-green in the United Kingdom and white in the tropics. Buttons, badges and the patent-leather belt worn by other ranks are all black. A distinct black pill-box hat is worn on parade but replaced by a dark green beret or slouch-hat at other times. Due to their diminutive size, Gurkhas are issued with the United States' M 16A1 Armalite rifle rather than the heavier British SLR and carry the world-renowned kukri knife so feared by their enemies. Versatile, light and razor-sharp, the curved kukri is the traditional knife of Nepal and lethal in close combat fighting.

What will happen to the uncomplaining and loyal Gurkha in the future is unknown. If Britain does sever her links, as many fear will be the case, she will be denying herself the services of arguably the finest close-quarter fighters in the world.

The Gurkhas are not only fighting soldiers but also capable of the highest standards of ceremonial duty. UK-based Gurkhas regularly provide detachments for the guard at Buckingham Palace; in this instance they are from the 6th Queen Elizabeth's Own Gurkha Rifles.

THE BRITISH INFANTRYMAN

The new helmet is still in the process of being issued. Made of plastic, it has been found to be lighter and more comfortable than the steel helmet which it is replacing

The new-issue 5.56mm SA 80 rifle is now entering service with the infantry. The SUSAT sight with its x4 magnification has greatly increased standards of marksmanship sight with its x 4 magnification has greatly increased standards of marksmanship

Originally produced for duties in Northern Ireland, the so-called 'NI gloves' are now on universal issue

The heavy canvas '58-pattern' webbing is now being replaced by a nylon system featuring a quick-release plastic buckle

After years of dissatisfaction, new boots are at last being introduced to the British Infantryman

The British infantryman has been described as the best trained but worst equipped in NATO. Whether or not this is true, he is certainly the most versatile. During battalion service he may find himself stationed in areas as far apart as Belize, Northern Ireland, Hong Kong or Berlin, with little time for acclimatization between.

Promotion within the infantry is slow but steady, the best soldiers attaining the rank of sergeant, with all the attendant privileges of the WOs' and Sergeants' Mess, after about eight years.

Selection for the infantry is fierce, with a sizeable minority of potential entrants failing either the stringent medical or the subsequent three-day selection course. The successful recruit undertakes an 18-weeks course at a Divisional Depot, during which time he is taught not only the rudiments of soldiering but the regimental traditions of the battalion which he will be joining. The professional infantryman takes a deep pride in the history and traditions of his battalion, with inter-unit rivalry encouraged at all levels.

Typically the young recruit will be posted to West Germany where he will form part of the 53,000 strong British Army of the Rhine. His mechanized battalion will form an important part of 1, 3 or 4 (Armd) Divisions based at Verdun, Zoeste and Herford, and as such will take part in a series of annual brigade and divisional exercises geared to test every facet of the individual soldier's training. Initially he will probably be attached to a rifle section where he will learn to work closely with an S man team although subsequently he may be transferred to the support company to give him experience in the handling of mortars and anti-tank weapons. After two or three years, if considered good enough, he will attend a battalion NCOs course and be promoted to the rank of lance-corporal and thereafter to corporal at which time he will be expected to command his own rifle section.

The Battalion may well find its tour of duty in Germany interrupted by a four-month posting to Northern Ireland. Understandably this is not always popular with married men who are forced to leave their wives and families at home. A spell in Northern Ireland is nevertheless surprisingly popular with the younger soldiers who seemingly regard the attendant dangers a small price to pay for the welcome break in routine. Accommodation has improved considerably since the Spartan days of 1969 when the first units on the streets were forced to live in appalling conditions. Food is usually good although recreational facilities are limited with the result that many regard a tour of Ireland as an ideal form of enforced financial saving.

On the completion of its tour in West Germany the battalion will almost certainly return to the United Kingdom where training will continue as before with perhaps more emphasis placed on ceremonial duties. In recent years it has become more common for line-infantry battalions to share royal duties with the Household Division and it is quite possible therefore that the young infantryman will be able to add to his experiences a spell of guard duty at Buckingham Palace.

At the commencement of his engagement the infantryman may sign-on for 3, 9, 16 or 22 years. Initially he will probably enlist for a minimum period to ensure that he is suited to military life but, if good enough, will be given every opportunity to extend his service at a later date.

All infantry regiments have their own cap badges and many their own distinctive service dress. A disruptive pattern uniform is worn by all units in the field. Despite claims to the contrary this is neither fully windproof nor waterproof and is at last being modified. 'Combat high' boots were introduced after the Falklands campaign but have proved less than successful. At present many infantrymen feel it necessary to purchase large quantities of often expensive clothing to supplement the inadequacies of that issued. Although clearly this is unsatisfactory there are at last indications that long overdue modifications are now being made to standard issue kit and hopefully in the near future the infantryman will be able to boast that not only is he the best trained but also the best equipped soldier in NATO.

Always alert while on duty, the British Soldier has nevertheless always had a reputation for showing kindness to children. Here a soldier of the Royal Welch Fusiliers attracts some young admirers while on patrol in North Belfast.

THE ROYAL ARTILLERY

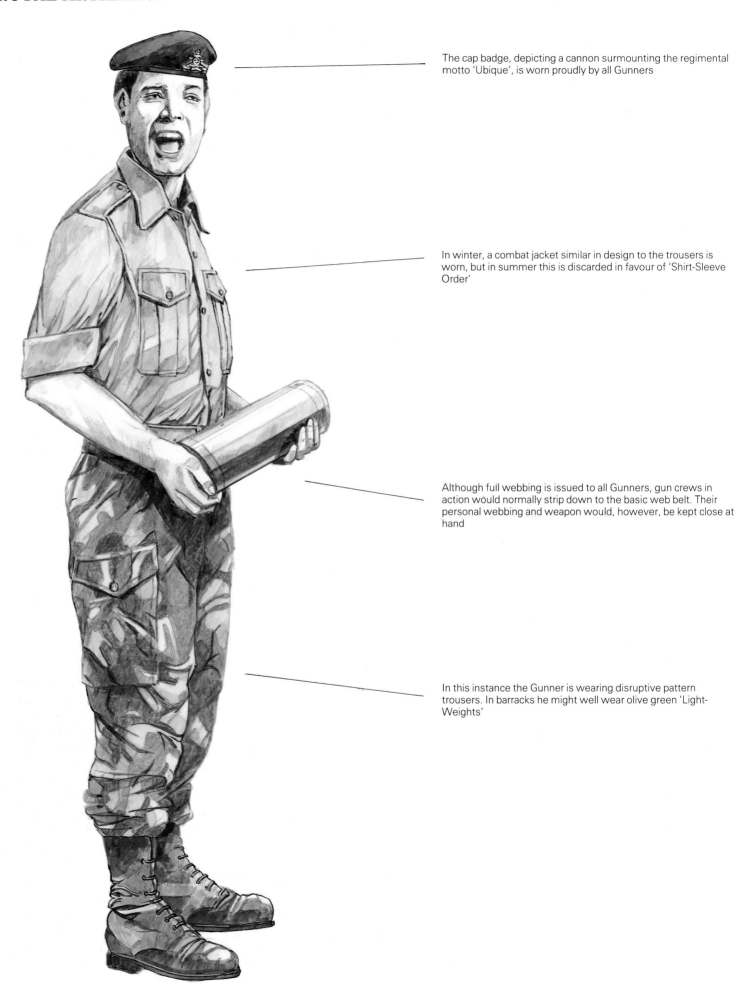

The cap badge, depicting a cannon surmounting the regimental motto 'Ubique', is worn proudly by all Gunners

In winter, a combat jacket similar in design to the trousers is worn, but in summer this is discarded in favour of 'Shirt-Sleeve Order'

Although full webbing is issued to all Gunners, gun crews in action would normally strip down to the basic web belt. Their personal webbing and weapon would, however, be kept close at hand

In this instance the Gunner is wearing disruptive pattern trousers. In barracks he might well wear olive green 'Light-Weights'

The role of the Royal Regiment of Artillery can be summed up by its motto 'Ubique', or 'Everywhere'. Since their creation as an independent force some 400 years ago, wherever the infantry or cavalry have gone the gunners have followed in close support, a tradition proudly followed in the Falklands when 105mm Light Gun batteries frequently engaged and destroyed much heavier Argentine ordnance.

The title 'Royal Regiment' is in many ways a misnomer as the Royal Artillery is in reality considerably larger than many Corps. To compound the confusion, 'The Regiment' is divided into a number of independent fighting units, themselves referred to as Regiments.

The modern Artillery is a powerful and complex branch of the Army. It is the only unit to employ battlefield nuclear weapons, in the form of the Lance missile deployed by 50 Missile Regiment RA in support of 1st (British) Corps in West Germany.

The vast majority of the Artillery is involved in conventional fire support. Modern gunnery is a matter of fire and movement as well as accuracy and, as such, mobility is of the essence. Despite the recent European failure to produce a domestic self-propelled howitzer capable of combatting the latest Soviet divisional artillery, the gunners can now boast a potential for destruction unsurpassed in their earlier history.

The bulk of the nine field regiments in West Germany are equipped with the M-109 A2 self-propelled gun, a rebarrelled version of the tried and tested United States' M-109 howitzer, although some still retain the elderly 105mm Abbot. Nominally, each regiment is attached to a designated brigade. In practice, overall control is so flexible that if necessary the massed fire of several, and on occasions all, regiments can be directed simultaneously against a single target. The effect of over 150 guns firing into an area little bigger than a football stadium would clearly be devastating.

It is anticipated that with the coming of the Multi Barrel Rocket Launcher (MBRL) in the next decade, long-range artillery warfare will be revolutionized. Based in Dortmund, 5 and 32 Regiments have been designated 'depth fire' regiments and will be equipped with the launchers when available. In the interim, each consists of two 6-gun batteries of the massive 175mm M-107, a Headquarters battery and a Locating battery. Locating batteries, of which there are four in the Royal Artillery, contain among the most specialist soldiers in the entire Army. Each battery consists of four totally independent troops: Survey, which supplies details of the exact position of all troops, friendly as well as hostile, on the battlefield; Meteorological, which forecasts weather throughout the entire Corps area; Sound Ranging, which locates enemy gun positions from the sound of their gunfire; and Drone. Although old and not always reliable, the Midge drone nevertheless forms an invaluable part of the 'depth fire' concept. Heavy artillery loses much of its impetus if it cannot be aimed accurately. The drone, which is equipped with a series of stereoscopic cameras,

overflies a potential target filming at pre-designated times. The drone returns on a set course, the film is processed, analysed and compared with the map, and targets designated. Although this operation is slow (it can take approximately 90 minutes from flight request to final analysis), it is reasonably accurate and will improve considerably with the coming of a new generation of remotely controlled vehicles in the next decade.

Artillery training is carried out at the Depot in Woolwich, South-East London, and at the Royal School of Artillery at Larkhill in Wiltshire. Due to its sheer size, and because it ordinarily operates in small units attached to large commands, the Royal Artillery does not have central battle honours nor conventional regimental colours. Uniquely, each battery incorporates the name of a battle honour into its full title and regards the guns themselves as its colours, affording them the same respect as an infantry battalion would its standard.

All ranks wear conventional working dress in the field. A distinctive red stable belt, with a dark blue central band and a yellow central stripe, is worn with barrack dress. A blue sweater may be purchased privately and worn as optional dress by officers and warrant officers. All gunners are proud of the white lanyard worn on the right shoulder of the No 2 (Parade) Dress. Originally issued in the mid-nineteenth century as a disgrace after a battery had deserted its guns, it is now regarded as an integral part of the uniform and is unlikely to be changed in the future.

Above and below: Battle proven during the Falklands campaign, the 105mm Light Gun has since been adopted by the US Armed Forces. It is capable of very high angle fire and the firing platform permits the rapid engagement of targets through 360°C.

KING'S TROOP, ROYAL HORSE ARTILLERY

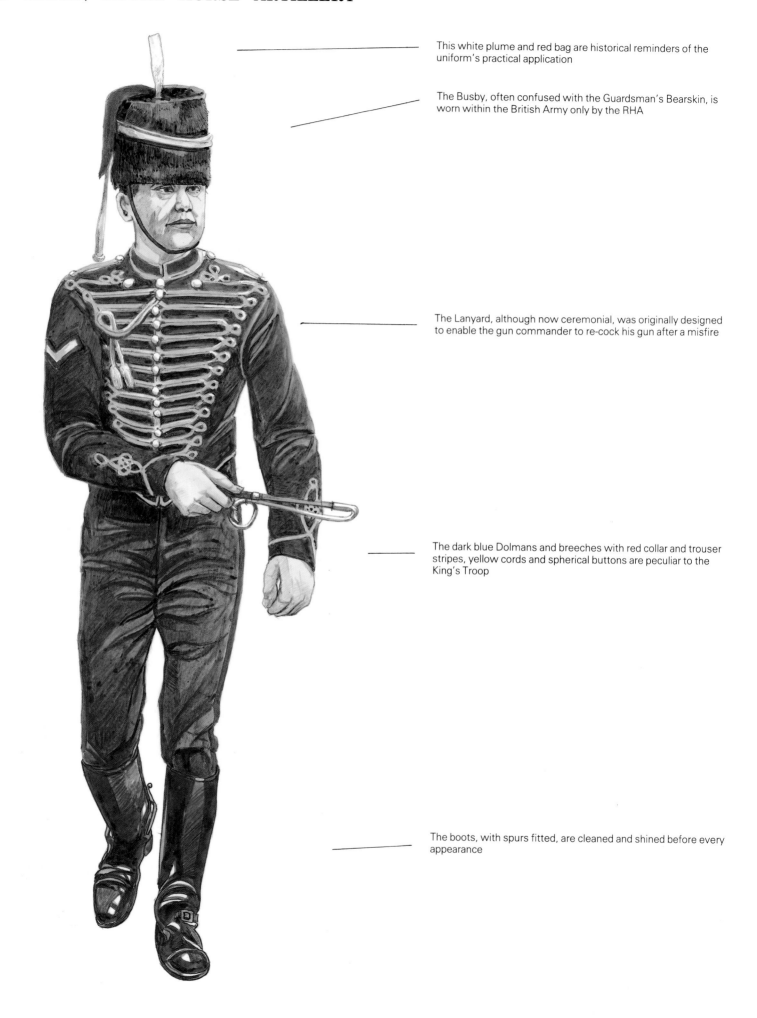

This white plume and red bag are historical reminders of the uniform's practical application

The Busby, often confused with the Guardsman's Bearskin, is worn within the British Army only by the RHA

The Lanyard, although now ceremonial, was originally designed to enable the gun commander to re-cock his gun after a misfire

The dark blue Dolmans and breeches with red collar and trouser stripes, yellow cords and spherical buttons are peculiar to the King's Troop

The boots, with spurs fitted, are cleaned and shined before every appearance

The King's Troop, Royal Horse Artillery, is the only purely ceremonial unit in the British Army. Although members of the Guards Division and Household Cavalry both undertake public duties and are responsible for guarding the Monarch and Royal Family on State occasions, they are also front-line fighting soldiers and when not based in London or Windsor can expect to train in a combat environment.

The Troop was formed in 1946 when it was decided to preserve a riding troop for ceremonial occasions. King George VI bestowed upon it the title King's Troop and, upon his death in 1952, Queen Elizabeth II decreed that it would retain the title as a mark of the esteem in which her late father had held it.

Recruits to the King's Troop make a conscious decision to join its unique and totally independent ranks prior to attending the formal Army Recruitment Selection Course at Sutton Coldfield, which they must nevertheless pass.

Potential troopers are invited to an initial interview at the Troop's purpose-built barracks in St John's Wood, situated in the centre of one of the most affluent areas of North West London. If successful, they subsequently spend two or three days as guests of the Unit to ensure that they are really suited to its gruelling lifestyle. Although at this stage some will not be able to ride, all will have a love of horses and most will be from a rural background.

Recruits undergo initial basic training with the rest of the Royal Artillery at Woolwich, in South East London, where they learn to take care of their uniform, to march, and the basics of gunnery and weapon handling. Although the troop has no formal combat role, in time of crisis it would relinquish its ceremonial status and become part of the London home defence force. It is therefore crucial that its members are trained to handle the full spectrum of British Army infantry weapons.

Whereas the majority of private soldiers, or troopers as they are known, serve for three years before returning to civilian life, the officers and NCOs are seconded to the Troop, returning to a conventional artillery regiment at the end of their tour. Competition is extremely fierce and, in the case of officers, based exclusively on merit rather than social background. Although only approximately 250 strong, the Troop has its own Regimental Sergeant-Major responsible for discipline and turnout. He is not, however responsible for mounted drills and on occasions in the past troops have been horrified to discover that a newly posted RSM could not actually ride!

In many respects, modern barrack routine has changed little since the Crimean War. The day begins at the crack of dawn as the 140 horses must be mucked out and exercised before breakfast. Each trooper is issued with two complete sets of riding tack (working and ceremonial) and must keep both immaculate. Horses are stabled in lines of approximately 20 under the command of a sergeant and again require hours of daily attention. Training for ceremonial events takes place on Wormwood Scrubs, close to the prison. The Troop takes part annually in the Royal Tournament and in many outdoor events both home and abroad throughout the summer months.

At the end of the summer season the entire Troop attends a fourteen-day 'rest and recreation' camp in the Aldershot area. Field craft and weapon training are brushed up and local gymkhanas organized, to which the families are encouraged to come and watch their men compete.

Full dress uniform worn for all ceremonial events has its supposed origins in practical application. It is said that originally the black busby could double as a water bucket for the horse, the white plume as a brush and the red bag worn over the right of the head dress as a pouch for dispatches, but as with so may of the best stories relating to ceremonial dress this must remain a matter for conjecture. Mounted troops wear dark blue dolmans and breeches, with red collar and trouser stripes, yellow cords and spherical buttons. The yellow cord attached to the busby and right breast of the dolman was worn originally to keep the dolman in place and to act as a makeshift bridle if need be.

For full ceremonial events such as the firing of Royal salutes in Hyde Park on the occasion of Royal birthdays, the Troop parades with six guns each pulled by six horses. The guns themselves are 13 pounders, all of which saw service in the Great War.

As well as firing ceremonial salutes, the King's Troop give mounted displays at many public events during the summer months. These soldiers are about to demonstrate their skills at a 'local' fair only some 10 miles from their London barracks.

THE ROYAL ENGINEER

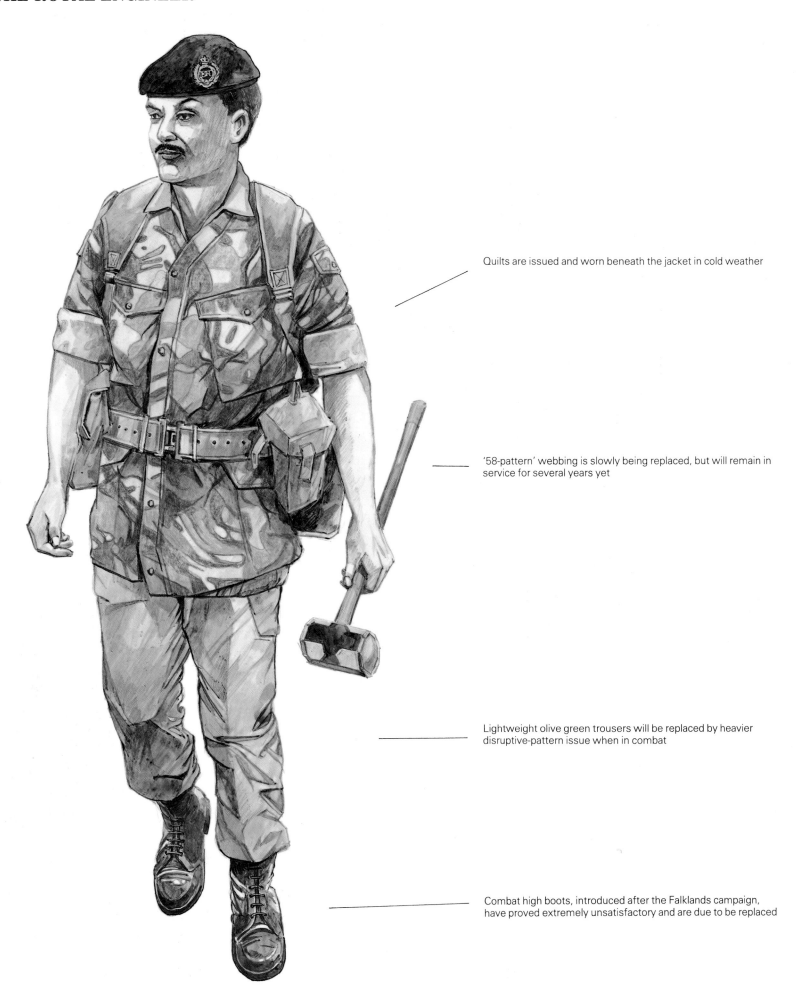

Quilts are issued and worn beneath the jacket in cold weather

'58-pattern' webbing is slowly being replaced, but will remain in service for several years yet

Lightweight olive green trousers will be replaced by heavier disruptive-pattern issue when in combat

Combat high boots, introduced after the Falklands campaign, have proved extremely unsatisfactory and are due to be replaced

The multi-capable Combat Engineer Tractor (CET) can excavate a tank fire position in a matter of minutes, using its large 'dozer blades.

The prime task of the Corps of Royal Engineers is to provide military support to the Armed Forces whilst simultaneously attempting to frustrate the enemy's ability to fight, live and move. The modern Engineer is not only a skilled technician capable of carrying out a variety of tasks with minimum support and equipment but also a trained soldier well-schooled in basic infantry tactics.

The majority of Engineers are attached to Combat Regiments supporting 1 (BR) Corps in West Germany. Others, however, undertake more exotic duties such as manning the Postal Courier and Communications unit (PCCU) responsible for the safe delivery of forces mail around the world, airfield construction, and bomb disposal, a responsibility shared with the Royal Army Ordnance Corps (RAOC).

Not only are the Royal Engineers among the first troops into battle, planning routes and clearing obstacles for the tanks and APCs to follow, they are invariably among the last out. Long after the withdrawal of 3 Commando and 5 Brigades from the Falklands in 1982, units of the Royal Engineers remained on duty on the Islands, painstakingly clearing the uncharted minefields scattered indiscriminately by the retreating Argentine Army.

Combat Engineers provide specialist support to front line formations and as such have to be fully capable of defending themselves against attack. They undertake tasks as diverse as route and mine clearance, demolition, building and bridge construction, map making and underwater reconnaissance. Combat engineers serving with BAOR are attached to one of three types of regiment.

As the name would suggest, the three Armoured Division Engineer Regiments support 1, 3 and 4 (Armd.) Divisions which comprise the bulk of the British NATO commitment to Germany. Each regiment has a self-contained headquarters, capable of moving and operating on its own, and three field squadrons. In defence, the squadrons would lay fields of anti-tank Bar mines and anti-personnel Ranger mines in an attempt to slow the enemy and force his advance into pre-selected killing zones. They would also extend natural obstacles, flood waterways and make rivers uncrossable by amphibious vehicles by weakening the banks. For political reasons it is most unlikely that the Engineers would be allowed to start the demolition of civilian facilities prior to the declaration of War. To prevent the possibility of the enemy overcoming key positions before their destruction, great emphasis is placed on speed and mobility during training.

Although of limited use on their own, certain obstacles when linked together create a formidable barrier. Thus, when time permits, trenches are often dug through the middle of minefields to force the enemy to commit obstacle-crossing as well as mine-clearing resources to a single area.

During an offensive, Engineers help maintain the momentum by filling ditches and bridging waterways, clearing routes through minefields and constructing roadways to the rear to facilitate the movement of supplies and reinforcements. Equipment required for the above tasks is held by the support squadron of each regiment. During the course of a battle a young Engineer, or Sapper as he is known, could be called upon to use any part of the equipment and it is imperative therefore that he is fully trained to use all of it.

There are two further specialist regiments within 1 (BR) Corps. 32 Armoured Engineer Regiment is equipped with a mix of Chieftain Bridge-layers (AVLBs) and Centurion Assault Vehicles (AVREs). 28 Amphibious Engineer Regiment is equipped with 72 West German M2 amphibious vehicles, capable of acting independently as ferries or in unison to create a bridge able to support the heaviest tanks.

A further four field regiments, six TA regiments and a number of independent squadrons are based in the United Kingdom as support. Small construction units are provided for the four RAF Harrier squadrons, whilst 9 Parachute Squadron RE is attached to 5 Airborne Brigade and 59 Independent Commando Squadron to 3 Commando Brigade, Royal Marines.

Few troops can boast skills as ubiquitous as the Royal Engineers. Whether building a defence or destroying it, laying a minefield or clearing it, they have a reputation for displaying the highest technical merit whilst constantly remaining first class front line soldiers.

The fully-amphibious CET is also in service with the Indian Army.

ROYAL MILITARY POLICE

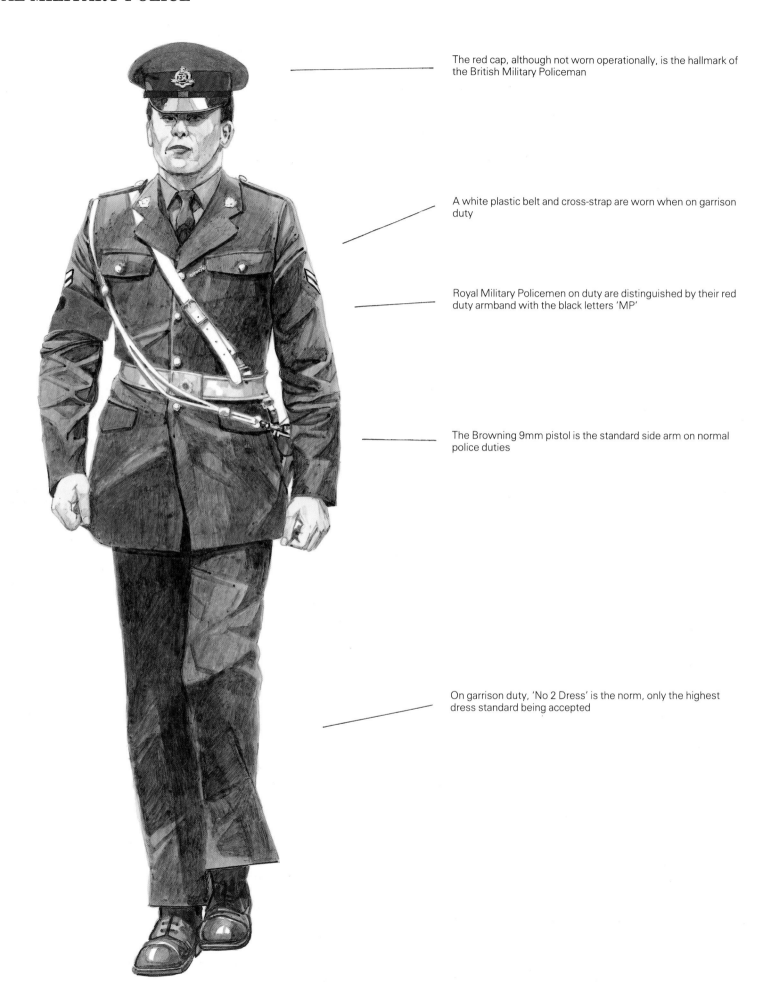

The red cap, although not worn operationally, is the hallmark of the British Military Policeman

A white plastic belt and cross-strap are worn when on garrison duty

Royal Military Policemen on duty are distinguished by their red duty armband with the black letters 'MP'

The Browning 9mm pistol is the standard side arm on normal police duties

On garrison duty, 'No 2 Dress' is the norm, only the highest dress standard being accepted

The Royal Military Police are a constituent part of the Provost Services and one of the best known Corps in the British Army. In practical terms, the RMP undertake totally different roles in peace and wartime. In time of peace, the Military Policeman (or Policewoman) performs a wide spectrum of duties similar to any civil police or law enforcement agency. These may vary from traffic control to the upholding of the law and military discipline within barracks, or, thankfully rarely these days, the rendering of assistance to the civil authorities in containing trouble among off-duty personnel. In time of war the MPs remove their distinctive red berets and service dress caps, don anonymous navy blue berets, and take responsibility for traffic control, reconnaissance, refugees and the rounding up of stragglers. The physical guarding of headquarters complexes is delegated to the Royal Pioneer Corps and not, as might be expected, to the Military Police.

Until 1955, officers were seconded for a tour of duty with the Royal Military Police, returning thereafter to their parent regiments. Since then, direct entry has been permitted to the extent that there are now 149 full-time officers serving in the Corps. Upon commissioning, young officers are seconded to the infantry for one year to gain a thorough grounding in basic soldiering before taking up a formal appointment in the Corps. Promotion is steady although competitive, with plenty of potential for high achievers to attain the rank of lieutenant colonel in their early 40s.

The men of the Royal Military Police are formed into two main branches. As soon as the young soldiers finish their basic training they are promoted to the rank of lance corporal (there are no qualified private soldiers in the RMP) and attached to the General Police Duties Branch (GPD). Here they practise the general concepts of policing together with military law, signals, first aid and photography. Driving (both vehicles and motor cycles) and the use of the 9mm pistol and sub-machine-gun are also taught.

Once trained, the soldiers of the GPD branch are then assigned to a Provost Company. One Company is attached to each of the three Divisions based permanently in West Germany, four to the rear area, where responsibility is taken for movement and security, and seven are stationed in the United Kingdom. The basis of the Company is the platoon, with its small headquarters section commanded by an experienced Staff-Sergeant and two field sections each consisting of a sergeant and four corporals. The number of platoons per Company varies greatly, depending on local needs. The Provost Company is kept extremely busy on a day-to-day basis. As well as its policing duties, it spends a considerable time training for its wartime role, playing an important part in all the major exercises.

Members of the General Police Duties Branch may apply to join the Special Investigation Branch, or SIB, which forms the other, but much smaller, main branch of the Corps. Once trained, a suitable candidate will be posted to a small detachment and may well find himself responsible for the administration of a huge area. The primary responsibility of the SIB is the prevention, investigation and detection of all serious crimes committed by, or against, the military, its property or interests. It is thus comparable to any detective agency attached to the civil police. More unusually, it acts as the coroner's office for the Army, dealing with all cases of sudden death. It deals with smuggling and drugs abuse, blackmail and breaches of security, in which instance it liaises closely with the local national security agencies.

A small team of RMP officers and senior NCOs is detached for close protection duty. Close Protection Teams are stationed around the world, guarding ambassadors, senior army officers and visiting politicians and have gained universal respect for the unobtrusive but firm way in which they have dealt with many incidents, invariably defusing them before serious diplomatic harm could be done.

A small mounted troop is based at Aldershot and undertakes ceremonial duties such as the Royal Tournament, the Edinburgh Tattoo and Trooping the Colour. Tours of duty are for three years and entry is extremely competitive.

All members of the Royal Military Police must meet stringent height, weight and fitness standards and must have a clean criminal record. Once trained, the military Policeman is segregated from the rest of the Army, even messing separately in the case of junior NCOs. On duty the distinctive red-topped service dress cap or beret is worn, together with a red armband, whistle and chain. If armed, the pistol will be holstered in a white belt with cross-strap.

The Royal Military Police provide the British element manning the infamous 'Checkpoint Charlie' crossing point between East and West Berlin.

THE TERRITORIAL ARMY VOLUNTEERS

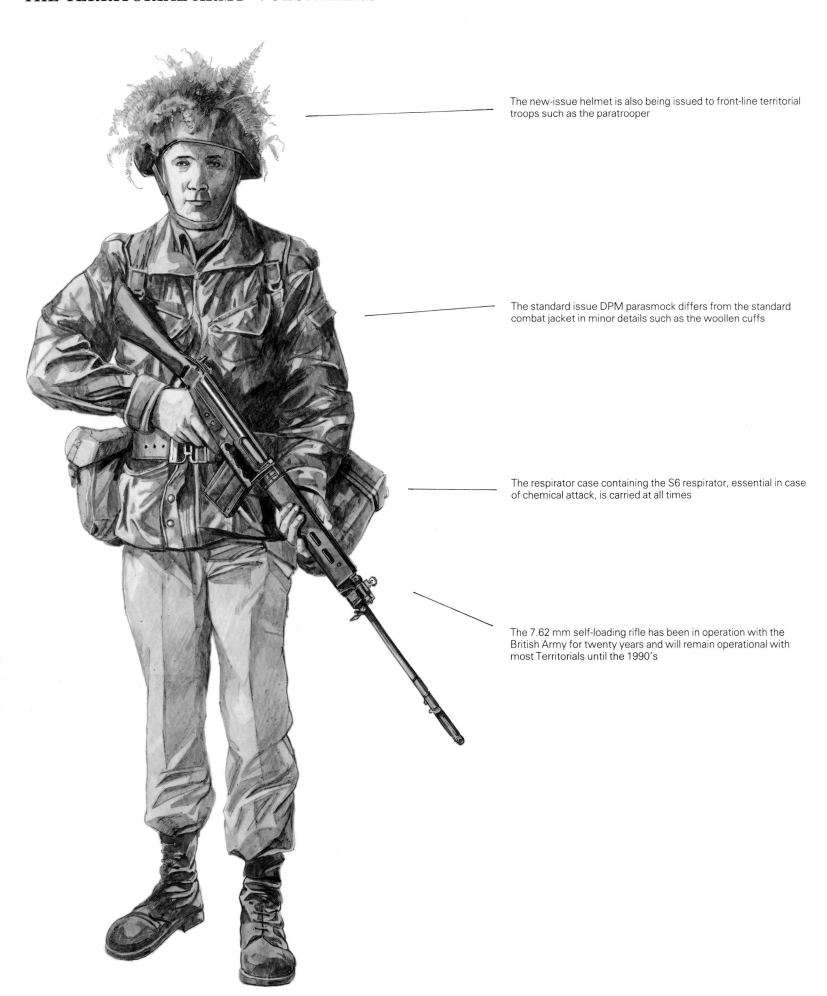

The new-issue helmet is also being issued to front-line territorial troops such as the paratrooper

The standard issue DPM parasmock differs from the standard combat jacket in minor details such as the woollen cuffs

The respirator case containing the S6 respirator, essential in case of chemical attack, is carried at all times

The 7.62 mm self-loading rifle has been in operation with the British Army for twenty years and will remain operational with most Territorials until the 1990's

The Territorial Army has a long tradition stretching back to the trained bands of the Middle Ages. Many Units are the direct descendants of Yeomanry regiments formed in the early nineteenth century to counter the threat of invasion from Napoleonic France whilst others, notably the Honourable Artillery Company (at full battalion strength despite its name) and the Royal Monmouthshire Royal Engineers, are far older.

The modern Territorial Army dates back to its restructuring along regular army lines in 1906. The new TA was not universally popular with the chiefs of staff at the time and did not form part of the British Expeditionary Force sent to France at the outbreak of war in 1914. It did, however, take part in the Battle of Loos in 1915 and in every major engagement thereafter.

TA units served throughout World War II, showing particular gallantry in the Middle and Far East. In the opinion of many, the post-war TA lost its direction somewhat, becoming more of a social organization than a military reserve. A second major restructuring was undertaken in the early 1960s, in which many units were scrapped and others streamlined. Although the reforms were undoubtedly unpopular at the time, there can be no doubt that without them the present day Territorial Army would not have attained the very high standards that it has.

The very cost-effectiveness of the TA (it provides one-third of all Army personnel yet accounts for only 3 per cent of the annual defence budget) makes it extremely popular with the Government, who are presently expanding it. Six new infantry battalions are in the process of being formed and it is estimated that by 1990 the entire force will be 86,000 strong.

The main strength of the modern TA lies within its infantry battalions, presently expanding in number from 38 to 44. In addition there are a total of 17 fighting units ranging from Gunner and Engineer formations to two Yeomanry Armoured Reconnaissance Regiments equipped with Fox armoured cars. There are even three battalions of the Parachute Regiment and two regiments of SAS.

Over 50 per cent of the above units have been assigned a wartime role with 1 (British) Corps in West Germany and regularly take part in NATO exercises alongside their regular army counterparts. With the exception of their small headquarters elements, two brigades of 2 (Infantry) Division, based in York but committed to Germany, are comprised exclusively of Territorials.

Despite attempts at introducing a 'one army' concept, TA equipment is invariably of a lower standard than that on issue to the regular forces. Due to difficulties inherent in driver training and maintenance, great emphasis is placed on wheeled rather than tracked personnel carriers, which will leave units very vulnerable in an action against a well-equipped and mechanized enemy.

In addition to its main fighting elements, the TA can provide nearly 250 minor units, a number of which are comprised of civilian specialists who are happy to offer their professional skills to the armed forces on a limited basis.

Territorial soldiers are drawn from all walks of life. Every soldier enlists for a limited period of three years, although many extend their services thereafter. Attendance is purely voluntary, although members who undertake a 15-day camp and attend a number of training evenings and weekends are entitled to a tax-free annual bounty. Pay and allowances, based on regular army rates, are good, but even so it is considered that the vast majority of territorials train for the fun and commitment and not for the money. Potential officers join their chosen units initially as private soldiers, after which they attend a District Selection Board. If successful, they attend a series of gruelling weekends culminating in a fortnight at Sandhurst, at the end of which they are awarded their commission.

Most Territorial Army units are attached to a parent regiment of the regular army and as such wear its uniform and cap badge. Others retain their own unique badges, some of which are centuries old in design. It is difficult to differentiate between regular and territorial soldiers in the field as each wears the same disruptive pattern uniform and carries the same webbing.

Despite its lack of heavy equipment, there can be no doubt that the Territorial Army will continue to play a crucial part in the organization of the British Army for decades to come.

Physical fitness is an important aspect of TA training. These soldiers are taking part in a military skills competition contested between TA units in Northern Ireland.

THE ULSTER DEFENCE REGIMENT

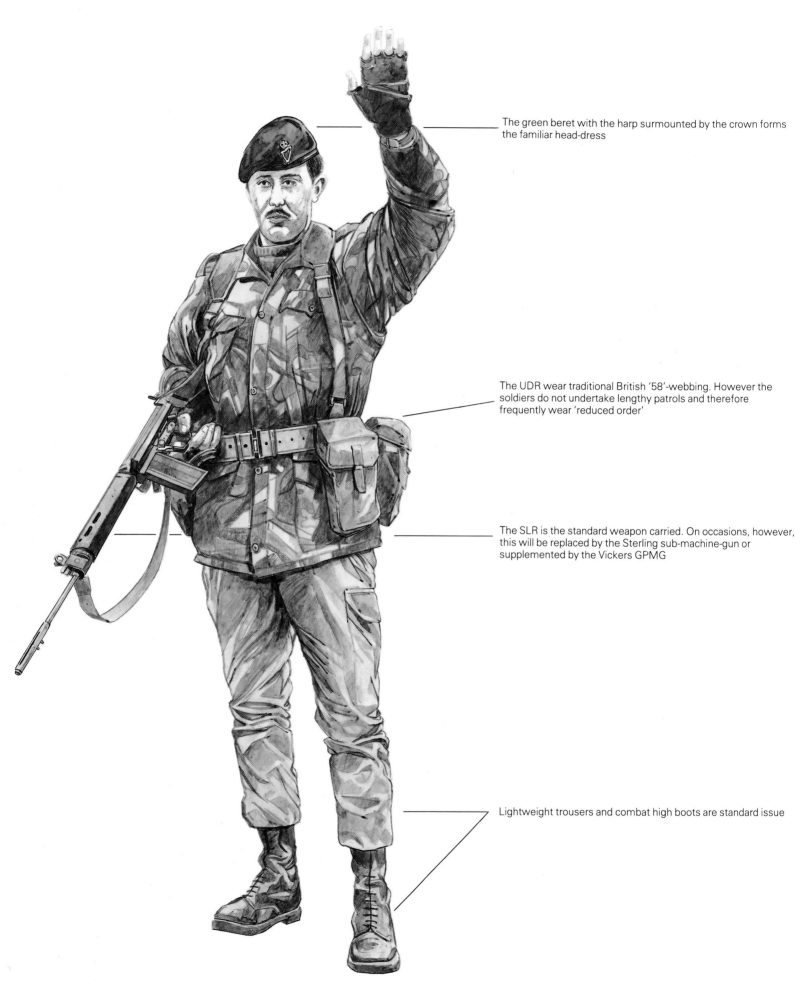

The green beret with the harp surmounted by the crown forms the familiar head-dress

The UDR wear traditional British '58'-webbing. However the soldiers do not undertake lengthy patrols and therefore frequently wear 'reduced order'

The SLR is the standard weapon carried. On occasions, however, this will be replaced by the Sterling sub-machine-gun or supplemented by the Vickers GPMG

Lightweight trousers and combat high boots are standard issue

An Ulster Defence Regiment Patrol prepares to move out from their barracks. Sniffer dogs are used for locating hidden weapons and explosives.

The Ulster Defence Regiment is unique for many reasons. It is the largest, youngest and only part-time Regiment of the British Army. Formed on 1st April 1970 to replace the politically discredited reserve police force known as the 'B' Specials, its only role is the maintenance of security in Northern Ireland.

Strenuous and genuine attempts were made in the early days to recruit across sectarian lines, but unfortunately a large part of the Roman Catholic minority is still suspicious of the Regiment with the result that few have joined. To compound the problem, a large number of Catholics who did join were ostracised by their own communities and in some instances physically threatened, to the degree that many subsequently felt it necessary to resign.

Each of the nine battalions of the Ulster Defence Regiment is administered by one of the regular army divisions based in mainland Britain. The Prince of Wales Division, for instance, would furnish its 'adopted' UDR battalion with administrative support, providing it with a regular training cadre drawn from the nine regular infantry battalions under its command. It would also supply the commanding officer.

Initially the UDR was envisaged as a virtually complete part-time organization in which the volunteer would give up the occasional evening and weekend. However, due to the high level of unemployment in the Province and to the increasing responsibilities undertaken by the Regiment, its full-time nucleus has grown increasingly during the last few years to 6,600 of the total membership of 10,300. A number of full-time members of the UDR have served in the Armed Forces, in many instances for the full term of 22 years, and have brought with them a wealth of experience which would otherwise have been lost.

Women play a crucial and, once again, unique part in the life of the Regiment. The 1,000 women serving are recruited direct and are not an attachment from the Women's Royal Army Corps (WRAC). The 'Greenfinches', to use their nickname derived from their call-sign, wear the same uniform and cap badge as the men. Although never armed, they man checkpoints and share the dangers equally with the men. Tragically, several have been killed in terrorist incidents but, if anything, this serves to have heightened their resolve and there is never a lack of female volunteers for any duty.

The UDR undertakes all routine anti-terrorist duties, particularly in rural locations where its members have the distinct advantage of intimate local knowledge, not just of the terrain but also of local troublemakers. Unapproved border crossing points are watched and random vehicle checkpoints manned in an effort to frustrate terrorist traffic.

Although potential recruits are carefully screened in an attempt to keep out political extremists, mistakes have been made and weapons passed to Protestant extremist groups, although fortunately incidences of this kind are very rare.

Once accepted by the UDR, the recruit is given a one-week basic training course before assuming Company duty. Further training takes place with the Company, including an annual 15-day camp on the mainland for the part-timer. The uniform and equipment issued to the UDR is similar to that in service with British-based infantry battalions. The individual soldier carries the SLR rifle or Sterling sub-machine-gun. Vickers GPMGs or Light Machine Guns, derived from the wartime Bren gun, are held and issued to patrols where necessary.

A member of the UDR with a 7.62mm LMG (Light Machine-Gun). The LMG is a development of the Bren gun.

RAF REGIMENT

No. 2 Squadron RAF Regiment is fully parachute-trained. Based at RAF Hullavingdon, it nevertheless deploys regularly on 'out of area' operations

This man wears standard parachuting clothing and equipment: a parachute helmet and smock, main static line PX 4 parachute [on his back] and a reserve parachute across his chest

A containerised Bergen rucksack as worn for parachuting, secured by clips to the parachute harness. The Bergen is lowered on a 15- ft rope during the descent in order to reduce speed on impact. The man's individual weapon is carried strapped to the Bergen in such a way that it lands above the container.

As with most members of the British airborne fraternity, 2 Sqn troops wear lightweight trousers. Boots are standard high combats - issued, not preferred

The RAF Regiment exists specifically to defend Royal Air Force bases and installations from ground and air attack. After completion of their formal training at the Regimental Depot at RAF Catterick, which all officers and men undertake immediately after initial Service training, most will be posted either to one of the nine Short Range Air Defence (SHORAD) Squadrons, equipped with the latest Rapier surface-to-air missile, or to one of the five Light Armoured Squadrons equipped with modern Scorpion AFVs and Spartan APCs.

Although the RAF Regiment does not have a Regimental Headquarters, it has its own Command Headquarters and Directorate in the Ministry of Defence.

As a Corps within the RAF, the Regiment adopts the same rank structure, chain of command and uniform regulations as its parent organization although its members wear standard issue combat suits, boots and protective clothing when in the field. When not wearing their distinctive dark blue berets it is therefore very difficult to differentiate them from the various Army units whom they closely support. The airmen are, however, extremely proud of their uniqueness and intensely dislike being referred to as soldiers.

The RAF Regiment is administered by the RAF Personnel Management Centre and forms part of Strike Command, Support Command or Headquarters RAF Germany dependent upon peacetime locations.

Four of the SHORAD Squadrons are stationed permanently in Germany, providing air defence for the major airfields of Bruggen, Laarbruch, Wildenrath and Gutersloh. Each has an Engineer Flight with attached mobile workshops and is capable of deploying up to eight self-contained Rapier fire units. Maintained on the airbase in time of peace, the fire units and their Blindfire Radars would be towed behind 1-tonne Land Rovers to pre-selected launch sites some kilometres from the airstrip in an emergency. Once deployed, they would engage enemy bombers and fighter ground attack aircraft before the latter had the opportunity to release their stand-off missiles. SHORAD units would be targets for Spetsnaz teams and as such must be able to defend themselves. Considerable time is dedicated to fieldcraft and weapon handling, with most exercises incorporating a lengthy element of NBC training, necessitating the wearing of protective suits, cumbersome rubber gloves and respirators. Above all, every airman must be skilled in aircraft recognition.

Only the Light Armoured Squadron is based permanently in Germany, at RAF Laarbruch. RAF Germany would however be reinforced by four squadrons from the United Kingdom and one from Cyprus in an emergency. Each squadron consists of a small headquarters with a Sultan command vehicle and Samson armoured recovery vehicle, and three combat flights of five Spartan APCs with up to six riflemen in each. There is also a support flight consisting of six Scorpion light tanks armed with the 76mm gun and co-axially mounted 7.62mm machine-gun. Squad-

rons are trained to operate for periods of up to 14 days without support and would deny the enemy access to areas immediately adjacent to the airfield. Although the two types of squadron operate independently and are not interchangeable, personnel are often posted from one to the other and are therefore trained to operate the equipment of both.

The Queen's Colour Squadron of the RAF Regiment is seen regularly on ceremonial occasions escorting the Queen's Colour of the Royal Air Force. It takes part most years in the Royal Tournament, where it never fails to thrill the audience with its breathtaking display of precision drill. The Squadron provides guards of honour for visiting heads of state and regularly provides the guard at Buckingham Palace. Although many of its members volunteer, others are posted for a period of two years during which they will attain standards of turnout and drill second to none.

As if to emphasize its military prowess, the RAF Regiment has provided several Squadrons for internal security duties in Northern Ireland since the outbreak of the present unrest in 1969.

RAF Regiment units in Germany are usually among the first to receive new equipment. This Regiment sergeant takes careful aim with the latest British anti-tank weapon – LAW 80.

FALLSCHIRMJÄGER, WEST GERMANY

The distinctive red beret with a cap badge showing a diving eagle is worn by all airborne soldiers

At present, the standard field-grey [feldgrau] uniform is issued. A new camouflage uniform will soon take its place

A modified helmet with special parachuting chinstrap and camouflage cover is carried

High cross-laced jump-boots are the norm

West Germany's 'Fallschirmjäger', as their paratroopers are known, are among the most highly trained of all NATO's airborne forces. Unlike the British paras or the US Army's airborne troopers, the majority of today's Fallschirmjäger are conscripts. However, like their NATO counterparts, they too volunteer to become airborne soldiers and are a vital element in NATO's strategic reserve.

Germany was one of the first countries to recognize the usefulness of airborne troops in modern warfare and was the first country to successfully employ paratroops in combat. In the early stages of World War Two the Fallschirmjäger, then part of the Luftwaffe, played an important part in the initial German offensives, including the invasions of Czechoslovakia, Poland, Denmark, Norway and the Low Countries. It was not until the invasion of Crete in 1941 that the use of German airborne forces was restricted. Although the massive airborne invasion was successful, the casualties sustained by the Fallschirmjäger (over 4,000 men) were so heavy that they spent the remainder of the war employed as conventional ground forces. In spite of this, the Fallschirmjäger continued with their exceptionally high standard of training which enabled them to conduct a number of extremely well-fought battles towards the latter stages of World War Two.

Today the Bundeswehr, West Germany's armed forces, contain three Luftlandebrigade – as the Fallschirmjäger brigades are known. These airborne brigades are part of the 1st Airborne Division and one brigade is attached to each of the three West German Army Corps spread across NATO's Central European Region. Each Corps has its own area of responsibility and the Luftlande Brigades act as their respective Corps' rapid deployment airmobile reserve. Each brigade has a headquarters and three Fallschirmjäger battalions, each consisting of two airborne infantry companies and two airmobile anti-tank companies. Both types of company can be deployed by aeroplane or helicopter and are particularly suited to anti-armour warfare.

The Fallschirmpanzerabwehr (airborne anti-tank) companies are equipped with vehicle-mounted TOW anti-armour missiles and 20mm guns. Capable of being flown into an area of operations by CH-53 transport helicopters, these weapon systems give the Army Corps a highly mobile and effective defence against enemy armoured thrusts. Over recent years new tactics have been developed in this area of airmobile anti-armour warfare and the Fallschirmjäger are highly trained for this demanding type of combat.

Training within the Bundeswehr is of a particularly high standard and this is especially true of the Fallschirmjäger. Volunteers for airborne training must pass a series of physical and psychological tests prior to joining one of the brigades for basic training. While with the brigade, the men are taught the rudiments of soldiering – fieldcraft, weapons handling and other basic military skills – before being sent to the Parachute Training School at Altenstadt. During the intensive four-week course which teaches basic

static-line parachuting, the recruits must complete a minimum of five jumps to qualify for their parachute wings. These descents include one night jump and one with full equipment.

On successful completion of the static-line parachute course, the newly-qualified Fallschirmjäger return to their parent battalion to continue their training. Most conscripts join either an airborne infantry company or an airmobile anti-armour company, and spend the remainder of their eighteen months national service learning the more advanced skills required for their role.

Conscripts serving with the Fallschirmjäger are among the best paid in the Bundeswehr, their additional parachute pay effectively doubling their monthly income. This is not the only incentive to volunteer however, for as with other airborne formations throughout the world the Fallschirmjäger have a particularly high 'ésprit de corps'. The traditional red beret with a diving eagle cap badge is worn by all West German airborne soldiers and serves to distinguish them from other types of infantrymen. Other identifying features include jump boots and a modified version of the standard helmet, with a special chin strap for parachuting. These helmets are usually worn with a camouflage cloth covering made from an old issue poncho, whereas most units use a simple netting cover. At present all units in the Bundeswehr wear a standard field grey (feldgrau) combat uniform, although a new camouflaged version is being currently tested. It is likely that when the new combat clothing is eventually issued, the Fallschirmjäger will be among the first to receive it.

This ultra-light transporter, made by Faun, is unique to the German Airborne Forces.

GRENZSCHUTZGRUPPE 9

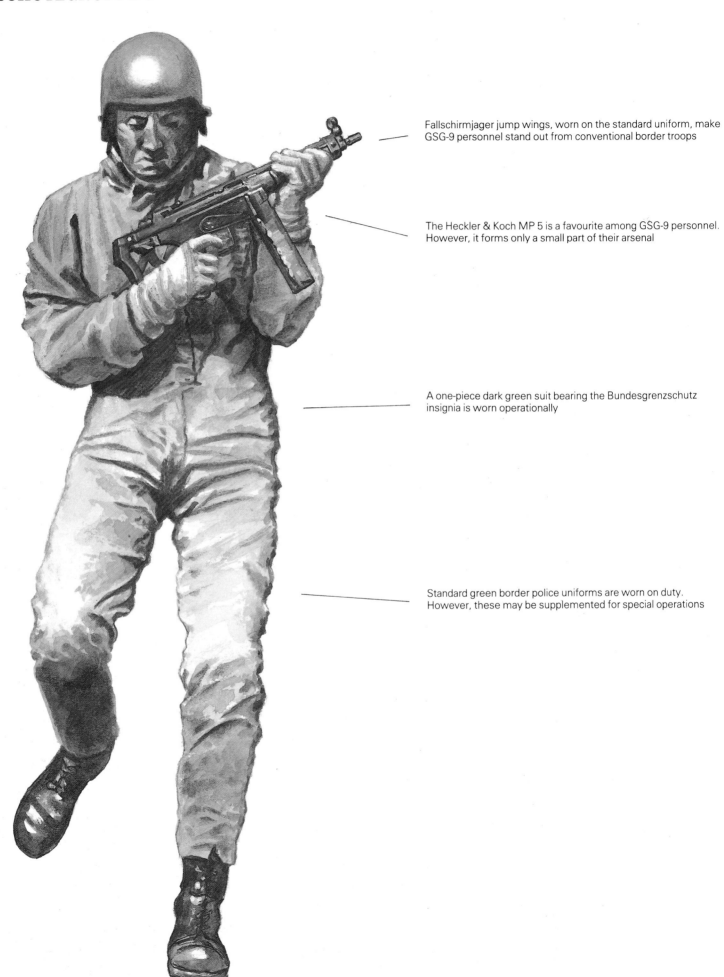

Fallschirmjager jump wings, worn on the standard uniform, make GSG-9 personnel stand out from conventional border troops

The Heckler & Koch MP 5 is a favourite among GSG-9 personnel. However, it forms only a small part of their arsenal

A one-piece dark green suit bearing the Bundesgrenzschutz insignia is worn operationally

Standard green border police uniforms are worn on duty. However, these may be supplemented for special operations

The Grenzschutzgruppe 9 (GSG 9) is a highly trained West German counter-terrorist unit. Formed after the massacre of Israeli athletes by Palestinian terrorists at the Munich Olympics in 1972, GSG 9 is a specialist group within the Bundesgrenzshutz – the West German Border Police. The term 'Grenzschutzgruppe' can be translated as 'border marksman group' but this is a misnomer as GSG 9 is far more than a unit of sharpshooters.

After the massacre at Munich the West German government realized the need for a small, specialized counter-terrorist unit capable of responding rapidly to similar hostage situations. Such a unit would be directly responsible to the Ministry of the Interior and so the Border Police, itself a para-military force, was chosen as the most promising organization to provide the necessary personnel and experience required to establish the new group.

Volunteers must first have served with the Border Police before applying to join GSG 9. If their application is accepted they must pass a series of physical and psychological tests before being accepted for the intensive 22-week training programme. The first 13 weeks of their training are designed to test the individual's basic and advanced police skills as well as teaching unarmed combat, marksmanship and weapons handling. Much emphasis is placed on physical fitness and general aptitude. If considered suitable, the volunteers go on to the second phase of the course in which they study all aspects of terrorism and counter-terrorist operations in great detail. Much time is spent learning about the various international terrorist organizations, their history and the tactics they employ. In addition to their studies the volunteers must also continue with their physical training, much of which takes place in specific scenarios. During these training exercises the volunteers must employ the specialist counter-terrorist techniques they have learned on a variety of targets such as cars, trains, aircraft, ships and buildings. The volunteers are closely monitored throughout their training and instruction. Each man is individually assessed by the experts running the course and only those who achieve a consistently high standard are selected for further training. The average pass rate for the 22-week course is around 20 per cent.

On passing the selection and training programme, the volunteers become provisional members of one of the four GSG 9 assault squads. Training is continuous with new skills, such as the use of electronic 'eavesdropping' equipment or vehicle anti-ambush drills, being taught as time allows. While undergoing their further training the 'provisionals' also take part in the operational standby duty of their assault squads. At any one time there is an assault squad on standby to deal with any terrorist threat either within the Federal German Republic or outside.

One of the GSG 9's successes took place in October 1977 when a Lufthansa Boeing 737 was hijacked while on a flight from Palma in the Mediterranean to West Germany. After a number of unscheduled stops, the aircraft finally ended up at Mogadishu. It was here that the plane was assaulted by a GSG 9 team who, with the help of an officer and a sergeant from Britain's SAS Regiment, successfully released the hostages unharmed after killing three of the four terrorists.

GSG 9 maintain close links with other counter-terrorist groups throughout the world. Intelligence is exchanged and a number of courses are attended by overseas groups. Advice about equipment and tactics is also exchanged and it is generally agreed within the counter-terrorist community that GSG 9 has some of the best equipment available. In fact one of GSG 9's standard personal weapons, the Heckler and Koch MP 5 machinepistol was used by members of the SAS during the Iranian Embassy siege in London and is currently being used by the police security teams at Heathrow airport. GSG 9 officers usually wear standard Border Police uniforms when on duty. These are of a dark green material with Bundesgrenzschutz insignia. It is only that most of the men wear Fallschirmjäger jump wings that makes them look any different from the average Border Policeman.

Training is rigorous and all-embracing. Of those who volunteer for GSG-9, only twenty percent are accepted.

The conventional green border police uniforms may be modified to suit particular circumstances. The Heckler & Koch MP5 seen here is a favourite weapon.

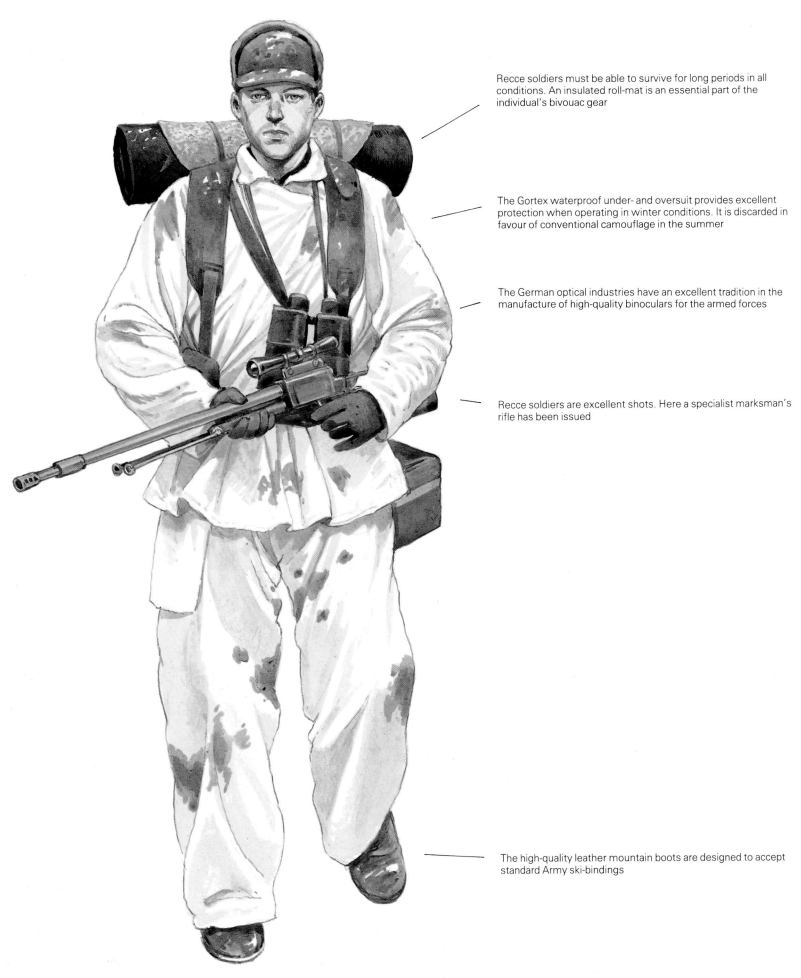

Recce soldiers must be able to survive for long periods in all conditions. An insulated roll-mat is an essential part of the individual's bivouac gear

The Gortex waterproof under- and oversuit provides excellent protection when operating in winter conditions. It is discarded in favour of conventional camouflage in the summer

The German optical industries have an excellent tradition in the manufacture of high-quality binoculars for the armed forces

Recce soldiers are excellent shots. Here a specialist marksman's rifle has been issued

The high-quality leather mountain boots are designed to accept standard Army ski-bindings

All Long Range Reconnaissance Patrol troops must be at the peak of physical fitness. Much of the selection and training is carried out internally, although members will regularly attend courses at the world-renowned LRPS School in Weingarten.

No German will ever forget the atrocities committed by the Soviet invaders in 1945 and therefore will never willingly allow a foreign invader on German soil again. Whereas certain of her NATO allies advocate the virtual surrender of the border strip in favour of the creation of strong defensive positions in more strategically convenient areas 15 or 20 kilometres to the West, the Bonn Government is adamant that every centimetre of national soil shall be defended to the hilt.

The execution of so forward a concept of defence requires timely and complete intelligence, covering not only the exact position of front line hostile troops but also detailed information of the whereabouts and strength of the reserves who will ultimately be responsible for exploiting any breakthrough.

Although satellites and pilot in-flight reports are able to give an overall perspective of the enemy in depth, and remotely-piloted drones and sound locating equipment provide a more detailed analysis of his activities immediately behind the front line, both concepts leave a void in the Corps Commander's knowledge which can only effectively be overcome by men on the ground.

In conjunction with the majority of NATO countries, the Federal German Republic operates Long Range Reconnaissance Patrol Troops (LRRPs), or Fernspähetruppen, trained to operate for long periods behind enemy lines. All LRRPs must be at the peak of physical fitness, totally self-assured and have an intimate understanding of the countryside which may on occasions supply them with their only sustenance. All will be parachute trained and most will be drawn from airborne or alpine divisions.

The Bundeswehr operates three LRRP companies, one each of which is attached to 1(Ge) Corps at Munster, 2(Ge) Corps at Ulm and 3(Ge) Corps at Koblenz. Administratively each company (Fernspähekompanie) is organized along traditional Federal German lines with a company headquarters providing logistics, supply, intelligence, transport and communications but in other respects it is unique. LRRP companies have two operational platoons, each approximately 30 strong.

Much of the selection and training is carried out within the company although specialist areas are catered for at the International Long Range Reconnaissance Patrol School at Weingarten, Southern Germany. Long distance marches, often with heavy loads, play an important part in basic training as does covert observation, escape and evasion. It is not the role of LRRPs to engage the enemy in hostile activity but nevertheless a high degree of unarmed combat is taught to enable the soldier to extricate himself from a dangerous situation if need be. Personal camouflage, navigational ability, enemy tactics and, above all, equipment recognition are taught. All reports are made by long-range radio, possibly with Morse burst-transmission, and it is essential therefore that every member of a patrol has first-rate communications skills.

Full details of LRRPs' methods of entry behind enemy lines are necessarily secret but may be presumed to include parachuting, either static or free-fall, possibly with an element of HALO (High Altitude, Low Opening), air transport at low level, delivery by armoured personnel carrier driven by specially trained troops or by the utilization of stay-behind parties who would remain in hides as their own forces withdrew, allowing the enemy front line to roll over them before emerging.

Members of the Fernspähetruppen wear clothing suitable for the environment, which will vary drastically according to the area and time of year. Where appropriate, full snow suits are favoured, worn in conjunction with thick alpine gloves, cap and boots. As the role of LRRPs is non-offensive, only standard West German small arms are carried. Kit and equipment are carried in a large Bergen, although life-saving essentials are normally carried in an 'escape belt', which the soldier carries at all times in case he is forced to abandon his Bergen in an emergency.

Troops are taught to keep their equipment dry and in good order, even when crossing rivers. The ability to swim is a prerequisite to selection.

WEST GERMAN MOUNTAIN TROOPER

The Gebirgsjager are the best-equipped mountain troops in NATO. Every man is issued with Gortex waterproof under- and oversuits.

Winter camouflage consists of a two-piece snow suit manufactured in white with green splashes

Belt equipment is standard throughout the West German Army, although the mountain troops use special mountain rucksacks

Gortex gaiters with zip-fronts are standard issue. Boots are specially designed for both winter and mountain warfare

The Gebirgsjäger, as West Germany's mountain troops are known, are a special breed of soldier. Operating in the high alpine regions of Bavaria in Southern Germany, the Gebirgsjäger are capable of conducting a guerrilla-type war in some of the most inhospitable terrain in Western Europe.

Formed during the First World War, the Gebirgsjäger went on to earn repute as tough fighting soldiers during the Second World War, where they fought with distinction in several campaigns, seeing action in the Balkans, Norway and Crete. During the invasion of Poland, the 1st, 2nd and 3rd Mountain Divisions which had deployed in the south of the country, moved forward in three separate columns and succeeded in outflanking the Polish defences.

Later, in Norway, the 2nd and 3rd Mountain Divisions linked up to fight their way to Narvik, seeing action at Trofors, Eisford and Rognan. In 1941 the newly-formed 5th and 6th Divisions deployed to the Balkans where they helped to open up the route into Greece. The 5th Mountain Division went on to further distinguish itself during the airborne invasion of Crete, where its ability to operate in mountainous terrain made it invaluable. The 1st and 4th Divisions were heavily involved in the drive into the Caucasus before being trapped on the Kuban peninsula after the German disaster at Stalingrad in 1942. The 3rd Mountain Division fought throughout the long withdrawal from the Soviet Union after the Battle of Kursk in 1943, while the 1st and 4th Divisions took up defensive positions in the area of Odessa.

History and tradition are important to the Gebirgsjäger. Unlike most West German army formations, with the exception of the Airborne units, the Gebirgsjäger have maintained strong links with their historic forebears. This fact, coupled with local recruitment, has allowed these mountain troops certain independence, as the resulting 'esprit de corps' of today's 23rd Gebirgsjäger Brigade testifies.

The 23rd Gebirgsjäger Brigade is part of the 1st Mountain Division and is the sole remaining specialist mountain formation with the West German Army. Based in Bad Reichenhall, five kilometres from the German/Austrian border, the Mountain Brigade consists of four battalions (231, 232, 233 and 234). These battalions are located between Bad Reichenhall in the east and Garmisch-Partenkirchen in the west. Between these two major towns are the highest peaks in Germany, and this area is the home ground of the Gebirgsjäger.

Although equipped with the latest in modern weaponry, Germany's mountain troops nevertheless use the traditional method of transport, as did their World War Two predecessors – the feet being the primary means of getting around the mountains. During the summer months, the Gebirgsjäger still use pack mules to move some of the heavier equipment and the Division has a total of 54 animals. In winter, movement is conducted either by skis and sledges or, weather permitting, by helicopter.

In order to cope with the climatic extremes and terrain, the Gebirgsjäger have one of the broadest training spectrums within the West German Army. The training is tough but, in spite of this, a high proportion of the conscripts (who make up around 60 per cent of the total strength) actually volunteer to serve with the Gebirgsjäger. Units are located in areas having the highest number of days with snow and around 45 per cent of their annual training is carried out in the mountains.

The Gebirgsjäger are well-equipped and highly-trained to carry out their assigned task. Their skis, made by Atomic, are the best available and far superior to those issued to other NATO ski-troops. All the men have waterproof Goretex suits over which they wear a reversible camouflage snow suit. This two-piece uniform is white on one side for snow, and white with green splashes on the other side for operations near the tree line. Although a special camouflage suit for summer is presently being tested, the standard dress for working in warmer weather remains field grey knee-length breeches, thick socks and heavy black leather mountain boots. It is not difficult to tell the difference between a Gebirgsjäger and a standard infantryman. In addition, the mountain troops have managed to keep the traditional long peaked cap worn by their forebears. This is worn with all uniforms, including combat clothing (except when a steel helmet is worn), and the 'Edelweiss' emblem on the left side of the mountain cap has been retained. The edelweiss is a wild flower that has been the insignia of these mountain troops since 1915, and like the Gebirgsjäger, is to be found high in the Alps.

The Gebirgsjager provide NATO with excellently-trained mountain troops capable of operating in the most inhospitable of conditions. In summer, the pack-mule is still used for porterage, but in winter this is abandoned in favour of the traditional back-pack and skis.

WEST GERMAN PANZERGRENADIER

The green beret, with its Marder cap badge, distinguishes the panzergrenadier from the conventional infantryman

The 7.62mm MG3, based on the wartime MG 42, remains a popular and reliable support weapon

Ample ammunition can be carried in the belt pouches when fighting dismounted

The high-quality double leather Bundeswehr boots are highly prized by other NATO soldiers

Recent years have seen an increased need for highly trained mechanized infantry in modern warfare and West Germany's Panzer Grenadiers are just such troops.

Germany was the first country to develop the mechanized infantryman as we know him today. At the beginning of World War Two the German Army, Das Heer, had a total of 39 Infantry Divisions, including four mechanized divisions designated the 2nd, 13th, 20th and 29th. These divisions were among the spearhead of the German fighting machine and an important part of the 'Blitzkrieg' offensive philosophy. The Panzer Division was the hitting power of the German Army and at the beginning of the war there was a total of ten such divisions. Each Panzer Division initially consisted of two complete tank regiments (totalling some 400 tanks) plus a small infantry complement and service support elements. During the successful invasion of France in 1940, the Panzer units far outran the infantry units, to such an extent that the latter units were unable to keep in contact or support the Panzers. The situation was soon redressed so that by the end of 1940 the Panzer Divisions had been reorganized to include one tank regiment, two motorized infantry regiments plus stronger and more mobile artillery.

In addition to the motorized infantry with the Panzer Divisions, the order of battle included Panzer Grenadier Brigades. These specialized formations consisted of two mechanized infantry regiments, normally of two companies each. Soon after the fall of France, when the lack of mobility was realized, one company from each regiment was equipped with armoured half-track vehicles. In addition, these armoured mechanized infantry companies had a large allocation of heavy weapons. These included mounted 20mm anti-tank/AA guns and 75mm self-propelled close support weapons. Highly mobile and heavily armed, these mechanized infantry companies were the forerunners of the modern Panzer Grenadiers.

The current West German Army has a total of 64 armoured infantry battalions. These battalions are divided among the Army's Panzer and Panzer Grenadier brigades, each of which consists of four battalions. A Panzer Brigade consists of two tank battalions, one armoured infantry battalion, and one 'mixed' battalion of armoured infantry and tanks. The Panzer Grenadier Brigades are the reverse, being heavier in infantry than in tanks. They consist of two mechanized infantry battalions, one tank battalion and one 'mixed' battalion. Both types of brigade offer a valuable mix of armour and infantry, designed with modern highly-mobile warfare in mind.

The Panzer Grenadiers are equipped with the Marder 'schutzenpanzer' or armoured personnel carrier. This was the first purpose-built mechanized infantry combat vehicle in the world and entered service in the early 1970s. Unlike most armoured personnel carriers, the Marder was designed as a platform from which to fight as well as being an infantry vehicle – in short, the troops could fight either mounted or dismounted. Armed with a 20mm cannon with a coaxial 7.62mm

machine-gun, and a second 7.62mm machine-gun mounted to the rear of the vehicle, the Marder is a formidable weapon system in spite of its age. The recent addition of a Milan anti-tank missile system has improved its capabilities still further.

However, it is not just the weapons and equipment that make a fighting unit, but also the soldiers within it. The West German Army enjoys a high standard of training and the Panzer Grenadiers are no exception. Not only do they have to master the complicated weapon systems but they must also learn the tactics of their employment. Although they ride into battle and fight from their vehicles, they must also be capable of going into combat on foot. This is especially the case when fighting in an urban or wooded environment, areas in which the Panzer Grenadiers are particularly well suited.

Operating in platoons consisting of three vehicles, each with a crew of three plus a six-man fire team, the Grenadiers can fight dismounted in built-up or wooded areas while their colleagues provide fire-support from the Marders. This type of warfare is extremely arduous and a high standard of physical fitness is required. Although many of the Panzer Grenadiers are conscripts, they nevertheless take their role seriously, and there is a special camaraderie which comes from operating in small groups. Each man has his own individual skill such as driver, gunner, commander or fire team member, while at the same time being part of a team. Highly trained in mechanized warfare, the Panzer Grenadiers (distinguished from other infantrymen by their green berets with a Marder badge) play a vital role in West Germany's defensive operational concept in the framework of Forward Defence in the NATO Alliance.

Although Panzergrenadiers ride into battle, they must be capable of dismounting and fighting as conventional infantry. Here a section practises house-clearing, one of the most difficult aspects of urban warfare.

A young Panzergrenadier mounted in his Marder 'schutzenpanzer' pauses for thought before ordering his vehicle into action.

FEDERAL GERMAN NAVY DIVERS/COMBAT SWIMMERS

A wet suit is normally worn to insulate against the cold waters in which the divers often operate

In this instance the diver is unencumbered. In hostile waters he would carry a variety of other equipment

Powerful underwater surveillance equipment is issued to enable the diver to work in the murky waters of Baltic port and harbour installations

As standard with all divers, a substantial knife is always carried, largely for safety purposes

The coastal minesweeper/hunter *Weilheim* (M 1077). The mine divers normally operate from smaller craft, but for longer distance training they can operate from coastal 'Lindau' class vessels.

The West German coastline is as crucial as it is short, controlling as it does access to the industrial heartlands of Northern Europe. The 200,000 tons of shipping which pass through Federal German territorial limits every day would prove a tempting target to an enemy in time of war, particularly as the shallow coastal waters lend themselves ideally to mining.

The Mine Defence Force (MDF) is tasked with securing shipping lanes to German and neighbouring harbours and with ensuring the safety of the ships once docked. Formed immediately after the reconstruction of the Federal Armed Forces in 1955, the MDF now employs 2,500 officers and men and constitutes the biggest flotilla in the Federal German Navy.

The 60 mine divers who constitute the elite of the Squadron are based in the small Baltic town of Eckernfoerde, approximately 15 miles (24 km) North East of Kiel. The Mine Diving Company, to give it its formal title, is under the command of the Naval Mine Warfare Force and is divided into a headquarters, two operational platoons and a training platoon. Two mine diving boats, the 'Hansa' and 'Stier', with a complement of 40 men, are permanently attached.

Mine divers operate specifically in harbours, coastal waters and inland waterways too shallow or narrow for the deployment of conventional mine sweeping boats. Their task is to search for, locate and identify mines, to neutralize, dismantle and if possible salvage explosives, to police dock and harbour areas in case of sabotage, to carry out underwater demolitions and explosions and to search for missing ordnance. In peacetime they will also assist in underwater rescue, for which their exceptional skills are particularly useful.

Training is long and strenuous. Not only must all divers be extremely fit but also able to work for long periods alone in constant danger and under considerable pressure. An initial eight weeks basic course, in which all aspects of practical and theoretical diving are covered, is followed by four weeks predominantly physical training, ten weeks tactical and operational procedure, including practical diving in the Baltic ports, and an academic course covering matters as diverse as medical aid, ordnance and weapon training. The course culminates in fourteen days demolition training with the Navy Weapons School followed by a 60-metre (196.8 feet) dive.

Trained divers are expected to undertake further courses in boat handling, communications and ordnance dismantling. Some will even attend parachute and Ranger courses to extend their breadth of experience. Constant 'on the job' training is provided by the large numbers of World War II mines, torpedoes and bombs which are still being located.

Many foreign Explosive Ordnance Disposal (EOD) courses are attended to ensure that the divers are equipped with the most up-to-date knowledge together with the finest equipment possible to enable them to fulfil their hazardous task.

The Naval Combat Swimmer Company was formed officially in March 1964, although in practice it had existed since 1959. The present Company, consisting of three operational platoons, a training platoon and service support group, about 50 combat swimmers in all, is based at Eckernfoerde alongside the mine clearance divers. Trained to operate in hostile waters and behind enemy lines, the combat swimmer must be equally at home on land as in the water. Trained in harbour and coastal reconnaissance, intelligence acquisition, beach clearance and demolitions, combat swimmers may approach their target by underwater swimming, cross-country – perhaps after a trek of many miles with heavy equipment – or by parachute.

A Westland Sea King Mk 41 helicopter of the Federal German Navy. Naval divers can operate from both fixed-wing aircraft and helicopters.

FRANCE, PARATROOPER

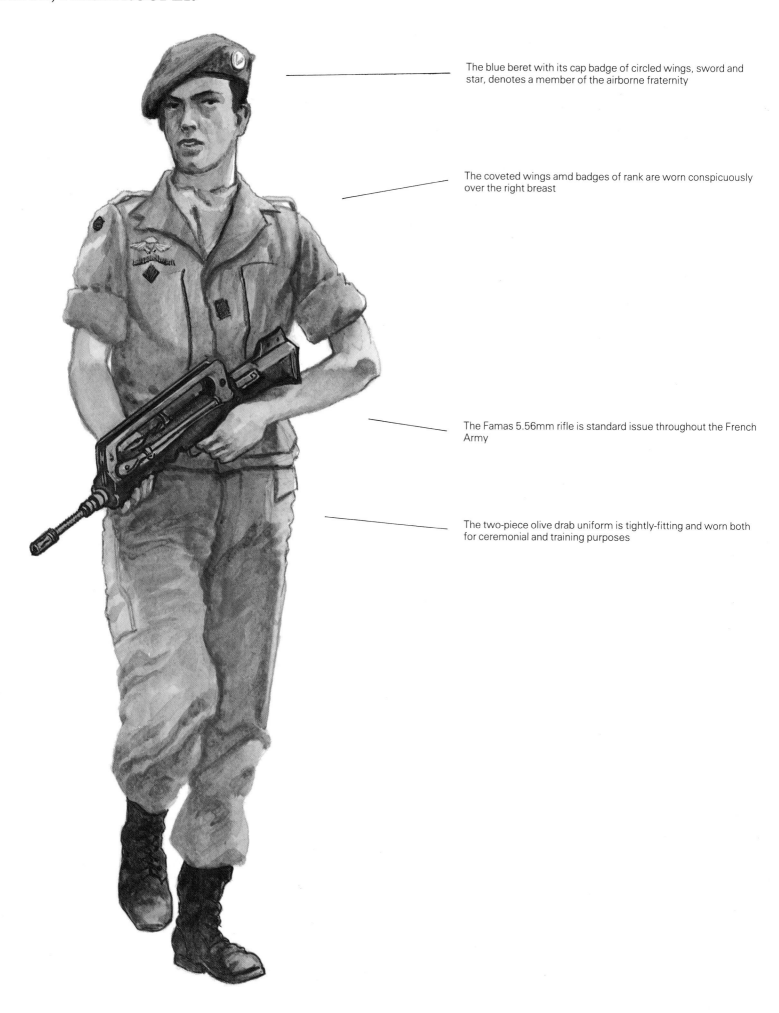

The blue beret with its cap badge of circled wings, sword and star, denotes a member of the airborne fraternity

The coveted wings amd badges of rank are worn conspicuously over the right breast

The Famas 5.56mm rifle is standard issue throughout the French Army

The two-piece olive drab uniform is tightly-fitting and worn both for ceremonial and training purposes

France has one of the largest airborne forces in the world, and over the last quarter century 'les paras', as the French paratroops are known, have earned themselves a reputation as tough fighters.

Prior to the Second World War, France's paratroopers were a part of the French Air Force. L'Armee de L'Air, and the Army's first airborne units were not formed until 1956. Since then, French paras have seen service in Egypt, Indo-China, Algeria and Central Africa.

France's present airborne division, the 11e Division Parachutiste (11e DP), was formed in 1971 from the 11e Division d'Intervention and the 20e & 25e Parachute Brigades. The new Division gave the French a complete airborne formation with its own command, transport and support facilities. Since 1971 the 11e Division Parachutiste has continued to evolve and has adopted the role of the advance force in France's out-of-area (OOA) operations, as part of the Force de l'Action Rapide (FAR) – France's equivalent to the US Rapid Deployment Force.

The 11e Division Parachutistes has two main missions, the first being OOA operations and the second to provide a strategic reserve force. The paras are well suited to this second role, being highly mobile and air transportable, and equipped to engage and destroy enemy armour. The Division consists of over 13,000 men, 570 wheeled vehicles, 36 armoured vehicles, 54 artillery pieces and 168 Milan anti-tank missile systems. These assets are divided between six airborne infantry regiments (not including 2e REP which comes under Divisional control), one light armoured cavalry regiment, one engineer regiment, one artillery regiment, and two command and supply regiments.

French paratroops include around 70 to 75 per cent conscripts undergoing their national military service. However, unlike most conscript soldiers, 'les paras' have volunteered to undertake a more hazardous and demanding role – that of the airborne soldier. There is little difference between airborne infantry and the various specializations such as light armour or artillery. All the men, regardless of whether they are conscripts or professional soldiers, undergo the same training and wear the same cap badge on their 'berets rouges' – their red berets.

In order to qualify for their parachute 'brevets', the French para wings, the volunteers must first pass through the intense training course at ETAP Pau, in southern France. Courses are run all the year round in all aspects of military parachuting, from basic static-line descents to advanced freefall and heavy drop (cargo resupply). The training is tough and the standards high. France's paras are some of the most qualified military parachutistes in the world and it is not unusual for a soldier to make up to eight parachute descents in a year.

All equipment used by the Division, with the exception of that directly relating to airborne operations, is similar to that used by the rest of the French armed forces. All officers and men in 11e DP wear the 'tenue de combat 1963', a two-piece olive drab combat uniform that is worn through-

out the French Army for both barrack and field dress. Like almost all combat uniforms, this is loose fitting. However, in the Parachute Division, as in the French Foreign Legion, it is traditionally tailored to be 'close' fitting. Standard French Army webbing is worn, which consists of a belt with two magazine pouches (each containing three 25-round magazines), a fighting knife/bayonet, and one or two canteens. The belt is supported by suspenders, the left of which usually has a first aid pouch attached. Other equipment is carried in a frameless rucksack.

When parachuting or in the field, French paratroopers wear the Mle 56 para version of the Army's Mle 51 helmet. This is usually worn with a green cloth cover, on the back of which are sub-unit identification signs, and rubber retaining band to secure local foliage for camouflage. The FAMAS 5.56mm rifle is the standard issue weapon for all troops with the exception of senior officers, and fills the roles of sub-machine-gun, rifle and section support weapon.

The French airborne soldier has traditionally gone into battle equipped with the minimum and this is still the case. Extra equipment, weapons and ammunition are carried in by jeep and light truck, with which 11e DP is adequately equipped. Everything the Parachute Division needs can be parachuted in by C-160 Transall transport aircraft, leaving the individual paratrooper unencumbered in order to carry out his immediate task.

Before emplaning, a rigorous pre-jump safety check is carried out by a senior NCO or instructor.

FRANCE, AIR COMMANDO

Whereas most armies rely on a variant of the standard helmet, French Paras and Air Commandos are supplied with a purpose-designed parachuting helmet

Unlike conventional paratroops, who wear their rank insignia on the chest, Air Commandos wear standard shoulder epaulettes

Equipment required by the paratrooper immediately upon landing is stowed conspicuously below the reserve 'chute

High quality leather paraboots feature a special shock-absorbing flat sole, developed specificallly for parachuting, and have proved a firm favourite with the wearers

The 'Fusiliers Commandos de l'Air', France's Air Commandos, are responsible for the security of French air bases both at home and abroad. There are nearly 9,000 commandos, most of whom are trained paratroopers, manning air defence weapon systems or providing vehicle-mounted rapid response units. There is also a crack squadron known as EPI (Escadron de Protection et d'Intervention), which is trained in both static-line and freefall parachuting. This small unit, composed of professional rather than conscript soldiers, is responsible for attacking or reinforcing airfields rather than defending them.

The Air Commandos were France's first airborne unit. Formed in 1936 by a French Air Force Captain named Geille who had trained in the Soviet Union, the Air Commandos began with a total strength of 150. France was one of the first countries to realize the possibilities of airborne forces and the Air Commandos continued to grow until the French defeat in 1940. Many commandos managed to escape to England, where they formed the nucleus of the two French Special Air Service Regiments. Reformed again into the French Air Force at the end of World War Two, the Air Commandos saw action in Indo-China and Algeria. After being disbanded for taking part in the Algerian coup, they were again reformed in 1965 and in 1972 expanded to become one of the Air Force's eight Commands.

The Headquarters of the Air Commandos is in Nîmes in the South of France. It is here that all commandos, whether national service conscripts or professional soldiers, are trained. Like almost all units in the French armed forces, the Air Commandos are composed of around 75 per cent conscripts and 25 per cent regulars. Not all the conscripts volunteer to parachute, however, but the inducement of parachute pay (which almost doubles their monthly income) persuades over 95 per cent of the 'non-volunteer' intake to jump. Furthermore, such is the esprit de corps of the Air Commandos, that many national servicemen sign on for two years as short service volunteers.

The EPI commandos are all either professional or short service volunteers. All members of the battalion-sized squadron must pass the standard 16-week basic training course in Nîmes before undergoing an arduous EPI selection course designed to test the individual's mental and physical stamina. Only those who possess a high degree of ability and motivation succeed in passing the selection course. Selection is followed by the no less gruelling continuation phase, which concentrates on advanced military skills and tactics. The EPI commandos are expected to be able to operate behind enemy lines with little or no support and therefore both group and individual skills are considered to be of paramount importance.

Another aspect of EPI training taken seriously is unarmed combat, a mixture of various Oriental martial arts, which is taught by the group's non-commissioned officers – all of whom are black-belts in one form or another. Other skills such as signalling and support weapons are taught in conjunction with the Army.

The EPIs role is very different from that of army paratroops. Men in the Squadron specialize in small unit, rapid-response operations rather than the large scale drops of the army's paras. However, the air commando's equipment is much the same as the paratrooper's. The combat uniforms are similar except for the pocket arrangement on the jackets – horizontal press studs instead of vertical zips. Another difference is that the air commandos wear Air Force badges of rank, worn on the shoulder rather than on the centre of the chest as they are in the Army.

In spite of the various differences between the paratroopers and air commandos, the blue beret worn by the EPI, with its circled wing, sword and star cap badge, signifies to all that the wearer is one of the airborne fraternity.

A short-service junior NCO of the EPI participates in a river crossing. The beret badge and Air Force rank insignia are clearly visible.

LEGIONNAIRE, 2e REP

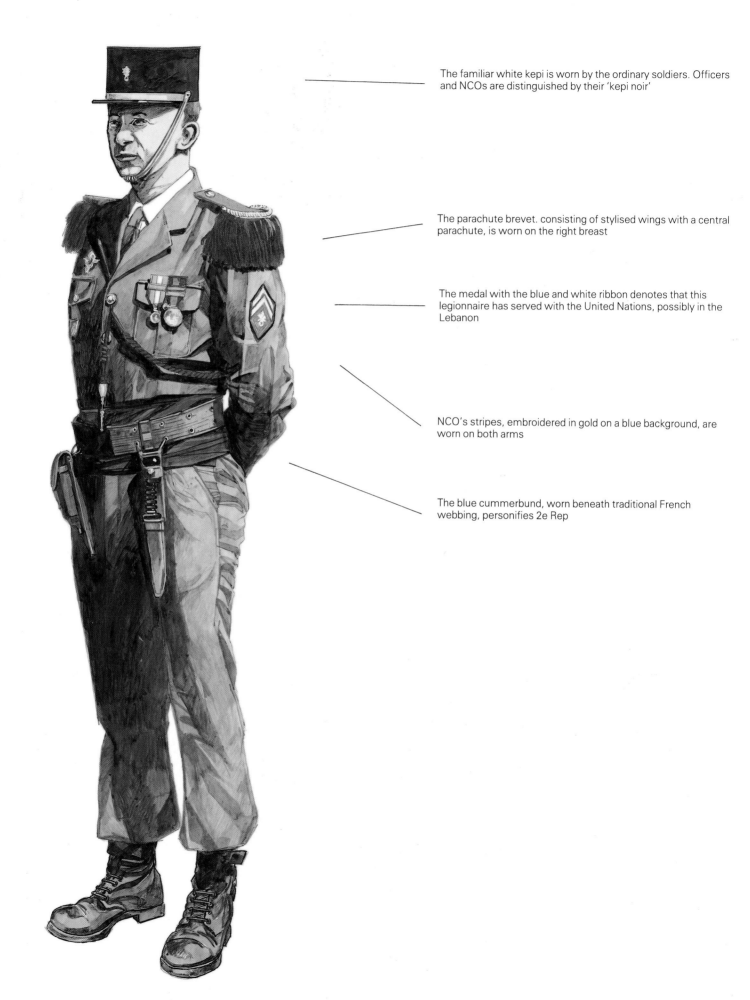

The familiar white kepi is worn by the ordinary soldiers. Officers and NCOs are distinguished by their 'kepi noir'

The parachute brevet. consisting of stylised wings with a central parachute, is worn on the right breast

The medal with the blue and white ribbon denotes that this legionnaire has served with the United Nations, possibly in the Lebanon

NCO's stripes, embroidered in gold on a blue background, are worn on both arms

The blue cummerbund, worn beneath traditional French webbing, personifies 2e Rep

One of the most legendary military formations in the world, the 'Légion Etrangère', the French Foreign Legion, came into being on March 9, 1831. Composed of foreign nationals rather than French citizens, the Legion soon proved itself to be one of the most capable and effective fighting forces in the world.

Today the French Foreign Legion comprises a highly trained, well-equipped modern armed force, with its own infantry, armour, engineers and support units. These are totally professional and none more so than the Legion's own Parachute Regiment – 2e Regiment Etranger de Parachutistes.

The Regiment's history dates back to French campaigns, during the 1950s in Indo-China (now Vietnam) where the unit, then known as 2e Bataillon Etranger de Parachutistes, was virtually wiped out during the siege of Dien Bien Phu. After being reformed, the Regiment saw extensive service in the Algerian war before being posted back to the French island of Corsica in 1963. Until this time 2e REP had been a conventional airborne infantry regiment, but shortly after their arrival at the new base near the town of Calvi, the Regiment adopted a different and more exacting role – that of Para-Commando. Reorganized, re-structured and re-trained, the Regiment quickly adapted to their new role. Selection into 2e REP became more stringent and the training became more diverse. All volunteers to the Legion must serve a minimum of five years and begin with basic infantry training at Castelnaudary, on the French mainland. Only those who pass sufficiently well out of their intake will be chosen for further training with 2e REP and only three out of ten make the grade. A large percentage of these are English speakers, mostly British, but with a number from the United States, Canada, South Africa and Australia. All orders are given in French which, considering that there are over fifty nationalities represented in 2e REP at present, makes life less complicated than one might expect as most legionnaires adapt to the new language quickly.

The 2e REP has retained the same basic organization since it first adopted the Para-Commando role. The Regiment's 1,300 officers and men are divided into six companies. These consist of the CCS, a service and support company; the CEA, a reconnaissance and tactical support company; and four combat companies, each with their own individual operational specialization. These are essentially as follows: Company No. 1 – urban warfare, night and heliborne operations, including behind-the-lines commando raids; Company No. 2 – mountain warfare, including skiing, climbing and pathfinding; Company No. 3 – amphibious operations, including underwater swimming; and Company No. 4 – sabotage and demolition, with a secondary role of supplying stay-behind parties and snipers.

Together these combat companies include most special operations force unit specializations. One sub-unit in particular, the Commandos de Renseignement et de l'Action en Profondeur (known as CRAPs), is trained in special forces warfare techniques. This unit of platoon strength is part of the CEA and all its men are trained in military freefall (HAHO/HALO) parachuting.

All the men in the Regiment are trained paratroopers regardless of their other specializations. Unlike other French paratroopers, who are trained at Pau in the south of France, 2e REP conducts its own parachute training in Corsica. The legionnaires wear the distinctive parachute 'brevet' on all their uniforms including their combat kit, which they also use as their day-to-day working dress. The standard French paras 'brevet' consists of stylized metal wings with a parachute in the centre and is worn on the right breast. One feature that distinguishes the para-legionnaires is the green commando beret (worn throughout the Legion), which in 2e REP is worn with the traditional French para cap badge.

Medals proudly displayed, members of 2e REP exhibit as much *élan* on parade as they do in the field.

Legionnaires of the mortar detachment bring their weapon into action within moments of clearing the DZ.

FRENCH MOUNTAIN TROOPER

The 'tartine', worn in barracks, is discarded as impractical during operational training.

The French still retain their preference for leather belts and pouches, rarely if ever resorting to webbing

The domestically-produced MAT 9mm sub machine-gun is carried generally by the French military, gendarmerie and police

High gaiters provide an excellent snow-proof seal between the specially-designed boots and the breeches normally worn under the white ski-suit

Mountain troopers spend over twenty percent of their time training in the field. They are completely self-reliant and think nothing of covering vast distances by ski. All equipment required is carried in their large back-pack.

The French Army has its own specialist mountain warfare formation – the 27th Alpine Division. Created from the merger of the 17th and 27th Mountain Brigades in 1976, this relatively new Division became a part of the Force de l'Action Rapide on its formation in 1983.

The 27th Alpine Divison comprises around 20,000 men, over 2,500 of whom are mountain infantrymen. The Division has its own integral armour, artillery, and engineer elements, plus divisional support assets, and is capable of fighting alongside armoured and airmobile units, or on its own. Specializing in mountain warfare, the various divisional sub-elements are also capable of fighting in built-up or forested areas, and are especially suited to winter warfare. Located in the French Alps, the Division is spread out over an area of nearly 18,000 square kilometres with major units based in the regions of Haute Savoie, Savoie, Isère, Haute Alps, and Alps & Haute Provence.

In the main the units are based in the valleys, but each of the six 'Chasseur de l'Alpin' battalions has its own mountain training centre which can accommodate up to one combat company. 'Chasseur de l'Alpin' means literally 'mountain hunter' and the five battalions, numbered 4, 6, 7, 13 and 27, spend much of their annual training cycles working high up in the mountains in both summer and winter.

Around 70 per cent of the Division's total manpower is made up of conscripts undergoing their national service. These men are drawn from all over France but in order to serve with the 'Chasseurs' must be able to meet certain criteria. As with all military formations specializing in mountain warfare, a high standard of physical fitness is essential, but just as important is the correct mental aptitude necessary for operating in climatic extremes. Training is hard and intensive, and at any one time over 18 per cent of the Division's total strength are deployed in the field or on training cadres. Not only must the men be capable of operating in the mountains (the Chasseurs must be competent skiers and mountaineers), but also in forests and villages. Anti-armour warfare is considered an important part of the Alpine Division's role and it has a total of 600 anti-armour weapons, including 108 Milan missile systems.

Capable of moving through rough terrain by day or night, the combat companies of the Chasseurs Alpins can carry with them everything they need to fight and survive. When operating during the winter months, the battalions can call on the Division's 36 tracked over-snow vehicles to move their heavy equipment or, during daylight hours, receive helicopter support. However, like mountain troops throughout the world, the Chasseurs Alpins rely first and foremost on themselves when it comes to getting from A to B.

Depending on which time of year a recruit joins the mountain troops, he will spend between three to six months on an alpine training cadre. At the end of this training, and if the recruit succeeds in passing, he will go on to join one of the combat companies. One of the obvious characteristics of the mountain soldier is the intense 'esprit de corps' which one often sees in men from more traditionally 'elite' units such as paratroops or commandos. When operating in the mountains, the officers and men share the same hardships and the same dangers, and this is evident in their attitude to themselves and their task.

Fiercely independent, the Chasseurs Alpins still maintain their regimental customs and tradition. They still wear the large flat black beret, known as the 'tartine', which distinguishes them from the basic infantrymen. Other differences in uniform include climbing breeches, long socks and heavy mountain boots. In addition, those who have passed the six month specialist alpine course at Briançon wear the 'brevet alpine militaire', a highly valued qualification badge composed of an ice pick, a circle and a star.

THE FOLGORE BRIGADE

All members of the Brigade wear a maroon beret with parachutist's cap badge, whether they are para-qualified or not

The green, brown and sand camouflage provides excellent cover for most conditions

Gathered at the wrists, ankles and waist, the uniform is both comfortable and practical

The AR-70 is rapidly replacing the Beretta BM 59 depicted here as the standard personal weapon

Knee and elbow pads have been built into the uniform

Italy was among the pioneers of military parachuting, having a fully trained parachute company as long ago as 1938. Two battalions each of 250 men fought in the unsuccessful Libya campaign and were joined in 1940 by a third battalion. All three battalions joined with their logistic support to form the Folgore Brigade in 1942. The Brigade was not exploited fully by the Italians and it was not until after their surrender in 1943, when part of the Brigade reformed as 'F' Squadron, part of the British 8th Army, that it saw strenuous service.

After the War the Italians retained a nucleus of airborne troops, using them to reestablish the Parachute School at Tarquiniar in 1946. A Parachute Brigade was created in 1952 and it was from this that the present Folgore Brigade evolved.

Although the majority of the Italian Army is committed by NATO to the defence of the Gorizia Gap in the North East, the defence of the South, with its long and vulnerable coastline, remains crucial. The FIR ('Forza di Intervento Rapido') consisting of the Folgore Brigade, the Friuli Brigade and elements of the San Marco Marines is based in Central Italy and tasked with the defence of the South.

The FIR has recently enjoyed a considerable enhancement of its anti-air and anti-tank capabilities with the introduction of 150 US Stinger surface-to-air missiles and 500 APILAS anti-tank rocket launchers. Two new personal weapons, built respectively by Beretta and Franchi under licence from Heckler & Koch, are being tested by the 2nd and 5th Parachute Battalions and will be issued as a priority to the Folgore Brigade as soon as trials are completed.

With a few exceptions, the personal weapons and equipment of the Folgore Brigade are essentially the same as those used by the rest of Italy's land forces. The Beretta BM59 7.62mm selective fire rifle is gradually being replaced by the much improved and lighter AR-70, whilst air-defence will soon be further enhanced by the introduction of the four-barrel 25mm self-propelled air-defence vehicle currently under construction by OTO Melara and Oerlikon and due to enter service during 1988.

All members of the Folgore Brigade are volunteers. Training, which lasts for 16 months, is very intense with great emphasis being placed upon physical fitness and personal reliability. An initial 18 weeks is spent in fitness training, after which the recruit spends 10 weeks studying communications, 15 weeks mastering underwater operations including demolition, six weeks in parachute training, 12 weeks with the artillery and eight weeks in alpine familiarization and skiing.

Both the 9th 'Colonel Moschin' Assault (Saboteur) Parachute Battalion, the special forces of the Italian Army, and the Alpini Parachute Company are formally part of the Folgore Brigade, although the latter carry the same arms and equipment as other Alpini units with whom they train and operate. The 9th Assault (Saboteur) Battalion, with an approximate strength of 225 men, comprises a headquarters,

training company and operations company with a third company authorized in wartime. The battalion normally operates in groups of from 2 to 20 men and keeps itself at the peak of readiness. Although not as proficient as many special forces in the application of general unit skills, the Saboteur is nevertheless regarded as one of the most able specialists in NATO.

Members of the Brigade wear a maroon beret with parachutist's beret badge. The highly practical camouflage uniform has built-in knee and elbow pads and is gathered at the wrists, ankles and waist. The Folgore brigade badge is worn with badges of rank on the left shoulder and parachutist's badges on the right breast, although none of these are worn on operations.

The distinctive maroon beret may be discarded in favour of more practical headgear when on exercise. The well-designed uniform with its tapered waist, sleeves and ankles provides excellent cover whatever the conditions. Here soldiers can be seen patrolling through a coastal village and deplaning from a helicopter.

ALPINI TROOPS

The black eagle feather and pompon, the hall-marks of the Alpini, are worn on all headgear including the helmet

The Beretta BM 59 Alpini Rifle, with folding stock, is standard issue

The Italian flag is worn on the right upper sleeve

The trigger mechanism is specially adapted to enable the weapon to be fired by a gloved hand

The all-white two-piece snow suit provides excellent camouflage in Alpine conditions whilst at the same time offering warmth and freedom of movement to the wearer

The major land threat to Italy comes from the mountainous areas abutting her Northern and North-Eastern borders and it is therefore essential that she maintains elite formations capable of operating in such areas. At present this task is excellently fulfilled by five brigades of Alpine Troops ('Brigata Alpina'); the 'Taurinesse', 'Orobica', 'Tridentina', 'Cadore' and 'Julia'. all Brigades are strategically placed, one with III Corps in Milan, three with IV Corps based at Bolzano and responsible for the defence of the crucial Brenner Pass, and one with V Corps based at Vittorio Veneto and responsible for the North Eastern border with Austria and Yugoslavia. One Alpini battalion on rotation is permanently assigned to the Allied Command Europe Mobile Force (Land), responsible for the defence of the Northern Flank, and is regularly deployed in Norway.

Each of the Alpini Brigades is fully self-contained, consisting of a regiment of three or four mountain infantry battalions and an APC company, signals and engineer companies, an artillery regiment with three battalions of 105mm pack howitzers (mule-portable and especially designed for mountain warfare) and a battalion of 155mm howitzers, an aviation flight and parachute-ski platoon. The Logistics Regiment, responsible for the resupply of food, ammunition and equipment, relies on mules for transportation. In addition each brigade has a carabinieri platoon of para-military police and a Fortress battalion trained to fight from pre-prepared defensive positions.

Alpini Brigades consist largely of conscripts, most of whom are local men born and bred to a mountain existence. All are extremely fit, self-motivated and exellent skiers able to survive and fight in the unforgiving environment in which they operate. An initial three-month training course, run by the 2nd Alpini Regiment and based in part on US Ranger training, is undertaken by all, after which most are posted to their brigades where they undergo a further four months' platoon and company training. Only then are they regarded as fully competent Alpini. A few attend the Alpine Warfare School in which gunnery, communications and engineering are taught in the context of mountain warfare.

An initial problem arises in the fact that conscription in the Italian Army is for 12 months only, of which the Alpini spend seven months in training, leaving little time for formal active service. This is however balanced in part by the fact that under this system a large number of men are trained who could in an emergency be recalled to the colours. Most continue to live and work in the mountains and by and large retain their fitness and skills, being competent therefore to return to their old units with the minimum of delay.

Alpini are armed and treated as light infantry, all their equipment with the exception of the 155mm howitzers being man- or mule-portable. The standard-issue personal weapon is the 7.62 Beretta BM59TA ('Truppe Alpini') rifle. Specially modified for the conditions, the TA weighs 4.6 kg (10 lbs) and has a range of 600 metres (656 yards).

A tubular metal folding butt, pistol grip and enlarged trigger capable of being operated by a gloved hand are standard. A variant with a removable flash-illuminator and grenade launcher is issued to the paratroop platoons. The 9mm Beretta 38/49 sub-machine-gun, a replacement for the excellent World War Two 38/42 model in service until recently, is issued in limited numbers.

All ranks are instantly recognizable by the famous grey-green felt mountaineer's hat worn with a black eagle feather and pompon on the left-hand side. Both feather and pompon are worn on the steel helmet. The black metal cap badge depicts an eagle above a light infantry bugle containing the regimental number. All ranks wear a green collar-patch. Combat dress varies with the conditions, ranging from a grey suit with black boots and grey soft cap to an all-white hooded overall and trousers with white gloves, webbing and overboots to provide excellent camouflage in the snow.

Top: Even mules are issued with snow shoes when serving with the Alpini.

Above: The Italian 105mm pack howitzer can be rapidly broken down into mule-loads. It has proved ideally suited to mountain warfare and airborne operations.

SAN MARCO MARINES

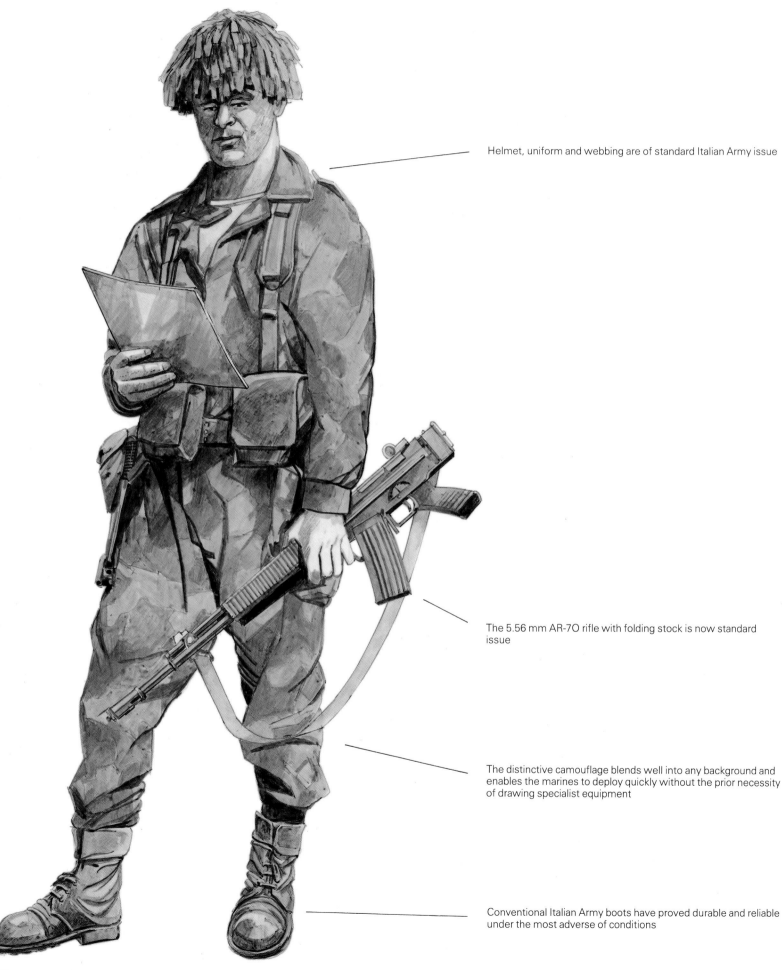

Helmet, uniform and webbing are of standard Italian Army issue

The 5.56 mm AR-70 rifle with folding stock is now standard issue

The distinctive camouflage blends well into any background and enables the marines to deploy quickly without the prior necessity of drawing specialist equipment

Conventional Italian Army boots have proved durable and reliable under the most adverse of conditions

The San Marco Battalion comprises the major combat element of the Italian Marines and, as such, spearheads her naval and maritime forces. In compliance with her NATO obligations, Italy has stationed the majority of her armed forces in the North, leaving her long and vulnerable coastline with few obvious defences. It is crucial therefore that units stationed in the South, which include the San Marco Marines, are comprised of men of the highest standard.

All members of the battalion attend a course at the Military Paratroop School, Pisa, and become experts in beach assaults, coastal demolition, cliff climbing and reconnaissance. The very best are attached to the 'Demolitori Ostacoli Antisbarco' (Shore Demolition Unit) prior to which they undertake a 10-week course at the Incursion School, run by the COMSUBIN or naval special forces, at which they master the arts of tactics and equipment, ordnance and weapons, climbing, diving and unarmed combat.

Administratively the Marines are divided into three groups; operations, training and logistics. Despite its lack of numbers, the operational element, which comprises four companies organized along traditional military lines, is responsible for the provision of the amphibious capability for NATO warships operating in the central Mediterranean.

Until recently the battalion's amphibious capability was severely limited by the lack of suitable shipping. Integral sea transport consisted of two ex-USN De Soto County-class Landing Ship Tanks (LSTs), the 'Caorle' and 'Grado'. Although each could carry 500 men, their vehicles and equipment were both old and unreliable. The launching recently of the 'San Giorgio', a 7,662-ton Landing Platform Dock (LPD), has improved the situation immeasurably. The 'San Giorgio', with its helicopter landing deck, extensive roll-on roll-off facilities and ability to launch the MTP 9733 loading craft much favoured by the Marines for beach assaults, can now allow the entire battalion to approach its potential destination together and in relative comfort and safety.

In addition to the domestically produced MTP 9733 landing craft, the Battalion has ten LVTP-7s (landing vehicle, tracked, personnel) each capable of carrying 25 fully equipped Marines or up to 4,550 kg (10,000 lbs) of cargo. These amphibious monsters, used by the Argentinians during the invasion of the Falklands, are capable of landing in running surf as high as 3 metres (10 feet) yet can travel along made-up roads at a speed of 64kph (40mph).

With a few exceptions, the San Marco Battalion is issued with conventional army weapons. The Marines were among the first to receive the new 5.56mm AR-70 rifle, capable of firing single shots or automatically at the rate of 700 rpm.

San Marco Marines wear the usual distinctive camouflage uniform and World War Two vintage helmet. When non-operational, a black beret is usually worn, although this may be replaced by a plain grey soft-peaked cap. The golden San Marco lion badge, with its distinctive red backing, is worn on the right sleeve cuff. Uniquely the

Marines wear the combat uniform of the Army but the Parade Dress of the Navy, embellished in the case of the latter by the lion badge worn by officers on the left breast above the medal ribbons and by the Marines on the tunic shirt cuffs.

The potential worth of the San Marco Marines was proved in 1982 when they provided the Italian peace-keeping contingent in the Lebanon. Although in political terms the mission was unsuccessful, the Marines nevertheless earned world-wide acclaim for their discipline, forbearance and sheer professionalism in the face of the most atrocious provocation.

San Marco Battalion marines form up with their kit prior to an amphibious landing.

A mortar team prepared to give fire support from a well-concealed position.

COMSUBIN

The woollen hat can be pulled down to conceal the skin tone as an additional aid to camouflage

A variety of European-produced weapons is issued, including this Heckler & Koch pistol capable of firing underwater as well as above

The mottle-green uniform lends itself ideally to night operations, a field in which the COMSUBIN excel

Little additional space is available for the carriage of essential items. Pockets are therefore at a premium

The 'Commando Raggrupamento Subacquei ed Incursori' or COMSUBIN was formed in 1952 and today continues the proud traditions of the Italian mini-submarine crews who wrought havoc among the ships and installations of the British Mediterranean Fleet between 1940 and 1943.

COMSUBIN is based at Varignano, near La Spezia on the North West coast, is under the direct control of the Navy Chief of Staff and is commanded by a Divisional Admiral. Administratively it is divided into five Units, two in support and three operational.

Support consists of the 'Gruppo Scuole' (Special Group) and 'Centro Studi' (Research Centre). The 'Gruppo Scuole' trains all underwater specialists including the police and is itself sub-divided into the Underwater, Incursion and Installation Defence Schools.

The Underwater School, which is the only organization in Italy competent to issue a military diving licence, is responsible for the training of frogmen and deep sea divers. Frogmen, all of whom are conscripts undergoing 18 months national service, attend an 18-week course. Ominously, naval conscription is soon to be reduced to 12 months in line with the Army and Air Force, with the result that standards will inevitably fall unless recruits are to spend one-third of their entire service in training. Deep sea divers, all of whom are professional soldiers, undergo a far more comprehensive six months' instruction. The 9th 'Colonel Moschin' Battalion, Italy's special forces unit, completes an intensive, diverse and secretive 10-week course at the Underwater School.

Nowhere within the COMSUBIN are the traditions of the Italian 'human torpedoes' of World War Two more revered than in the Incursion School, where future 'Incursore' are selected from among officer and NCO volunteers of the regular navy. The 10 months training which follows initial selection incorporates lessons on tactics and equipment, ordnance and weapons, climbing, diving and unarmed combat. HALO (High Altitude Low Opening) and HAHO (High Altitude High Opening) techniques are taught at the Military Paratroop School, Pisa. Training is so intensive that of those originally accepted for the course only five per cent can hope to pass out successfully. Even then the fledgling 'Incursore' must spend 14 months undergoing 'in-house' training before being considered fully qualified.

The Installation Defence school trains conscripts in ground base defence in a one-month course covering matters as divergent as the physical security of buildings and the countering of attacks by Soviet Naval Spetsnaz frogmen.

The operational group consists of the Underwater Operational Group, the Special Naval Group and Incursion Operational Group, the first two of which work in close conjunction.

Underwater divers are trained not only in the defence of domestic bases but also provide the nucleus of Italy's submarine rescue resources. Divers are trained in the use of conventional respirators and air lines together with diving bells, deep diving systems and even mini-submarines,

thus ensuring that rescue attempts can be undertaken at any depth regardless of conditions.

The 'Incursori', the offensive arm of COMSUBIN, is small, consisting of less than 200 men of all ranks and necessarily extremely secretive. Divided into logistics and operational cells, the 'Incursori' works in small teams of between two and twelve. Its base at Varignano affords excellent training facilities with its integral shore and underwater training areas. Friendly, but invariably unsuspecting, naval and merchant ships around the coast provide excellent material for the numerous simulated mine and sabotage attacks made by every 'Incursore' each year.

Training is carried out at night, with most exercises split into the three distinct stages of infiltration, attack and escape. Often live ammunition is used. Although fully trained for every contingency, each 'Incursore' specializes in a particular skill which may be free climbing, deep reconnaissance, communications or demolition.

COMSUBIN, with its excellent support and resources, is armed and equipped to a standard second to none. Although most weapons are of standard issue, certain highly specialist aspects of kit and equipment remain secret. Most personnel carry the Beretta 92 pistol, Beretta M-12 machine-gun or the Heckler & Koch MP-5 9mm sub-machine-gun. The MP-5SD, the silenced version of the MP-5, is occasionally carried, as is the versatile Franchi SPAS-15 pump action rifle. The Heckler & Koch P-11, as capable of firing underwater as on dry land, will soon enter operational service.

As well as infiltrating by sea, Incursori must be capable of scaling coastal cliffs to carry out their operational tasks.

The training of frogmen at the Underwater School takes 18 weeks.

CANADIAN PARATROOPER

The beret, worn in barracks, will be discarded in favour of more practical headgear when in the field

The Canadians have a unique layered system of uniform dress in order to accommodate the wide temperature range encountered in local conditions

The 9mm sub machine-gun is a Canadian variant of the British Sterling

Snow shoes are a must for normal snow operations when not skiing

The Canadian Airborne Regiment is Canada's sole formation of military parachutists, and is the core of the Special Service Force. Tasked with the role of providing 'a combat-ready, quick-reaction force in support of national security, North American defence and international peacekeeping', the Airborne Regiment has a total strength of around 750 personnel, and is composed entirely of volunteers. All members of the Regiment, whether infantrymen, cooks or drivers, are trained parachutists, a distinction which separates them from a number of other NATO airborne formations.

The origins of Canada's Airborne Regiment can be traced back to the Second World War and to two separate units – the 1st Canadian Parachute Battalion, and the 1st Special Service Force. The 1st Canadian Parachute Battalion was formed in 1942 and trained at Fort Benning, Georgia, and at the Parachute Training Wing at Camp Shilo, Manitoba. The Battalion's first operation was during the Normandy landings on D-Day and it continued to fight as a part of the 6th (British) Airborne Division until the end of the war. Included in its battle honours are the Dives Crossing, The Rhine and North-West Europe 1944-45. During the Rhine Operation, Corporal F. J. Topham won the Battalion's first Victoria Cross.

The second formation to which the present Airborne Regiment owes its existence was the 1st Special Service Force, or the 'Devil's Brigade' as it becomes more commonly known. This unique force was formed in 1942 from both Canadian (2nd Parachute Battalion) and US personnel. The SSF was first deployed to the Aleutian Islands in 1943 and later distinguished itself in the successful assaults of Monte La Difensa and Monte La Remetanea in Italy. The Force saw further action at Anzio and became the first Allied troops to enter the Eternal City. The 1st Special Service Force was disbanded in December 1944.

The Canadians maintained a small airborne formation in the years immediately following the Second World War. In 1946, parachuting skills were revived with the formation of a Canadian SAS Company which was trained and located at Rivers, Manitoba. Between 1948 and 1958 various elements of infantry with supporting arms and services formed a Canadian Airborne Brigade which was based throughout Canada at the parent unit's home station. This Brigade, known as the Mobile Strike Force, was tasked with the defence of Canada, with special responsibility for the North. Trained in both parachuting and Arctic warfare, the Brigade was drastically reduced in size in 1958. Whereas previously whole battalions, such as the Royal Canadian Regiment, Princess Patricia's Canadian Light Infantry and Royal 22e Regiment, have undergone airborne training, the parachute-trained contingents were now reduced to company size and support elements were severely cut. This much smaller force was renamed the Defence of Canada Force.

The present Canadian Airborne Regiment was formed in 1968 and consisted of two infantry Commandos (one French-speaking), one artillery battery, one engineer field squadron, one signals squadron and a service support company. Over the years the organization has changed and the Regiment has lost its own artillery and engineering sub-units, their roles being taken up by E Battery (Para) RCHA and 2 Combat Engineer Regiment respectively. In addition, the two existing airborne Commandos were reduced in strength and a 3rd Airborne Commando was raised, bringing military parachuting back into its own within the Canadian Armed Forces.

Clothing and equipment is the same as that issued to the rest of the Canadian Army but with a few exceptions, the most notable of which is the maroon beret. This is worn with the Canadian Airborne Regiment badge, which consists of a pair of stylized wings around a parachute over a maple leaf, under which is a scroll bearing the words 'Airborne Canada' in both English and French. Other differences include a camouflaged parachute smock similar to that worn by British Paras, with the winged dagger badge of the present Special Service Force (of which the Airborne Regiment is a part) worn on both arms. The SSF insignia bears the motto 'Osons', which translated means 'We Dare', presumably derived from that of the SAS. In addition to the SSF flashes, the Canadian 'jump' wings are worn on the right breast by all members of the Canadian Airborne Regiment.

The new 5.56mm weapons adopted by the Canadian Armed Forces are the C7, a version of the M16A1, which replaces the 7.62mm C1 rifle, and (left) the C8 light machine-gun version of the Belgian Minimi.

CANADIAN HELICOPTER PILOT

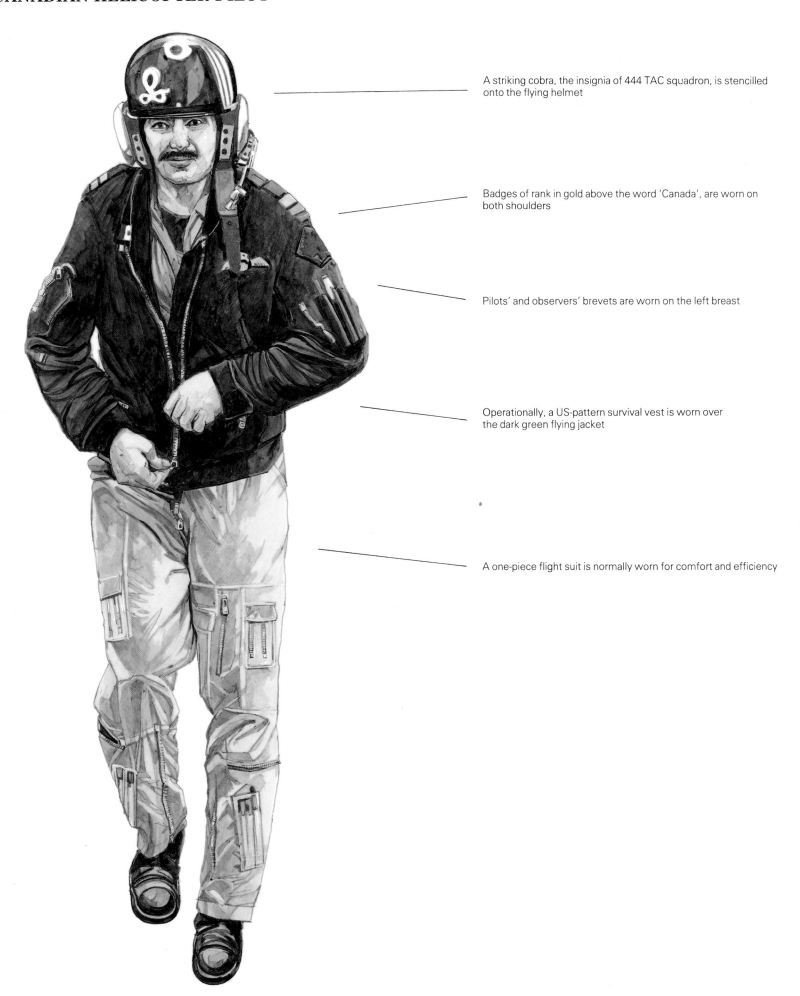

A striking cobra, the insignia of 444 TAC squadron, is stencilled onto the flying helmet

Badges of rank in gold above the word 'Canada', are worn on both shoulders

Pilots' and observers' brevets are worn on the left breast

Operationally, a US-pattern survival vest is worn over the dark green flying jacket

A one-piece flight suit is normally worn for comfort and efficiency

The Canadian Armed Forces have a long tradition of providing highly trained aircrew which dates back to the Second World War, when British aircrew were trained in Canada and thousands of Canadian servicemen flew from RAF airfields in Britain.

Today the Canadians continue to train their own aircrew to the same high standards and, although the aircraft have become far more sophisticated, the various squadrons have managed to maintain their individual identities. With the increased need for helicopters on the battlefield, some units have changed from jet aircraft to helicopters, and one such squadron is 444 Tactical Helicopter Squadron. Known as 'Triple Four', this squadron provides the West German-based 4 Canadian Mechanised Brigade Group with helicopter support.

The Squadron is based in Lahr in the Black Forest Region of West Germany. The Brigade Group to which it is assigned is the only permanently based Canadian military formation of its size in Western Europe and is tasked with supporting the 7th (US) and 2nd (German) Corps in this vulnerable area close to the Inner German Border.

444 Tactical Helicopter Squadron is tasked with a number of vital missions. It can be used in the Command and Liaison role to provide the Brigade with a major command and control asset. It can be used for general area reconnaissance or in-depth reconnaissance in conjunction with the Brigade's ground forces, and finally it can be used to control and adjust artillery fire or provide forward air control for friendly ground attack aircraft.

Equipped with Kiowa OH–58A helicopters (Canadian designation COH–136), Triple Four is a combined unit of both army and air force personnel. The aircraft are flown by air force officer pilots while the observers are army non-commissioned officers. These two-man teams, despite their apparent differences in background, combine to produce an effective unit to carry out their various missions.

The Kiowas themselves are unarmed, but nevertheless are expected to go into combat with attack helicopters should the need arise. As in Vietnam, these Kiowas can form the observation element of a 'Pink Team' and the aircrew of Triple Four regularly exercise with US and German attack helicopters.

Although the aircraft are unarmed, the men themselves are not, and when deployed carry their personal weapons – 9mm Browning semi-automatic pistols or, in some cases, privately purchased handguns. When in the field, the aircrew are also responsible for local area defence while on the ground and often draw 9mm Sterling sub-machine-guns in addition to their pistols. These additional weapons, together with the individual's personal webbing, can be carried in the rear of the Kiowa if space and weight allow.

The aircrew normally wear a dark green one-piece flight suit with standard Canadian Armed Forces insignia. Pilots' and observers' wings are worn on the left breast. A matching dark green

flying jacket is worn while flying and, when operational, a survival vest of the US pattern is worn over the jacket. These vests are modified to individual requirements but usually include a pistol holster and a survival knife. They contain everything necessary to sustain survival should the aircrew have to put down in an emergency.

Canadian Tactical Helicopter Squadrons such as Triple Four are extremely self-sufficient and are used to operating independently when deployed in the field. They rely on their own skill to camouflage their aircraft and vehicles when on the ground, and their flying ability to keep them out of trouble when in the air. The Tactical Helicopter Squadrons are combat units and, above all, tactical.

Although the Kiowa OH-58A helicopters with which the Squadron is equipped are unarmed, the aircrew who fly them are not.

NETHERLANDS MARINE

The marine is wearing standard combat dress consisting of olive green trousers, stone-coloured shirt and heavy wool jersey

The Belgian 7.62mm FN FAL is the standard personal weapon

The cut and colour of the combat uniform cause the Marines to stand apart from the Army

Unlike the conventional Army, which wears brown boots, the Marines wear black

The Royal Netherlands Marine Corps (RNLMC) is a Dutch amphibious force tasked by NATO and is capable of deploying anywhere in the world. In addition to this role the Corps has a UN commitment with units on 24 hours standby, ready to deploy overseas for 'peacekeeping' duties, while other units are responsible for the security of the Netherlands Antilles. The RNLMC motto 'Quo Patet Orbis', which means 'wherever the world extends', accurately describes their area of operations.

The Corps is the oldest unit within the Netherlands armed forces with a proud tradition dating back to 1665, when it was formed to fight the English. The fact that a Dutch monarch once sat on the British throne bears witness to their success. The Dutch have a proud seafaring tradition and the RNLMC have supported their maritime fleet as far afield as the East Indies and China. More recently, Dutch marines were instrumental in delaying the initial German advance in 1940, when they blew the bridges crossing the Maas.

Many marines managed to escape to Britain following their country's defeat, including the Prince's Irene Brigade which contained a Marine element. The Brigade took an active part in the D-Day landings and distinguished itself during the drive through north-west Europe. At the end of the Second World War the Corps grew dramatically in size and saw further action in various campaigns in East Java.

At present the Corps Headquarters is in Rotterdam and consists of intelligence, operations and training sections. There are three operational commands – Home Command, Antilles Command and Corps Command. The Corps Command includes the headquarters and is responsible for both operations and training. Today the RNMLC has a total strength of 2,800 men, including 170 officers and 800 NCOs. One distinctive feature of the Corps is that it contains few conscripts, less than 10 per cent of the total strength. This means that it has a larger than average proportion of highly trained troops within its ranks, while at the same time having adequate reserves on which to call if required.

The RNLMC has two amphibious combat groups, the 1st and 2nd ACGs. The primary role of the Netherlands-based 1 ACG is to support NATO's Northern Flank and each year the Group deploys to Norway, where it spends three months conducting winter warfare exercises. While in Norway, 1 ACG comes under the command of Britain's 3 Commando Brigade Royal Marines, a situation unique within NATOs armed forces.

2 ACG, like its counterpart, has a total strength of around 700 men, divided into three companies. Based in the Netherlands Antilles, 2 ACG's marines are trained in jungle warfare, which means that as volunteers serve a minimum of four years, it is possible for a young marine to have experience of both the Arctic and the jungle.

The RNLMC is well equipped to carry out its various tasks. Depending on the area of operations, a Dutch marine can be found wearing Arctic, jungle or temperate clothing. The standard combat dress, however, consists of olive green combat trousers, a stone-coloured shirt and a heavy wool jersey similar to that worn by the British. When in the field, a combat jacket of the same material as the trousers is worn. Both the jacket and trousers are of a different cut, colour and material from that worn by the rest of the Netherlands armed forces. In addition, the marines wear black combat boots as opposed to the army's brown.

One unit within the RNLMC, Whisky Company, is an independent company permanently attached to 3 Commando Brigade. As such, much of its equipment is British, including combat clothing. The marines in Whisky Company wear British camouflage jackets and trousers but with their own badges of rank. These are similar to those worn by the Royal Marines but consist of shoulder slides for all ranks. However, regardless of what uniform the marines are wearing, they can usually be distinguished by their black beret with its anchor badge on a red cloth background.

A Dutch marine points out a target to a forward observer from a Commando battery of the Royal Artillery.

THE BELGIAN PARA-COMMANDO REGIMENT

2nd Bn Para Commando wear a green beret signifying their past affinity to the wartime Commando

The Vigneron M2 9mm SMG is a Belgian design and was adopted in 1953

Unlike conventional soldiers in the Belgian Army, Para-Commandos wear camauflage uniforms

In 1942 parachute and commando units were formed from the Free Belgian Forces then stationed in the United Kingdom. The first Parachute Company, drawn from the 2nd Battalion Belgian Fusiliers, was trained at Ringway, Manchester, and was subsequently incorporated into the British Parachute Regiment. Re-designated the Belgian Independent Parachute Company in January 1943, a year later it became the Belgian Squadron of the Special Air Service Brigade. As part of the SAS, the Squadron carried out covert missions against the encircled 7th Panzer Group in Normandy, at Beauvais, in the Ardennes, and deep behind enemy lines in Holland and Belgium. Boosted by domestic recruitment after the Liberation, the Squadron was raised to battalion status and in April 1945 was formally designated 5 SAS. After the War it was posted to Germany and Denmark for counter-intelligence duties, assuming the title 1er Regiment Parachutiste-SAS in April 1946.

The Belgian Commandos were formed on 30th April 1942 as 4 Troop of 10 (Inter-Allied) Commando, a composite drawn from all corners of Europe including Austria and Germany, and as such saw service with 2 Commando Brigade in Italy and Yugoslavia before entering Germany as part of 1 Commando Brigade. After the War the Unit, now based at March-Les-Dames, was renamed the Belgian Commando Regiment.

Belgium joined NATO at its inception and was one of the first nations to send a contingent in support of the United Nations to Korea. The Corps Volontaires Corea (CVC), formed from volunteers drawn from the Parachute and Commando Regiments, saw considerable action and in so doing sewed the seeds of amalgamation.

In February 1952 unification was agreed in principle, in April the Regiments were redesignated battalions and in May the Para-Commando Regiment was formed. Great care was taken to ensure that neither original unit lost its identity nor was forced to compromise its traditions, each retaining its coveted red or green beret.

The Para-Commandos were considered the ideal regiment to contain the problems then plaguing Belgium's African possessions, with the result that a company from each battalion was sent to Katanga in 1953. In September 1955 the 3rd Battalion was formed from veterans of the CVC and posted permanently to Central Africa. The Regiment grew considerably during the next few years but, with the withdrawal from Empire, in September 1960 was reduced to its present size of a headquarters, airborne and commando training centres, two parachute and one commando battalions, anti-tank, reconnaissance and artillery detachments and independent swimmer/canoeist and mountain leader groups.

In November 1964, in one of the most brilliant airborne operations in history, 320 members of 1st Parachute Battalion and 12th Company, 2nd Commando Battalion, with full medical support successfully parachuted onto Stanleyville airfield to rescue European hostages of the Simbas caught up in the bloody Congo Civil War.

Assigned primarily to NATO as part of the ACE Mobile Force, the regiment does however maintain itself in readiness to operate anywhere required of it in the world. The Equipes Speciales de Reconnaissance (ESR), the true successors of 5 SAS, maintain a presence at the International Long Range Reconnaissance Patrol School at Weingarten in Southern Germany, where they provide the Belgian quota of instructors.

Recruits are drawn either from the annual intake of conscripts, who serve for 12 months at home or 10 months in Germany, or from Regular Army volunteers who enlist for periods of two to five years with an option of extension thereafter. In 1976 a small group of women was enlisted. Required to undertake training identical to the men, those remaining in the Regiment now serve either in administration or in a training capacity.

Recruits undergo three months rigorous commando training at Wartet, near Marche-Les-Dames, during which their stamina and physical abilities are tested to the full. Thereafter they move to the training headquarters at Château d'Arenberg for one month's 'in-house' training in survival, patrolling, climbing and abseiling with a commando company to qualify for their brevets.

Training culminates with four weeks at the parachute training centre at Schaffen, after which the coveted wings are awarded and the soldier is posted to an operational unit where he is taught specialist skills prior to taking his place as a fully trained para-commando.

Unlike conventional soldiers, who retain the olive drab uniform, para-commandos wear camouflage. The 1st and 3rd Battalions wear the maroon airborne beret and the 2nd Battalion the green of the commandos. The 1st Battalion retains the winged dagger beret badge in commemoration of the Unit's SAS ancestry and the 3rd Battalion the CVC badge originally worn in Korea. The standard Belgian NATO helmet is worn, fitted with a double chin-strap, camouflage cover and netting.

This FN-designed ultra-light vehicle is ideal for para-commando operations, particularly the rapid movement of heavy weapons or logistic support.

NORWEGIAN ARMY

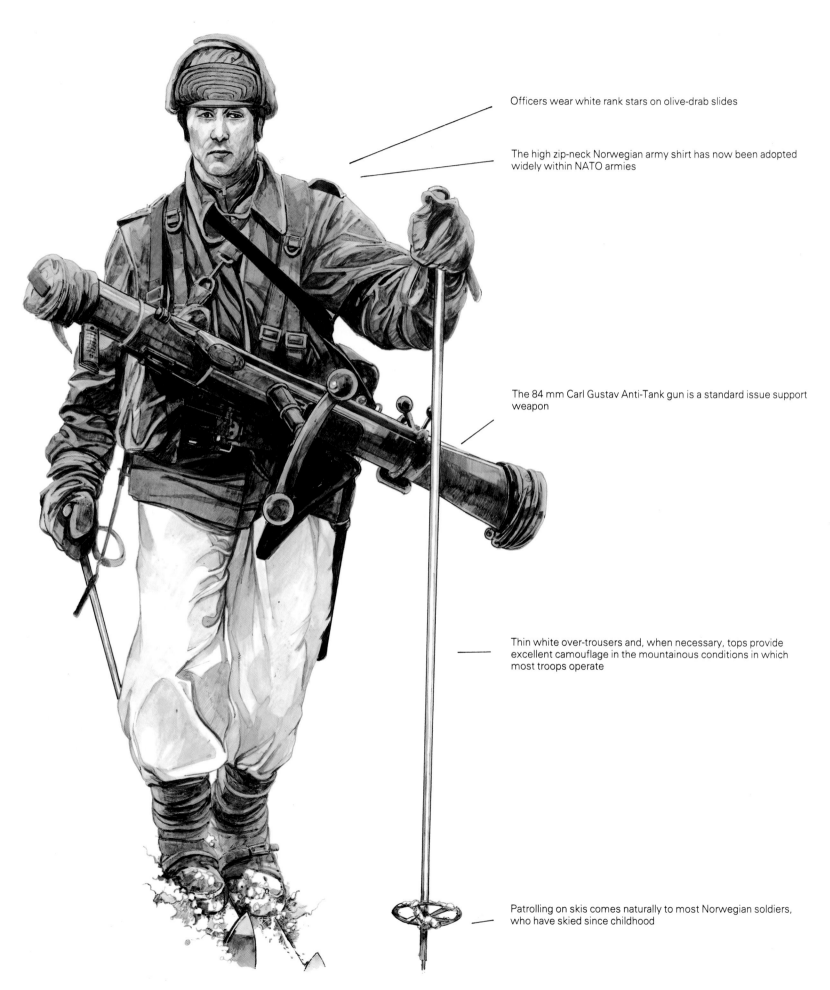

Officers wear white rank stars on olive-drab slides

The high zip-neck Norwegian army shirt has now been adopted widely within NATO armies

The 84 mm Carl Gustav Anti-Tank gun is a standard issue support weapon

Thin white over-trousers and, when necessary, tops provide excellent camouflage in the mountainous conditions in which most troops operate

Patrolling on skis comes naturally to most Norwegian soldiers, who have skied since childhood

Norway, the wartime anchor for NATO's Northern Flank, is of vital importance to the Alliance. Her territory comprises one-third of NATO's eastern frontage including a 123-mile (197-km) Arctic frontier shared with the Soviet Union. This is linked to the more populous South by 1,200 miles (1,920 km) of road skirting the coastline and therefore is vulnerable to landings by Soviet Naval Infantry attached to the White Sea Fleet, or to a mechanized thrust from Murmansk across neutral Lapland.

Although Norway would rely in part for her defence upon the arrival of allied troops, particularly the United States and British Marines, she nevertheless operates a highly effective, if small, domestic Army supported by a larger force of highly skilled and motivated Reserves.

In order to prevent a surprise attack and to enable her allies time to deploy, Norway retains a standing army of 19,000, including 13,200 conscripts undertaking 12 months national service. This force could be supplemented virtually overnight by a staggering 146,000 Reserves, all of whom undergo regular refresher training courses, most of whom are skilled cross-country skiers and many of whom are at home in Arctic conditions.

Conscripts spend between three and eight months undergoing specialist training prior to transferring to an active unit, with which they continue to exercise until transferred to the Reserve. All troops are mountain and Arctic warfare trained.

Norway has a small company-sized special forces unit, trained in tactical reconnaissance, sabotage and demolitions. All members are parachute trained, are combat swimmers and LRRPs experts. The company, which consists of a small permanent cadre supported by regular soldiers on two-year attachment, exercises regularly with United States and British special forces deployed in Norway, is closely associated with the Royal Marines Mountain and Arctic Warfare Cadre and is generally considered to be one of the best elite groups of its kind in the world.

The Army itself is presently undergoing its greatest period of restructuring since its post-war recreation in the early 1950s. In time of war, Brigade North, based at Heggelia near Tromso, would advance to the Finnmark border to engage a Soviet invasion force from Murmansk and, as such, forms the linchpin of Norwegian defence. Its present strength consists of a headquarters with integral signals, provost and armoured reconnaissance companies, three infantry battalions each with four companies, an armoured company with three armoured and one mechanized platoons, an anti-aircraft battery, and an artillery battalion with four self-propelled batteries. This is presently being enhanced by the addition of a mechanized battalion with 26 tanks and 32 APCs to give it an overall strength of 6,000 men – as large as the average Soviet division! Brigade South and 13th Brigade, which are also enhanced, would be airlifted in support of Northern Brigade as soon as possible after the commencement of hostilities.

The Norwegian Home Guard ('Heimevernet') was formed in 1946 from Resistance fighters. It is 74,700 strong, containing Army reservists, male and female volunteers and a small nucleus of approximately 350 Regular Army officers and senior NCOs. Divided between 18 districts, 84 sectors and 525 (parish) areas, its members keep their weapons at home, are able to mobilize in four hours and exercise an importance out of all proportion to their costs (approximately three per cent of the National Defence Expenditure).

Most members of the Home Guard are conscripted, having served for three to 18 months in the Forces (under certain circumstances the period of military conscription may be reduced from 12 to 3 months for those joining the Home Guard), and on transfer to the 'Heimevernet' are expected to undertake six days training per year.

British-style uniforms were adopted by the Norwegian Free Army during the War. Plain olive drab trousers are worn in the field together with a new-style camouflage jacket and 'Norwegian' shirt. Officers wear white rank stars on olive drab shoulder slides, edged gold for general and white for field officers, and NCOs wear white shoulder-board chevrons. In summer a distinctive non-camouflage field cap is worn, replaced in winter by a fur cap with a metal rank badge mounted in the peak.

Surveillance along Norway's extensive borders is a crucial element of the Army's role.

Norwegian soldiers are trained to patrol their country's myriad fjords to counter any enemy infiltrations.

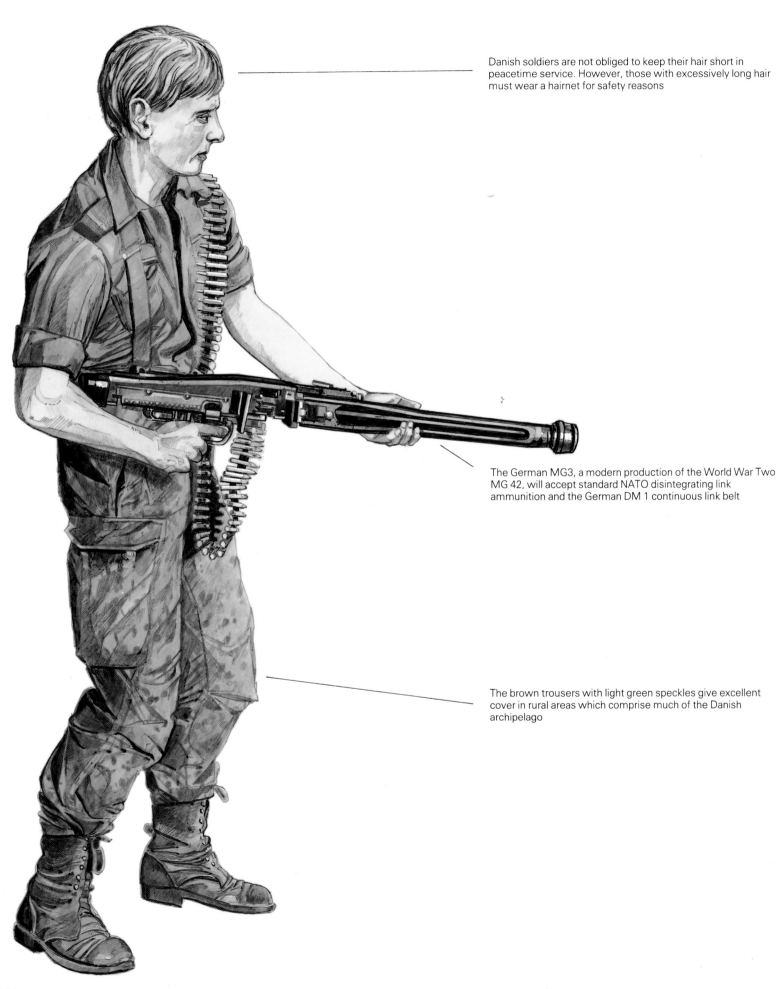

Danish soldiers are not obliged to keep their hair short in peacetime service. However, those with excessively long hair must wear a hairnet for safety reasons

The German MG3, a modern production of the World War Two MG 42, will accept standard NATO disintegrating link ammunition and the German DM 1 continuous link belt

The brown trousers with light green speckles give excellent cover in rural areas which comprise much of the Danish archipelago

Denmark has one of the smallest populations of any NATO country yet one of the most strategic borders, commanding as it does the Kattegat and Baltic approaches. Despite drastic attempts to preserve her neutrality, including the standing down of half her Army so as not to provoke the Nazis, Denmark was attacked and within four hours overrun by Hitler in June 1940.

Today Copenhagen, the capital, stands on the island of Sjaelland overlooking the Sound through which the Soviet Baltic fleet would have to deploy in time of crisis. The 7th Polish Naval Assault Division, the 5th East German Army and two Soviet motor rifle divisions are trained for operations in the peninsula and the Danes are fully reconciled to the fact that out of geographical necessity, their country would provide one of the first battlefields of any future East-West confrontation.

Since their liberation in 1945, the Danes have preferred to rely for protection on a strong and highly motivated force of volunteer Home Guard ('Hjemmevaernet') rather than the formal armed forces. The peacetime Army numbers only 17,000, of whom 6,800 are conscripts serving for nine months, one of the shortest periods of compulsory service in the world. 7,000 men are stationed in the permanent Standing Force, 4,000 in training units, 6,000 in schools, regional headquarters and in administration and up to 500 in a UN Battalion at present serving in Cyprus.

In time of war the Standing Force would be supplemented immediately by the 6,000 strong Augmentation Force consisting of a combination of serving regular soldiers and conscripts, some of whom would have recently completed their national service. The Field Army Reserve of 35,000 men would be activated as soon as possible thereafter, as would the 24,000-strong Regional Defence Force and 60,400 men and women of the Home Guard responsible for area and territorial defence.

The elite of the Danish Army serve in the independent reconnaissance battalions, divided into companies to provide tactical intelligence for the five mechanized infantry brigades and regimental combat teams.

A Special Operations Company, or Jaegercorps, was formed in 1961. Although Denmark has no airborne capability, all Jaegers are paratroop-trained. Selection, open to naval and air force personnel as well as the military, is extremely uncompromising.

Transferees undertake a series of courses covering the conventional special forces skills of demolitions, unarmed combat, communications and free-fall parachuting. Great emphasis is given to speed-marching over great distances, often carrying heavy loads, to patrol skiing and to survival in a hostile environment. SCUBA diving, surface swimming with or without a wet suit, and boat handling are all taught to a high standard. After two years of training, a volunteer will qualify to join one of the five-man Long Range Reconnaissance Patrol (LRRPs) teams and may then wear the Jaeger-bugle badge, paratroop wings and red beret.

The American TOW anti-tank missile is found throughout NATO. This Danish TOW launcher is mounted on a tracked APC to provide a highly mobile anti-armour capability.

The Danish Army equips itself from a variety of sources. This Danish soldier has a German G-3 rifle, American-pattern webbing, and is guarding a British Land Rover.

So as to ensure a high standard of leadership, Jaegercorps run a series of annual training courses for the Army as a whole, which must be attempted and passed by all officer cadets prior to their commissioning.

The Home Guard, more than twice the size of the armed forces, was formed in 1948 by former resistance workers suspicious of the regular army. Divided into seven regions, 37 districts and 540 Home Guard Companies, it is lightly armed but highly motivated and could be expected to give a good account of itself in any future conflict.

THE SPANISH FOREIGN LEGION

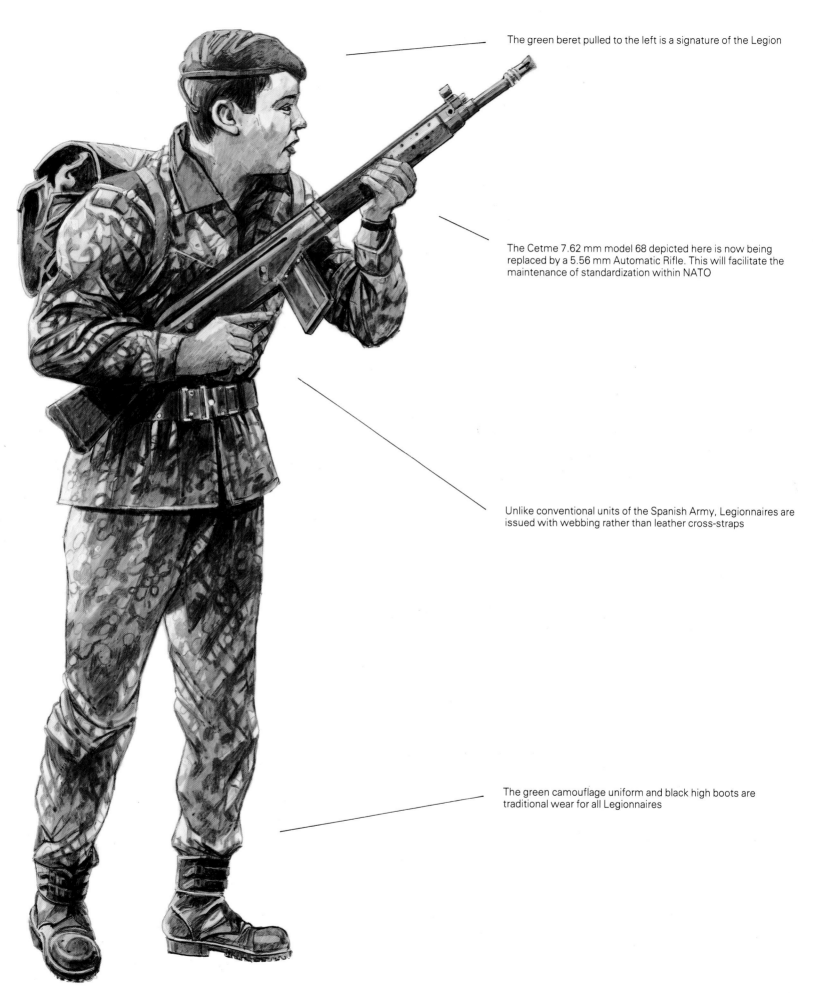

The green beret pulled to the left is a signature of the Legion

The Cetme 7.62 mm model 68 depicted here is now being replaced by a 5.56 mm Automatic Rifle. This will facilitate the maintenance of standardization within NATO

Unlike conventional units of the Spanish Army, Legionnaires are issued with webbing rather than leather cross-straps

The green camouflage uniform and black high boots are traditional wear for all Legionnaires

Unlike its older and better known French equivalent, the Spanish Foreign Legion has always been constituted almost entirely of natives and indeed since 1987 has completely ceased recruiting foreigners. Formed by the King of Spain in 1920, it drew its initial inspiration from a combination of French activity in North Africa and the actions of Spanish and foreign volunteers who had fought so valiantly in the nineteenth-century Carlist civil wars.

It was a prerequisite for all volunteers that they abandoned earlier allegiances in favour of the all-encompassing 'Credo of the Legion', which offered as a reward an uncompromising attitude of total military commitment with absolute forgiveness for all past deeds. Accordingly a mystique grew up around the Legion which survives to this day, and which is arguably the root-cause of the mistrust felt towards it by many post-Franco politicians.

Today's Foreign Legion has suffered severely from the latest round of domestic arms reductions. Not only is it presently being reduced from an overall strength of 8,500 to a proposed target of 6,500, but nearly 20 per cent of its battalion-sized units have been dissolved.

The Legion, although under the direct command of the Chief of Army Staff, retains its own headquarters and integral staff under the command of a brigadier. It operates three combat and one support regiments, or Tercios, each with its own full colonel. Although retaining its headquarters and depot at Ronda, in Southern Spain, the Legion's present commitments are currently mobile and there is the distinct possibility that once its internal reorganization has been completed it will form the backbone of Spain's new Rapid Deployment Force being formed for operations outside the Iberian Peninsula.

The 1st and 2nd Tercios, known as 'Gran Capitan' and 'Duque de Alba' respectively, are garrisoned in the North Moroccan towns of Melilla and Ceuta. Both have recently lost a motorized battalion, leaving each with a headquarters company, one motorized and one mechanized battalion and an anti-tank company equipped with TOW anti-tank guided weapons.

The motorized battalion, or bandera, withdrawn from the 1st Tercio has been reassigned to the Legion's main depot at Ronda and placed under the command of the 4th Tercio ('Alejandro de Farnesco'). It has been integrated with the Special Operations Platoons originally drawn from each bandera to form the elite Special Operations Battalion and now attracts some of the best personnel in the Legion. Scuba diving, military parachuting, unarmed combat, guerrilla and anti-terrorist operations are taught in conjunction with normal military training.

The 3rd Tercio ('Juan de Austria') is permanently garrisoned on the Canary Islands and is considered by many to constitute the highest operational readiness element of the Spanish Army.

The new streamlined Legion has recently been heavily re-equipped. The mechanized battalions now have new ENASA wheeled APCs, the Light

Cavalry Group (itself part of the 4th Tercio) has replaced its old AMC armoured cars with 48 new ENASA VEC wheeled reconnaissance vehicles mounting 25mm or 90mm guns and a new domestically produced 5.56mm automatic rifle is replacing the elderly 7.62 CETME model 68.

Enlistment into the Legion, which is relatively easy, is for an initial period of three years renewable thereafter. Training is short, severe and savage, including physical assault or imprisonment for relatively minor transgressions. Much time is dedicated to drill, fitness training, weapon familiarization and the completion of long route marches often over rough terrain. Generally Legionnaires are heavily dependent on their officers and are positively discouraged from using their own initiative. Officers and NCOs are trained at the Leaders Academy, a college run internally under the command of a Legionnaire lieutenant-colonel.

Traditionally the Legion wears a green camouflage uniform with black high boots and a green beret adjusted to the left. Webbing straps and belts are issued, as opposed to the less comfortable leather worn by the rest of the Army. In cold weather gauntleted gloves and a white-lined cape with fur collar and hood are worn.

Above: American influence is apparent in this soldier's equipment, but his 5.56mm CETME rifle distinguishes him.

Below: This soldier is equipped with the carbine version of the new CETME rifle, which features a shorter barrel and a collapsible butt.

PORTUGUESE ARMY

The deerstalker hat is a throw-back to Colonial days

Low visibility red badges of rank are worn on both shoulders

The traditional jungle-green camouflage was originally designed for Colonial service but has now been adapted for the European climate. A thick roll-neck jumper is issued for cold-weather use

The CETME 7.62 mm rifle is standard issue

Uniquely, the webbing is held in position by straps around the thigh

For centuries Portugal regarded herself exclusively as a sea power, maintaining both her empire and worldwide trading interests with the help of a large and efficient navy. With the exception of the Great War, when she sent two divisions to fight with the Allies on the Western Front, she ignored European intrigue whenever possible. She did, however, allow the Allies the use of the Azores from 1943 to 1945 and in 1949 joined NATO. The entire *status quo* changed drastically when, on 25th April 1974, a socialist-orientated military coup toppled the autocratic Salazar regime and granted independence to the warring and largely unsuspecting colonies within a matter of months.

Portugal immediately began to look upon herself once again as a part of Europe, determined to play a more realistic part in the defence of NATO. Her armed forces, which for decades had been geared towards the maintenance of order throughout the empire, were grossly outdated and ill-equipped by European standards. Initial attempts at improvement were frustrated by the precarious domestic economic situation, so much so that military expenditure declined steadily until by 1985 Portugal's defence expenditure as a percentage of her GNP was virtually the lowest in NATO. This has now changed and, although traditionally the role of the Navy is still regarded as paramount, Army weaponry and equipment are steadily improving.

Today the Army totals 39,000 soldiers, of whom 30,000 are conscripts undertaking 16 months national service. The largest unit, the 1st Composite Brigade, is assigned to NATO's Land Forces South Europe Command and would be stationed with the Italians on the Yugoslav border in time of emergency. Although the Brigade is virtually at full strength and exercises regularly in its combat area, none of its heavy equipment is pre-positioned, with the result that it would take up to 15 days for it to become fully operational, a time scale unlikely to be permitted in any future war. The 4,000-strong Brigade is classified as motorized, consisting of one mechanized battalion of three companies, two motorized battalions, a small armoured battalion, artillery group including a 155mm self-propelled battery, and reconnaissance engineer and signals companies with a support battalion with its integral maintenance and medical wings.

The elite Special Forces Brigade was formed in 1984 from 2,000 battle-hardened veterans of the African campaigns. Consisting basically of the Independent Commando Regiment with its headquarters, training battalion and two enlarged operational battalions, each of five companies, it would be enhanced in time of war by the Parachute Brigade and helicopter wing. Unusually, the Light Parachute Brigade, which comes under the jurisdiction of the Air Force, does not train as a single entity but is dispersed in time of peace.

Other military units, including the 14 infantry regiments, the elite 5th Rifles Battalion (Cacadores), the two armoured reconnaissance regiments and the five field artillery regiments,

are dispersed between the Military Regions and Zones.

Equipment issued is of general NATO origin, although the M–47 and M–48A5 tanks and M 109A2 self-propelled howitzers are all of United States construction. The field dress retains several African traits, particularly in the 'deer-stalker' cap with its long flap at the rear to protect the neck from sunstroke.

The Army, although small, is well-motivated and improving rapidly. Economic constraints permitting, it will soon be able to play the role within NATO so obviously sought for it by its new political leaders.

Distinctive free-fall parachute assemblies are being worn by the two jumpers nearest the camera.

Unusually, the Light Parachute Brigade comes under the jurisdiction of the Air Force. However, in time of war it would work closely with the Independent Commando Regiment.

TURKISH ARMY

Standard mass-produced US helmets have been adopted by the Turkish Army amongst many others

Unusually, conspicuous badges of rank are worn on both sleeves

The infantry is now being issued with up-to-date equipment, in this instance the Heckler & Koch G3 7.62mm self-loading rifle

DPM uniforms are a recent introduction, replacing the old olive-drab battledress

Both politically and economically, Turkey has moved increasingly towards the West throughout the second half of the twentieth century. Although she declined to declare war on Nazi Germany until the very final stages of World War Two, she formed a close alliance with the United States soon afterwards and became a formal member of NATO in February 1952. Prior to that, her troops had shown their tremendous combat potential when a full brigade had deployed with the United Nations forces in Korea. Not only did they prove themselves to be excellent fighters but also extremely hardy individuals. Although a number were captured by Communist forces, not one broke under interrogation or torture – a record unique to their contingent.

The modern Armed Forces enjoy great prestige among the general population and exercise tremendous political influence. The President, himself a retired Army General, is also Commander-in Chief of the Armed Forces and relies on the latter heavily to ensure that the civilian government does not stray excessively from traditional nationalist values.

The sheer size of the modern Turkish Army should be seen as a reflection of her traditional animosity towards her Greek neighbours rather than as a sign of her anti-Soviet commitment. Turkey and Greece nearly found themselves at war in July 1974, when Turkey invaded northern Cyprus, and more recently over disputed territorial waters.

The Army is 542,000 strong, of whom some 497,000 are conscripts undertaking 18 months national service. It is organized into four field armies, all assigned to NATO. The 1st Army, the largest and best equipped, is stationed in the Istanbul area and in time of war would be tasked with denying use of the Bosphorus to the Soviet Black Sea Fleet. The 2nd Army, stationed in Malatya, Eastern Anatolia, would respond to the Soviet threat from the north-east or to attempts at destabilization from Iran and Iraq, whilst the 3rd Army, based at Erzerum, would guard the 400-mile (640-km) long Soviet border. The 4th or Aegean Army contains only the XI Corps with two divisions and 25,000 men and is presently based at Kyrenia in Northern Cyprus.

Each of the 10 Corps controls up to five divisions, of which there are 17 in all, and a number of the 25 independent brigades, together with signals, armoured and engineer battalions, an artillery regiment of three battalions and two anti-aircraft battalions in support.

Only one division is truly armoured, consisting of three armoured brigades, each with one mechanized and two armoured battalions, a self-propelled artillery regiment and armoured reconnaissance. The majority of divisions are motorized, containing 12,000 men, two motorized regiments each of three motorized battalions, an armoured or mechanized regiment and a field artillery regiment. The elite Parachute and Commando Brigades, each 5,000 strong, have three parachute or commando battalions, an artillery battalion and support services.

The 125,000 strong Gendarmerie, or

'Jandarma', is divided into three mobile brigades and 67 regiments, one per region, and in time of war acts as a home defence force under military, but not NATO, command. These would be supplemented by the Civil Defence Force constituted by men aged from 16 to 60 and women between 20 and 45, mobilized to repel Soviet airborne or amphibious landings and to combat Spetsnaz operations.

Although the Turkish soldier has a justifiable reputation for toughness, his equipment is sadly lacking. With the exception of 77 German Leopard 1s, all tanks are elderly US M–47s or M–48s. Even allowing for the fact that the latter are now being re-engined and re-gunned, they are no match for the latest generation of Soviet armour.

At present, camouflage uniforms are restricted to commando, paratroop and Gendarmerie-Commando troops, the rest wearing a brown two-piece combat suit of trousers and blouse with a black beret (although more colours are now being introduced), a brass or black thread cap badge for officers and professional NCOs and a brown-coloured beret disc for conscripts.

These Turkish soldiers, pictured at the time of their invasion of Northern Cyprus, possess a great variety of weapons and equipment. Much of the older kit has been phased out, but the Turkish Army still retains much equipment regarded as obsolete by the rest of NATO.

An important part of Turkey's contribution to NATO is provision of this radar site in the mountains of Eastern Turkey. Part of the Nato Air Defence Ground Environment (NADGE), these radars provide essential cover for NATO's southern flank.

THE GREEK ARMY

Commandos and paratroopers are issued with a green beret, adorned by a cap badge depicting the Greek royal emblem

The domestically-produced webbing is strongly influenced by the standard US pattern

The ubiquitous PN 7.62 mm FAL, in this instance with folding butt, is standard issue

Only special forces are issued with camouflage uniforms. Conventional troops wear plain olive-drab

The Greek army has a strong tradition of military defiance against a numerically superior enemy. In October 1940 it successfully withstood an Italian attack from Albania, beating the enemy so decisively that they were forced to plead with their German allies for military assistance. Pockets of the Greek Army managed to escape before their country was forced to surrender in April 1941 and many subsequently joined the British 8th Army, with whom they fought valiantly throughout the North African and Italian campaigns. After the Germans were forced to evacuate Greece in October 1944, there followed five years of bitter civil war which ended with the complete defeat of the Communist-inspired ELAS guerrillas.

By December 1950 the Greek Government felt strong enough to send a battalion, later joined by a second, in support of the United Nations forces in Korea. In February 1952, Greece formally joined the NATO alliance and began at once to receive massive United States aid. Greece left the Integrated NATO command in August 1974 in protest at the Organization's failure to prevent the Turkish invasion of Cyprus, but returned in October 1980 more out of a fear of her growing isolation than in response to anti-Soviet sentiments.

The modern Greek Army is 165,000 strong, including 108,500 conscripts serving for 21 months and 1,400 women who mostly act as nurses. Command is delegated to three Military Regions – Salonika in the north, Kocani in the centre and Athens in the south – and to two territorial commands – Attika, which controls the offshore islands, and the Aegean responsible for the politically sensitive islands abutting the Turkish coastline.

The combat formations are divided between four main corps and a number of independent divisions. 'A' Corps, with three motorized infantry divisions, stands in Army reserve at Larissa whilst 'B' Corps, with three infantry division, guards the north-west frontier against the possibility of a Soviet flanking attack through Yugoslavia. 'C' and 'D' Corps, the best equipped with one armoured and three infantry divisions and one mechanized and two infantry divisions respectively, are assigned to NATO and tasked with the halting of a Soviet-Bulgarian invasion through Thrace.

The 20th Armoured Division, a part of 'C' Corps, is 13,000 strong and with its integral reconnaissance battalion, artillery, transport, signals and medical battalions, is without doubt the most potent force in the Greek Army. the 11 infantry divisions each have 14,000 personnel, split between an armoured battalion with one reconnaissance and three armoured companies, a field artillery regiment with three armoured companies, a field artillery regiment with three battalions and three motorized regiments.

Over 1,750 troops, including an infantry battalion, 350 commandos and 450 officers and NCOs on loan to the National Guard, are stationed in southern Cyprus to counter the Turkish threat from the north.

Anti-tank sections of the Greek Army, equipped with Jeep-mounted US TOW missiles, deploy on exercise.

Mechanics work on a Steyr APC now being produced under licence by Hellenic Arms Industries.

An elite Para-Commando Division, with a parachute regiment (two battalions), Special Raider Force Battalion, commando regiment (three battalions) and marine regiment (three battalions) is retained in reserve.

The Greek Army is well respected by the population. Its officers tend to be professional and its soldiers undemanding and reliable. Its equipment however is outdated and geared far more to overcoming the threat, real or imagined, from Turkey than to countering the latest generation of Soviet armour. To compound the problem, both Greece and Turkey look upon each other's rearmament with marked suspicion and do all in their power to dissuade potential donors such as the United States from giving or even selling replacement weapon systems.

With the exception of paratroopers, marines and commandos, who are issued with camouflage uniform, all ranks wear a plain olive drab combat suit. Commandos and paratroopers wear a green beret, the 'Evzones' or Presidential Guard a blue beret, and armoured troops black.

SOVIET PARATROOPER

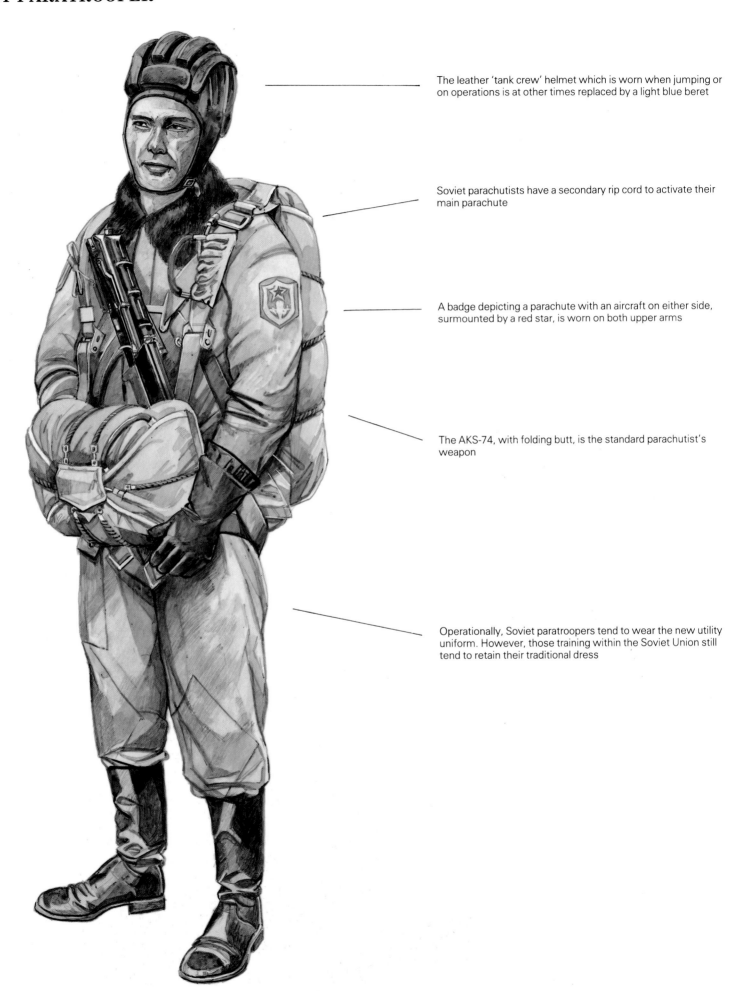

The leather 'tank crew' helmet which is worn when jumping or on operations is at other times replaced by a light blue beret

Soviet parachutists have a secondary rip cord to activate their main parachute

A badge depicting a parachute with an aircraft on either side, surmounted by a red star, is worn on both upper arms

The AKS-74, with folding butt, is the standard parachutist's weapon

Operationally, Soviet paratroopers tend to wear the new utility uniform. However, those training within the Soviet Union still tend to retain their traditional dress

The BMD airborne assault vehicle was specially developed for the Soviet airborne forces and is capable of being dropped by parachute. Together with command and artillery variants, the BMD adds considerably to the mobility and firepower of the otherwise lightly-equipped paratroops.

Whereas NATO has recently questioned the whole concept of airborne operations in conventional warfare, the Soviet Union has rarely expressed any doubt as to the value of an airborne élite in any future conflict and has steadily increased the size and potency of its airborne forces. Today these are in excess of 50,000 men deployed with nine divisions, seven combat-ready, one reserve and one training, stationed as far afield as the Baltic and Afghanistan. Totally enshrining the Soviet principles of mobility, surprise and aggression, the Soviet Airborne Forces ('Vozdushov Desantiye Voyska') have long been used by the Government as its iron fist whenever and wherever foreign policy dictates. For instance, the 103rd Guards Air Assault Division spearheaded the invasion of Czechoslovakia in 1968, supported the 105th Guards Air Assault Division in the capture of Kabul in December 1979 and is even today in the forefront of the struggle to contain the Mjuahideen.

Unlike their British or American equivalents, Soviet paratroopers are conscripts undertaking their two years of national service with an airborne division. Usually they will have learned to parachute with a civilian club sponsored by DOSAFF, which they will have joined during their final two years of school and where they will have established themselves as competent sportsmen before actually joining the airborne forces at the age of 18. Rejection during training, as high as 60 per cent in the British Parachute Regiment, is therefore kept to a minimum.

Initial basic training is regarded as character-building concentrating on fitness, battle technique and self-reliance, with surprisingly little emphasis placed on the actual art of parachuting. Political reliability among airborne soldiers is considered essential, considerable time being spent on propaganda. All training jumps are made with T-series parachutes similar to those used throughout NATO. However, whereas the Western recruit is only expected to jump cleanly, relying on his static line to open his parachute, the young Soviet, although attached to a static line, is expected to master the 'delayed-pull' ripcord from the outset. Although this complicates his basic training, it is of considerable advantage in the future as it enables the individual soldier to control the height at which he opens his 'chute if jumping under fire.

Once a recruit completes his training he must make ten jumps per year to retain his jump status with its attendant privileges.

Although a Soviet airborne division consisting of approximately 6,500 men is small by Western standards, its firepower and mobility are second to none.

The Soviets will only use airborne forces after careful consideration, as they have no wish to squander valuable men, equipment or aircraft in futile exercises. Airborne operations are usually deployed in support of a main army thrust and can take place anywhere between 500km and 50km from the front line. The size of the force used varies considerably from a single company to a full division, dependent on the size of the objective, its distance behind enemy lines, anticipated resistance and the potential for reinforcement.

Although airborne troops in Afghanistan have been seen in a new utility uniform, most continue to wear their own distinctive dress. A leather tank-crew helmet is worn while jumping or on operations, but at all other times is replaced by a light blue beret. Unusually, a red triangular badge is worn next to the main cap badge either on the left or right, dependent on local custom. Blue arm badges worn on both sleeves and the high-necked blue striped vest both denote élite troops. As all airborne units gained 'Guards' status in the Great Patriotic War, all wear the Guards badge over the right breast. Interestingly this honour has not been afforded Spetsnaz troops, who are immediately recognisable when disguised as airborne troops by the lack of this badge. A badge depicting a parachute with an aircraft on either side is worn on the collar tabs to complete the uniform.

SPETSNAZ

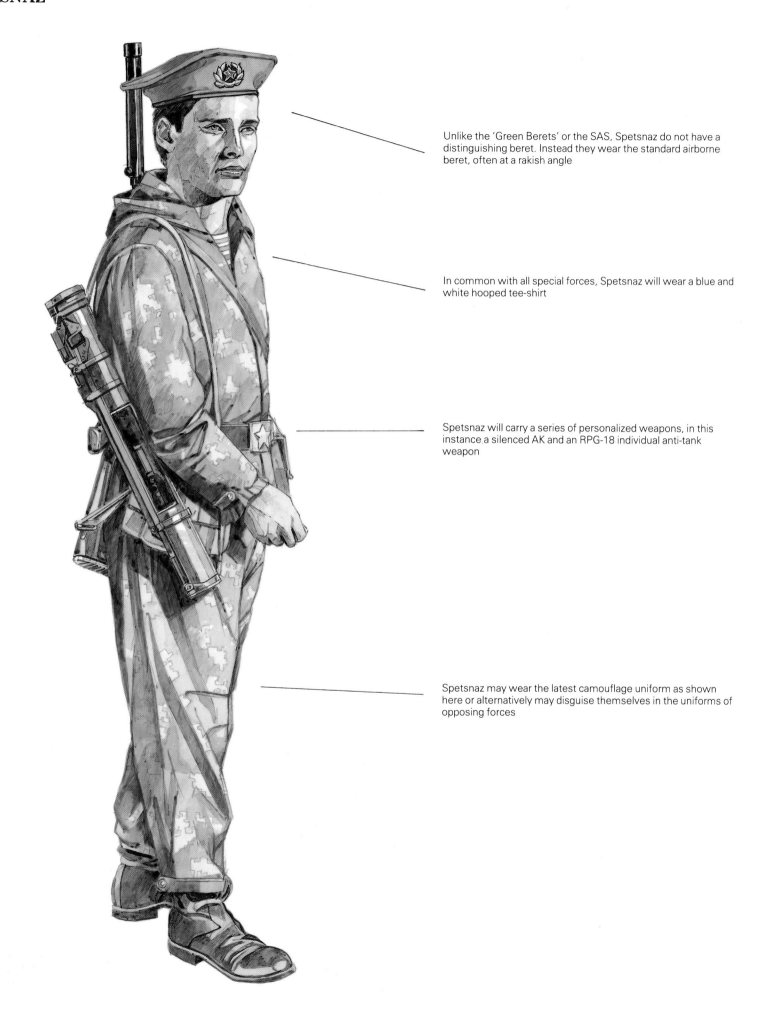

Unlike the 'Green Berets' or the SAS, Spetsnaz do not have a distinguishing beret. Instead they wear the standard airborne beret, often at a rakish angle

In common with all special forces, Spetsnaz will wear a blue and white hooped tee-shirt

Spetsnaz will carry a series of personalized weapons, in this instance a silenced AK and an RPG-18 individual anti-tank weapon

Spetsnaz may wear the latest camouflage uniform as shown here or alternatively may disguise themselves in the uniforms of opposing forces

The name Spetsnaz originates from the words 'Spetsialnoye Nazhacheniye' or Special Purpose and is used to describe the most secretive and feared military force in the Soviet Union. Subordinated to the 2nd Military Directorate of Soviet Military Intelligence (GRU), and not, as is sometimes thought, the Committee for State Security (KGB), Spetsnaz is an integral part of the Army.

Great precautions are taken within the Soviet Union to disguise the strength, structure and deployment of Spetsnaz, which is never referred to as such in the open press.

The vast majority of Spetsnaz soldiers are conscripts. Well before induction all will have been vetted for political reliability, most will be the sons of Party members and themselves members of Komsomol and all will have excelled as members of DOSAFF (the Voluntary Society for the Co-operation with the Army, Aviation and Navy).

Basic training is far harsher than that undertaken by the conventional conscript. It starts with a month-long intensive and highly physical course during which the natural leaders will be selected and sent to training battalions to become sergeants. Most qualified 'sergeants' will then be posted to their units as private soldiers, thus ensuring that any sergeant failing to maintain the superlative standards expected of him can be replaced immediately.

Brigade headquarters and three independent regiments are manned exclusively by professional soldiers whose activities are shrouded in even greater secrecy. Many of these professional soldiers are female and a notable minority are Olympic champions.

Training of conscript combat units, although based on conventional airborne forces training, is far more rigorous, so much so that officers and warrant officers receive 50 per cent additional pay, an allowance for every parachute jump and a 50 per cent increase in pension. Each soldier is likely to spend over half of each year on field exercises under simulated combat conditions. Training is made as realistic as possible; troops learn to live off the land and sleeping-bags are rarely supplied, however inclement the weather. Exercises often consist of long forced marches culminating in an attack on a well-defended target guarded by an experienced but unsuspecting 'enemy'.

The Special Operations Brigade ('Brigada Osobovo Naznacheniya') is the basic Spetsnaz unit. Allotted one per Group of Forces or Military District, each of the 16 brigades comprises a headquarters element and company, three or four parachute battalions and supporting units. Each brigade, consisting of between 1,000 and 1,300 fighting soldiers, is capable of operating either as a single entity or as a number of sub units, up to a total of 135.

In time of war, Spetsnaz would undertake several diversified roles, from the hunting down and assassination of political leaders to the destruction of command centres, airfields and key points. Operations rely on speed and mobility. All ranks are trained in the use of enemy weapons

and equipment, including tanks and APCs, and would seize and use these whenever practical.

It is highly likely that many Spetsnaz soldiers will enter enemy territory during the build-up to hostilities to facilitate pre-emptive strikes. Many will land by parachute or boat, others will disguise themselves as civilians (a large percentage speak excellent English or German) whilst some will infiltrate the enemy's lines wearing perfect replicas of its uniform.

When stationed abroad, Spetsnaz will usually disguise their presence by wearing the uniform of the nearest major communications unit. Unlike the British SAS or United States' Green Berets, they have no distinctive headdress or cap badge and when not disguised as another unit wear the standard uniform of the airborne and air assault forces. Airborne forces were however awarded Guards Division status in the Great Patriotic War and now wear Guards badges on their distinctive blue-epauletted uniforms. Thus, airborne soldiers wearing airborne uniform without the Guards badge will be either air assault troops or Spetsnaz. As the former never parachute, the proximity of a parachute will be an obvious aid to identification.

In Spetsnaz the Soviet Union has a dedicated force of approximately 30,000 men and women, all highly trained and motivated. Although neither are as highly trained nor as specialist as the SAS or Green Berets, their role in any future conflict would be significant.

Soviet special forces practise a wide variety of infiltration techniques on exercises. When operating as small patrols, they must be totally self-reliant in overcoming any obstacles between them and their objective.

Natural athletes are encouraged to develop their skills to the highest level. Foreign travel as a sportsman permits much greater freedom of action than travel as a 'diplomat' and also such opportunities are exploited for reconnaissance value.

SOVIET JUNIOR OFFICER

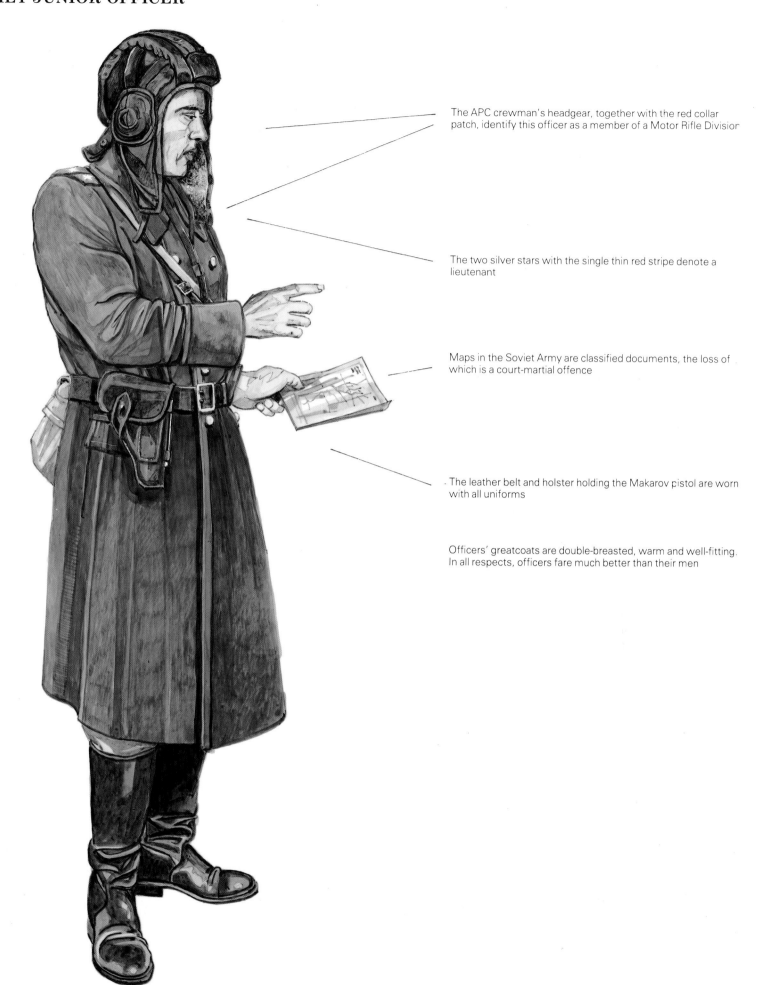

The APC crewman's headgear, together with the red collar patch, identify this officer as a member of a Motor Rifle Division

The two silver stars with the single thin red stripe denote a lieutenant

Maps in the Soviet Army are classified documents, the loss of which is a court-martial offence

The leather belt and holster holding the Makarov pistol are worn with all uniforms

Officers' greatcoats are double-breasted, warm and well-fitting. In all respects, officers fare much better than their men

The status and role of the Soviet officer is completely different from that of his European or United States equivalent. Gone are the days when an officer automatically enjoyed a lifestyle far above his civilian counterpart. Although conditions for the senior officer are good, those for the junior are tedious, living standards spartan, and the incidence of alcoholism high. Despite this, the young officer is being drawn increasingly from the upper strata of a theoretically classless society, with many even regarding the Army as an hereditary profession.

There are several methods of obtaining a commission. Most recruits, however, attend one of over 140 officers' schools situated throughout the country. Unlike the RMA Sandhurst or West Point Military Academy, each school specializes in a particular field of soldiering. Entry is by written examination, there is no central regular commissioning board, and standards vary greatly.

Pupils at a Military Academy will have attended either a State-run or secondary school, a Suvorov Military School or will have completed the first period of their two years' conscription. Conscripts will take the same written examination as school entrants, after which they will transfer directly to the academy. Although the Soviets deny the existence of a quota system, most successful conscripts will be of Russian origin and few, if any, will be from the Muslim south. The nine Suvorov schools, originally opened in 1943 for the children of servicemen killed in the war, offer the highest standard of education within the Soviet Union. Nowadays fees are subsidized and not – as might be expected in a Communist country – free, and entry is restricted to the sons of officers and Party officials.

Undergraduates will not be conscripted at the age of 18 but will be expected to complete a part-time military course whilst at university, at the end of which they will be awarded the rank of reserve junior lieutenant. All graduates are allotted their first employment which they may not leave for three years, and it is entirely possible that technical graduates will find themselves awarded short-service commissions and sent to the regular forces for this period.

Officers' Schools themselves are divided into Higher Command and Higher Engineering Schools. Courses run for a minimum of four years with 60 per cent of the time devoted to military subjects, 30 per cent to general education and 10 per cent to political study. Most newly commissioned officers are members of Komsomol (the Young Communist League) and many will actively be taking steps towards becoming full Party members.

Newly commissioned officers are assigned either staff or command positions and may later attend Higher Education Colleges, akin to Western Staff Colleges, if deemed suitable. Although pay and living conditions for young officers were once considered good, both have stagnated and are now markedly lower than those enjoyed by the young civilian professional classes who have gained considerably under Gorbachev. However,

allowances for those serving abroad are good, promotion is reasonable, pensions above average and access to well-stocked military shops always available.

Many tasks allotted to skilled junior NCOs in NATO armies are carried out by technically trained officers, with a resultant high ratio of officers to men. Sub-unit commanders are given no scope for discretion, are not encouraged to get to know their men and are under the constant eye of the political officer. A single political indiscretion can mean the end of an otherwise promising military career.

It is clear that the war in Afghanistan has taught the Soviets the need for more flexibility in command. Recent military publications have called for a far greater show of awareness and initiative from younger officers, but this will only be obtained if the whole educational structure changes. Change comes slowly within the Soviet Union and it is likely, therefore, that for the conceivable future the officer class will continue to offer excellent technicians but poor tacticians.

The difference in quality between the officer's uniform and that of his soldiers is clearly seen in this photograph, taken in the Siberian Red Banner Military District.

SOVIET CONSCRIPT NCO

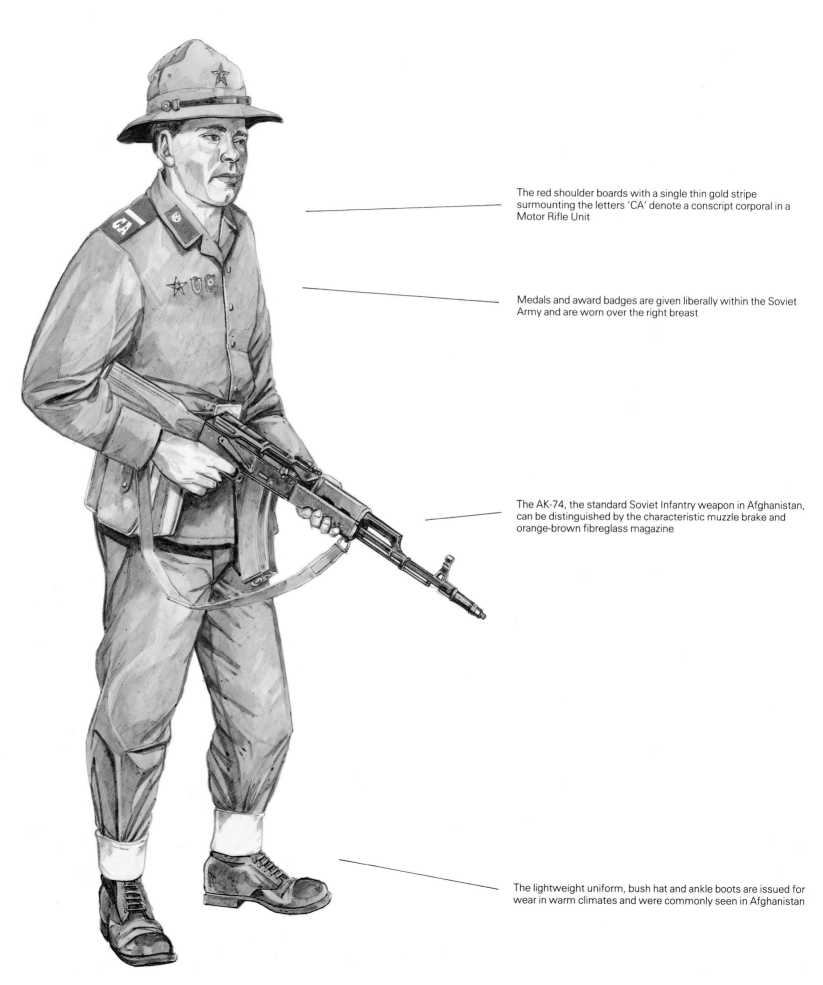

The red shoulder boards with a single thin gold stripe surmounting the letters 'CA' denote a conscript corporal in a Motor Rifle Unit

Medals and award badges are given liberally within the Soviet Army and are worn over the right breast

The AK-74, the standard Soviet Infantry weapon in Afghanistan, can be distinguished by the characteristic muzzle brake and orange-brown fibreglass magazine

The lightweight uniform, bush hat and ankle boots are issued for wear in warm climates and were commonly seen in Afghanistan

Historically the Soviet Union does not enjoy the West's traditions of a professional NCO cadre. Whereas a senior rank in the British or United States Army will be given a position of great responsibility within his unit, a Soviet sergeant will undertake only the most menial and repetitive of tasks. Discipline, training and the maintenance of equipment, all of which are at least in part the responsibility of NCOs within NATO, will be undertaken exclusively by officers.

The great majority of junior NCOs in the Soviet Army are sergeants (junior sergeants, sergeants and senior sergeants) who are selected on conscription. Selection is virtually at random, although reports from school and DOSAFF will probably be taken into account. The number of recruits selected at this stage is governed by the number of vacancies rather than by the potential of the intake, which may vary greatly.

Once selected, the potential NCO attends a six months course at a training division. If successful, he is then promoted for the remaining 18 months of his service to a combat unit. Each regiment within a training division specializes following a rigid curriculum. Once again, posting appears to be arbitrary with little or no effort taken to allot the recruit a trade to which he is most suited.

Training is intensive and discipline harsh. At the end of the fifth month each trainee sits an examination and, if successful, is promoted to the rank of corporal or junior sergeant, dependent in part on his ability but more specifically on the vacancy which he is being allotted to fill.

As 18 or 19-year-olds, the sergeants have no actual advantage of age or experience over the conscripts whom they control. Whereas an efficient NCO can hope to rise to senior sergeant during his 18 months of regimental service, a conscript, however good, will be lucky to attain the rank of corporal, with the result that there is often a high degree of resentment and friction between the NCO and his men.

The ratio of sergeant to private is far higher in the Soviet Union than anywhere within NATO. Whereas there is one sergeant per platoon of three sections in the British Army, all Soviet tank crews (bar the loader in older tanks) are NCOs. BTR-60 mounted infantry sections have one sergeant each and BMP sections an amazing three!

As the Soviet Army runs entirely on drills, the role of the sergeant in barracks is simply to supervise the endless repetition of section and platoon practices. Even drill parades are normally taken by officers. In battle his task is not to advise his officer but simply to obey orders unquestioningly and thereafter to ensure that they are carried out to the letter.

At the end of his first year a conscript may apply for entry to officer training college or for regular NCO service. If accepted for the latter, the recruit will receive a little extra money and such immediate privileges as use of subsidized military shops and possibly even leave.

Many young men opt for regular service as their only means of escaping the collective farm.

Conscripts are forced to return home on completion of their service, often to a backward area which they will not then be allowed to leave. Regular NCOs on the other hand are issued with internal passports after five years and regard military service for this period a reasonable price to pay for a chance to move to a city for the rest of their lives.

With the exception of senior sergeants who have opted for regular service, who are then issued with a parade walking-out dress, NCOs wear standard conscript uniform. Badges of rank, a single stripe for corporals, two for junior sergeants, three for sergeants and a thick band for senior sergeants, are worn on the shoulder boards above the branch of service designation. Collar-dogs are also worn, depicting the unit to which the NCO is attached.

Young tank NCOs take an impromptu musical break from their exercise to entertain local girls. Staging such propaganda exercises is part of the unit political officer's duties.

Most NCOs in technical positions will be directly supervised by an officer.

SOVIET INFANTRYMAN

The red shoulder board and letters 'CA' (Soviet Army) denote a conscript in a Motor Rifle Battalion

Unlike the majority of NATO armies, which now rely on webbing or increasingly on synthetic material, the Soviets still rely on leather belts and straps

The AK-74 is the standard personal weapon of the Soviet Infantryman

The high boots, although of reasonable quality, are rarely polished. Under-socks are not issued

The lot of the Soviet infrantryman is not a happy one. Life is hard, conditions brutal, pay virtually non-existent and punishment often collective.

Unless there are serious medical or domestic problems, or he has yet to finish his education – in which case enrolment will be deferred until the age of 27 – the young Soviet citizen will be drafted straight after his 18th birthday and will serve for a period of two years. Conscripts are called up *en masse* every six months, with the result that a highly undesirable four-tier society has evolved. 'Old soldiers' in their final six months of conscription (known as 'stariki') bully the young newcomers (or 'salaga'), often confiscating equipment and food whilst allotting them the most menial of barrack room tasks. The NCOs, none of whom have leadership experience, seem unwilling or unable to do anything about it.

Living conditions are basic, cramped and unhygienic. It is not unusual for an entire infantry company to sleep virtually shoulder-to-shoulder in a single barrack block with minimal, if any, privacy. If the camp is rural, which is usually the case, the latrine is often no more than a hole in the ground in the open air, or is situated in a shed outside the barracks. Many barracks do not have showers, only washbasins. Although the soldier will go with his entire unit to a banya, or steam room, once a week, there are few facilities for the laundering of uniforms. As he is usually required to retain the same uniform throughout the period of his service it soon becomes smelly and uncomfortable, particularly in hot climates.

Civilian clothes are never worn and the soldier is not allowed to wear anything non-government issue, even under his uniform. Foot cloths, known as portyankai, which are wrapped round the foot, are issued in lieu of socks. Although reportedly quite comfortable when worn properly, these must come as quite a shock to the young conscript.

As well as basic food and accommodation, the young soldier receives an allowance of between 5 and 8 roubles (about US $7.00 to US $10.00) per month.

Drinking and gambling are both strictly forbidden within the confines of the camp, with the result that the soldier's only chance of spending even this meagre sum comes at the weekend when, if he is lucky, he may be granted a pass to visit the local town. Once there, however, he may find that his conscripts haircut, utilitarian uniform (he will not be allowed to leave the camp in civilian clothes) and lack of money do not help him to attract local girls, who prefer the well paid factory workers. The fact that he will almost certainly be posted far from home, and will very probably therefore have difficulty in even understanding the local dialect, will not help.

The young infantryman gets no leave at all during his national service, although short periods may be offered as an inducement for joining Komsomol, on compassionate grounds, or on requesting transfer to the regular army (which is offered to the better recruits after their first year).

Training is both simplistic and repetitive, taking into account as it must the 25 per cent turnover of personnel every six months. Programmes are based on a five-month module and will include nothing more complex than a frontal company assault. This does however ensure that every soldier is highly skilled in the use of his personal weapon and will know exactly what will be expected of him in time of war.

Until recently, training was disrupted by the drafting every year of thousands of soldiers into the country to help with the harvest, but this now seems to be discouraged.

The Soviet infantryman has always been brave, obedient and tenacious. Despite the harshness of his service conditions, no one seriously doubts that he will prove a formidable enemy in any future conflict.

Soviet infantry attached to an armoured unit are seen leaving the protection of their T-62 tanks. Infantrymen may be attached to a number of different units and may well be expected to operate in the coldest of conditions.

123

SOVIET TANK CREWMAN

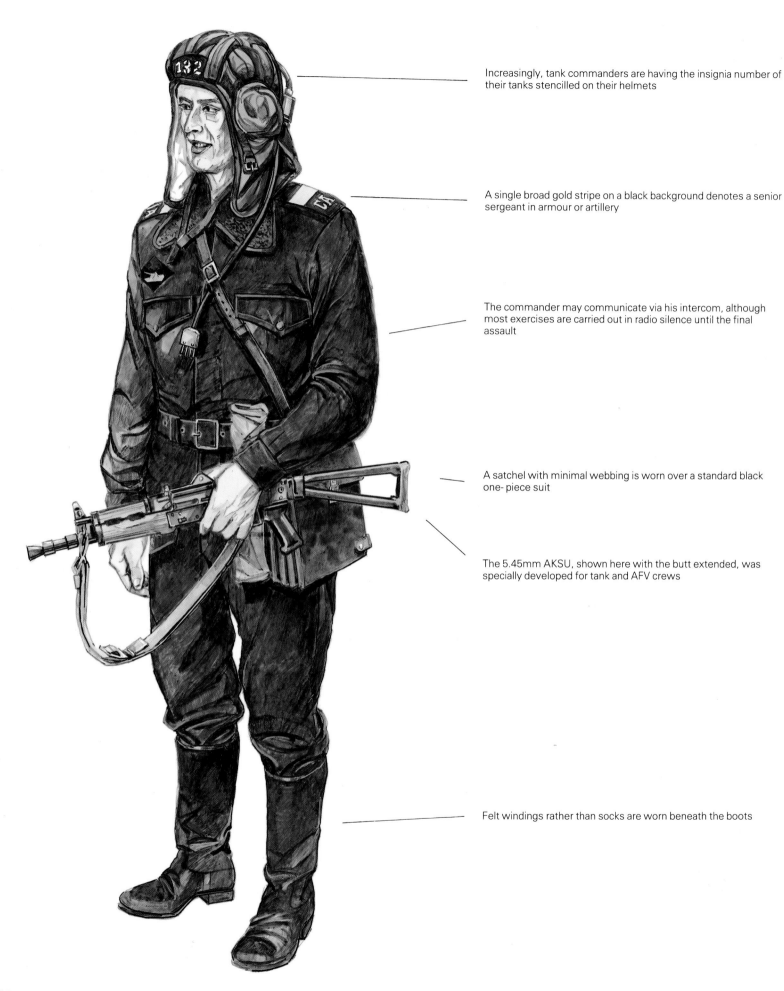

Increasingly, tank commanders are having the insignia number of their tanks stencilled on their helmets

A single broad gold stripe on a black background denotes a senior sergeant in armour or artillery

The commander may communicate via his intercom, although most exercises are carried out in radio silence until the final assault

A satchel with minimal webbing is worn over a standard black one-piece suit

The 5.45mm AKSU, shown here with the butt extended, was specially developed for tank and AFV crews

Felt windings rather than socks are worn beneath the boots

Massed armour has played a crucial role in Soviet military thought since the huge tank battles of the Great Patriotic War. Today the Soviet Union has some 53,000 operational tanks, including over 21,000 of the latest T-64s, T-72s and T-80s, spread throughout some 50 Tank Divisions.

The role of the tank as an aggressive exploiter of enemy weaknesses has, if anything, been enhanced by the advent of battlefield nuclear and chemical weapons. In any future Northern European war, it is likely that these would be used to smash a hole in the enemy's defences which would afterwards be exploited by massed armour.

Unless seconded to a reconnaissance role, in which case additional training is given, Soviet tank crews are never expected to operate below company, and rarely below battalion, level. Although the majority of tank soldiers operate within armoured divisions, a tank battalion is attached to each motor rifle regiment and a tank regiment to each motor rifle division to give it additional firepower.

The Soviet tank crewman is a conscript serving for two years. During his initial training he will have been designated the role of driver, gunner or commander and will have trained in that area to the exclusion of all others. Unlike his NATO counterpart therefore, a driver will have little idea of how to fire the gun nor the gunner how to drive the tank, with the result that an injury sustained by any one of the crewmen will effectively render the tank inoperative.

Despite the fact that all battle drills are rigidly pre-ordained, with the individual commander having absolutely no scope for initiative, tank training is regarded as so specialist that all crew members, other than the loader, are non-commissioned officers. As the latest generation of Soviet tanks have automatic loading systems (which frequently break down), only the older T-55s and T-62s, now relegated to reserve divisions and to the Far East, actually carry a loader. Astonishingly therefore, the lowest rank of any armoured soldier physically facing NATO troops in the Central European theatre is likely to be that of corporal. It must be remembered however that junior NCOs are allotted at random from among the new recruits and are given absolutely no training in leadership. It should not therefore be assumed that Soviet crews are better than, or indeed in any way as good as, the majority of their NATO equivalents.

Individual crew training places far too high an emphasis on simulators to be satisfactory. Tanks are usually restricted to no more than 250km of travel annually, far too little to keep the drivers proficient. Furthermore such training as there is concentrates on a few tanks only, with the majority remaining in storage, only seeing service during occasional battalion or regimental exercises. As British armoured units have found to their cost, equipment which remains idle too long soon deteriorates, and it is likely therefore that breakdowns are commonplace during such exercises. Soviet tank gunners fire only about a dozen rounds of main gun ammunition per year – about one-tenth of the United States' allocation and

The symbol on the turret identifies this T-72 as belonging to a 'Guards' division.

The black overall and the absence of webbing typify Soviet AFV crewmen. The officer on the right has his vehicle number painted on the front of his helmet.

even less than the British! Although firing simulators in the form of 23mm sub-calibre devices fitted into the tubes is adequate to maintain the gunner's accuracy, it cannot give him practice in target acquisition, loading or retargeting, all of which will be crucial in any future conflict.

The once-distinctive black overalls and helmet which typified Soviet tank troops are now also worn by the crews of APCs and self-propelled guns. Crewmen attached to armoured regiments will wear black shoulder boards bearing the letters 'CA' (Soviet Army) below the insignia of rank. Those belonging to tank battalions attached to motor rifle regiments will wear the red shoulder boards of the infantry. Commonly, the tank turret number will be stencilled onto the driver's leather helmet for ease of recognition.

The Soviet tank crewman enjoys none of the elitism or panache of his Western equivalent. Despite his outward rank superiority, neither his training nor equipment are as good. Nor is he expected under any circumstances to play more than the smallest of roles in a large, complex and, to him, probably incomprehensible scenario.

SOVIET RECONNAISSANCE TROOPS

Reconnaissance Troops can expect to operate in contaminated areas and so will often wear full protective kit from the outset

The rubber face-mask covers the entire head, is uncomfortable and cannot be worn for prolonged periods

Ordinary soldiers do not have a voice transmitter incorporated in the respirator. Only officers and specialist troops have the abliility to communicate when masked-up

Unlike the suit, which is rubberised and easy to decontaminate, the leather belt and webbing will absorb chemicals readily

The all-important filter is housed in a haversack. Should the air tube be breached, it would prove lethal to the wearer

The Soviet Union is well aware of the fact that it cannot hope to be successful in battle without timely and comprehensive reconnaissance. Their recce operations are large scale, exploit a wide variety of assets drawn from numerous arms of the service, and are intensive and continuous. Unlike British or United States commanders who rely on a single screen of fast, lightly-protected vehicles to probe to their front, the Soviets employ multiple patrols on all sides of their formations. Not only will a Soviet Divisional Commander be able to call upon a wide variety of Army-level air and electronic warfare assets but he will also have up to three layers of dedicated ground recce patrols under his absolute control.

As soon as possible after the initial breakthrough, a Soviet Divisional Commander will send up to 15 Divisional recce elements forward to establish the strength, proximity and, if possible, make-up of the enemy. Each patrol, which will operate up to 50km forward of the front line, will consist of from three to five vehicles drawn from the Divisional Reconnaissance Battalion. This battalion, which uniquely consists of a combination of specialist recce vehicles, motor cycles, armoured personnel carriers and tanks, is manned by a cross-section of the most able soldiers available to the commander. Its members will have trained exhaustively in the arts of stealth, fire and movement (rarely practised by conventional troops, who are expected to master little beyond the frontal assault) and map reading – a skill also lost on the average Soviet infantryman.

Every regimental commander has a dedicated recce company which can be called upon to examine in detail the terrain up to 30km beyond his front. Unlike its larger Divisional counterpart, Regimental Recce has no tank support and is consequently trained to avoid combat unless absolutely unavoidable.

With the exception of the officers and senior NCOs, reconnaissance troops are drawn from the ranks of ordinary conscripts. In the tradition of the Soviet Army they will wear the relevant shoulder boards of their parent arm (crimson in the case of troops manning the APCs and black for the armoured crews) but lapel badges depicting the arm of service of the regiment to which they are attached. Thus a tank crewman will wear black shoulder boards but red lapel badges!

It is likely however that, taking into account the physical nature of their role, the majority of recce troops will be among the first Soviet soldiers to be issued with the new DPM coverall which has no badges of rank or unit identification.

Engineer and Chemical Defence units each have their own specialist elements tasked with providing the divisional or army commander with details of the best potential axes of advance. Engineer Recce units include frogmen trained to assess the viability of assault river crossings and to scout water obstacles and bridges for mines. They are also supplied with primitive mine detectors not supplied to conventional divisional or regimental recce troops, who are presumably expected to ascertain the position of mine fields by trial and error!

Whereas deep physical reconnaissance remains the prerogative of Spetsnaz, each Soviet division has the capacity to insert small teams of five or six men up to 50km behind enemy lines. These teams, which are trained in sabotage as well as reconnaissance, will usually be inserted by helicopter under cover of darkness and will be tasked specifically to locate potential air or artillery targets, such as nuclear launch sites, command control and communications centres and troop reinforcement concentrations.

Despite the very high level of regimentation found at all levels of Soviet operational thought, no commander can hope to succeed unless he has a clear idea of his enemy's numbers and intentions. To this end, a great deal of thought and effort is dedicated to the field of reconnaissance. High losses among recce troops would be inevitable in the early stages of any battle, yet only the best potential soldiers are chosen to fulfil this role.

The motorcycle combination, based on a WW2 design, has a shaft drive to the sidecar wheel, giving it surprisingly good cross-country performance. This, combined with its small size, makes it a useful adjunct to the amphibious BRDM-2 recce vehicles which are following it.

STRATEGIC ROCKET CREWMAN

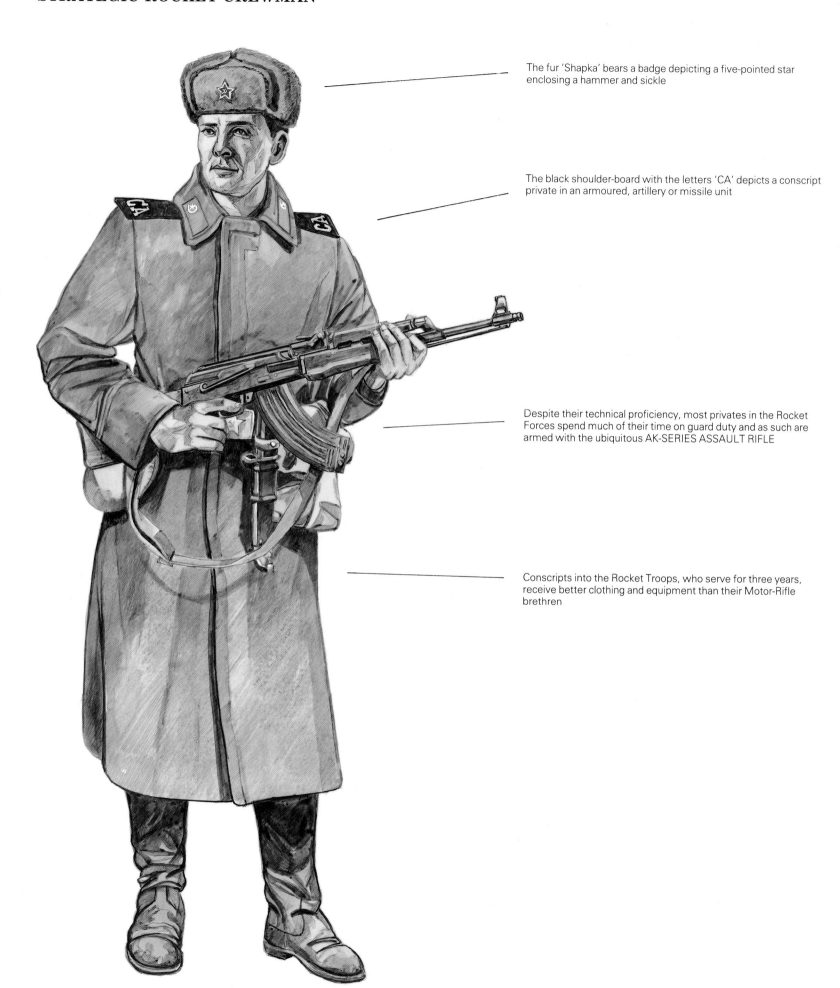

The fur 'Shapka' bears a badge depicting a five-pointed star enclosing a hammer and sickle

The black shoulder-board with the letters 'CA' depicts a conscript private in an armoured, artillery or missile unit

Despite their technical proficiency, most privates in the Rocket Forces spend much of their time on guard duty and as such are armed with the ubiquitous AK-SERIES ASSAULT RIFLE

Conscripts into the Rocket Troops, who serve for three years, receive better clothing and equipment than their Motor-Rifle brethren

First seen in 1965, the SCUD-B on its MAZ 543 transporter/launcher is regularly displayed at the big military parades in Moscow's Red Square.

The Strategic Missile Force ('Raketniye Voiska Strategicheskovo': RVSN) is the newest and smallest of the five Armed Services which make up the Soviet Army. Formed from the Artillery in December 1959, it is commanded by a full Marshal of the Soviet Union (the equivalent of a five-star general in the United States or British Field Marshal) who is directly responsible to the Kremlin for the maintenance of all intercontinental ballistic missiles.

The 500,000 officers and men attached to the RVSN are divided into three Rocket Armies each with 10 divisions. The division itself is divided into 10 regiments which will themselves control from one to ten launchers, dependent on the type of missile deployed. A missile regiment is very small, comprising between 250 to 400 men, most of whom are conscripts.

Conscription into the RVSN is for a period of three years, a year longer than for the rest of the Army, and is reserved for the academic cream of the potential intake. Russians, who are assumed to be brighter and more loyal than other Soviet citizens, predominate. Minorities account for no more than 10 per cent of the total and are invariably relegated to the more menial tasks.

For the young soldier, induction into the Strategic Rocket Forces has its advantages and disadvantages. On the one hand, pay and allowances are higher, promotion quicker and food and accommodation far superior to that enjoyed by the rest of the Army; on the other hand, most bases are situated far from the nearest habitation, precluding any opportunity for recreation. Furthermore, during his service the conscript will almost certainly learn secrets which will signifi-

cantly limit his chances of obtaining a foreign travel visa in later life.

Every regimental commander has a small staff of professional officers, five duty launch teams, an emergency repair battery and guard company. An underground command post, with a direct link to the Divisional and Army commanders as well as the Central Command post, is manned constantly by a hand-picked team of officers. In time of stress a further team deploys into a mobile command post in case of a pre-emptive strike.

The majority of non-technical conscripts are attached to the guard company and, as such, are told little if anything about the actual mechanics of the missile site.

Why it is found necessary to employ such highly qualified men in so tedious a role, when MVD Interior Troops could perform the task as well, if not better, is not known.

Repairs, maintenance and technical resupply are undertaken at divisional level, usually by the more fortunate technical conscripts.

The uniform of the Strategic Rocket Forces is indistinguishable from that of the conventional artillery. Black shoulder boards and collar tabs are worn, the latter bearing the crossed barrel insignia of the artillery. A black arm badge, worn on the upper left sleeve of the jacket and great-coat by all soldiers and NCOs, depicts cross cannon surmounted by a hammer and sickle within a five-pointed star.

Despite recent Soviet-American peace moves, there can be no doubt that international ballistic missiles, and with them strategic rocket troops, will remain a reality for years to come.

KGB CEREMONIAL GUARD

The rifle is carried unsupported while the soldier executes the ceremonial goose-step. At other times it is sloped more conventionally across the shoulder

The Kremlin Guard are the smartest soldiers within the Soviet Army. All wear tailored double-breasted officers' greatcoats, a luxury unknown to the ordinary conscript

The ornate gold belt and lanyard are hallmarks of the ceremonial soldier. Neither is issued to the ordinary conscript

The leather boots are highly polished, unlike those worn by most Soviet soldiers

The Komitet Gosudarstvennoi Bezopastnosti, the Committee of State Security, came into being on 13th March 1954 to replace the notorious NKVD, so feared during the era of Joseph Stalin. Today it regards itself as the guardian of the nation, the last bastion, the Praetorian Guard, of the Soviet Communist system. Under Andropov's leadership in the 1970s it began to dismantle much of the secrecy which had surrounded it and even published books for domestic consumption to explain its role to Soviet citizens. Rather ominously, however, it seems to be resisting all overtures of Gorbachev's Glasnost to relax its still extensive controls further, as if to intimate a deep-seated fear of real change.

Though not under military control, the KGB nevertheless operates its own uniformed and fully-equipped military force with integral armoured and artillery support.

The exact size of the KGB is unknown but is thought to consist of approximately 230,000 officers and other ranks, of whom a staggering 170,000 are conscripts. Young men conscripted into the overt military part of the KGB serve for three years, having been chosen from the political and physical cream of the bi-annual intake. They are not conscripted in the normal way and their service is in lieu of, rather than a part of, conventional military service.

The largest KGB formation is the Border Guard, which has 175,000 soldiers. Responsible for the protection of the Soviet Union's external and internal borders, and not the East/West border as is often assumed, it is recruited on the basis of competitive examination but has a marked Russian, Byelorussian and Ukranian bias. In time of peace it deals with internal security and the suppression of ethnic dissent. Border Guards man immigration checkpoints, crossings and airport controls (Soviet citizens must carry internal passports and require permission to travel from one state to another within the Soviet Union.) It is these immaculately dressed but unsmiling and clearly nervous young men who are the first to greet foreign tourists on their arrival in the Soviet Union. The tourist may feel a certain sympathy however when it is realised that the young guard's every action is monitored both visually and vocally to ensure that there is no fraternization.

The most photographed of all KGB soldiers are those who, day and night in all weathers, mount ceremonial guard over Lenin's tomb positioned between the outer wall of the Kremlin and Red Square. During the summer months the guard changes every hour on the hour, but this period of duty may be reduced in inclement weather, occasionally limited to five minutes in the depth of a harsh winter to avoid exposure. While on duty, these men wear immaculately tailored officers' uniforms with distinctive blue shoulder flashes which at once distinguish them from the equally smart but less politically motivated Honour Guard Unit, retained in Moscow for large ceremonial occasions. Armed with Great Patriotic War rifles, which are held unsupported in the left hand, the Guard goosesteps in public but is quick

to revert to a conventional march immediately upon turning right into the Kremlin gates.

Unlike the Household Division in London or the United States Marines in Washington, when not on ceremonial duty the KGB guards fulfil a very real security liability. The small number of guards on duty at any one time is drawn from an entire regiment based on the outskirts of Moscow. In the extremely unlikely event of the Politburo, any of the 70 government ministries, KGB headquarters, or the General Staff coming under physical threat, it would be this regiment, with its associated support, which would be tasked with restoring order.

Being selected for duty at Lenin's tomb is regarded as a great honour by members of the KGB Ceremonial Guard. However, the duties are quite onerous, particularly in winter when the temperature falls well below freezing.

BORDER GUARDS

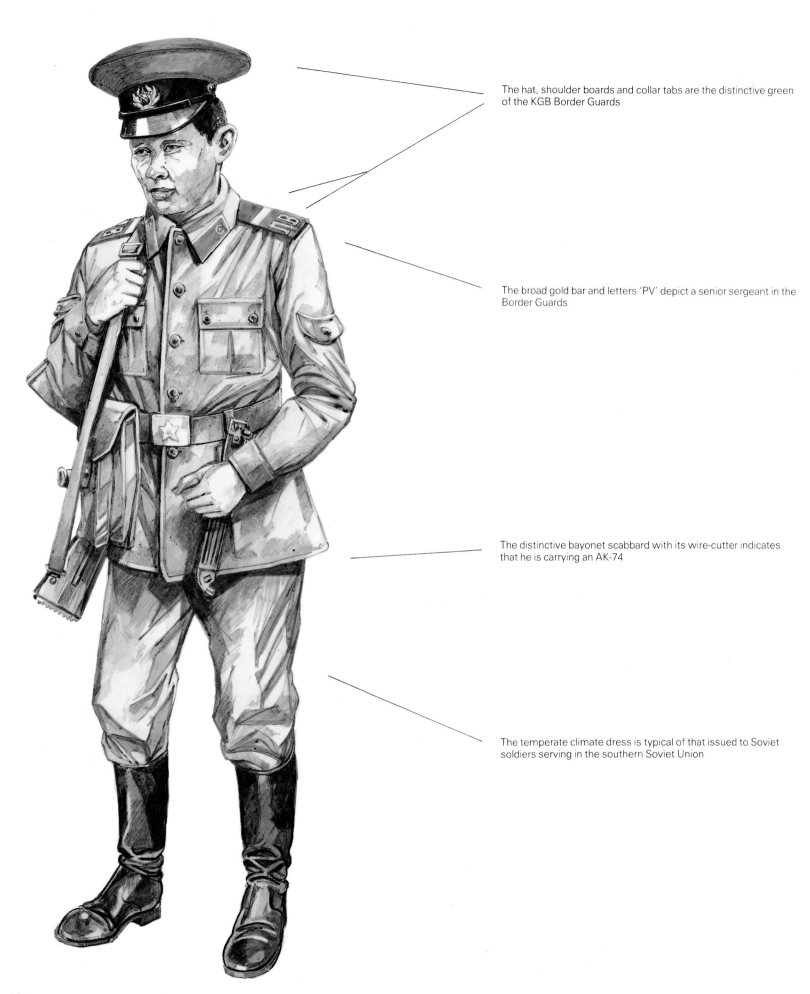

The hat, shoulder boards and collar tabs are the distinctive green of the KGB Border Guards

The broad gold bar and letters 'PV' depict a senior sergeant in the Border Guards

The distinctive bayonet scabbard with its wire-cutter indicates that he is carrying an AK-74

The temperate climate dress is typical of that issued to Soviet soldiers serving in the southern Soviet Union

It is perhaps not surprising that a country as xenophobic as the USSR should delegate the control and guardianship of its borders to the KGB or Committee of State Security. The 175,000 members of the Border Guard man immigration checkpoints, airport controls and border crossings, not only between the Soviet Union and its neighbours but also between its various constituent states. Rigid movement controls are exercised over Soviet citizens, who must carry internal passports at all times and obtain prior written consent, not always given, before travelling from one republic to another.

The majority of Guards are stationed on the national boundaries, or 'Districts', where they are organized on conventional military lines into mechanized or armoured elements. Small, completely integrated artillery, air and naval wings also exist to give the Guards units parity with local army elements in case of insurrection. Although the borders with Poland and Czechoslovakia are quiet, those with China and Afghanistan have been traditionally volatile. Border Guards were involved in pitched battles with the Chinese Peoples' Army over still-unresolved territorial disputes in the 1960s and are now regularly engaged in the suppression of smuggling and preventing attempts by the Mujahideen to infiltrate the Afghan border.

In time of peace, the Border Guards are organized into nine military border districts which vary in depth from 3 to 600km inland from the frontier. Individual detachments, each consisting of approximately 500 men, take responsibility for sectors of between 100 and 600km within each District. Each detachment has an independent headquarters, five platoon-sized outpost units consisting of rifle squads, machine-gun and dog sections, and a rapid deployment manoeuvre group. Helicopter patrols and mechanized units equipped with the latest APCs remain in reserve.

The role of the Border Guards in time of war is more ominous. Not only will they advance a small distance into enemy territory in support of the Army and to combat hostile partisan groups, but they will also suppress anti-Soviet activities, including mutinies within the Army if necessary, among domestic Soviet citizens. Whether or not they would copy the Army, shooting stragglers and deserters out of hand, as did their predecessors the NKVD in the Great Patriotic War, remains a matter of conjecture.

Entry into the Border Guards is highly selective and normally limited to applicants of Russian, Byelorussian and Ukranian descent. Service which is for three years (a full year longer than conventional conscription into the Army) is in lieu of military service and has obvious political rewards for the young man in later life. To join the Border Guards a recruit must have an unimpeachable political background. He will most probably be an active member of Komsomol (the Young Communist League) and will have earned an excellent reputation within DOSAFF. He will also have passed a gruelling written examination. At the age of 18 he will be considered too young for full membership of the Communist Par-

ty but may well be taking active steps towards joining it, possibly in his mid-20s.

Although a civilian organization, the KGB Border Guards are run on military career structure lines with regular NCOs and officers, the latter attending one of two KGB officer-training colleges for a minimum of four years.

When operational, Border Guards wear conventional military uniforms, including the new disruptive pattern dress when serving in Afghanistan, and are therefore often mistaken for soldiers. They do however wear the letters 'PV' on their dark green shoulder boards and, when practical, a similarly coloured band around their wide-rimmed parade hats.

Very high-powered binocular telescopes are used to keep watch on the frontier.

Tracker dogs are an invaluable asset to the Border Guards, especially in difficult terrain.

131

MVD

A russet band worn beneath the wide brim of the hat denotes MVD service

Three thin stripes, the letters 'BB' and a russet background, denote a sergeant in the MVD

Pistols are normally only issued to senior officers. Note the leather belt and holster for the Makarov Pistol

A double-breasted, well-fitting greatcoat worn by a soldier below officer status indicates that he is a member of a specialist unit

The standard of turn-out, and therefore the shine on the boots, will be well above average among MVD conscripts

In the best traditions of the Soviet Union, the Ministry of State Security, or MVD, maintains a completely separate armed force of some 260,000 troops totally independent of the Army. Known as the Interior Army, or Vnutrennie Voiska, the force with its own armour, APCs and artillery, is divided into regimental- and divisional-sized units and is stationed throughout the Soviet Union. Service, which is in lieu of military conscription, is for two years, during which time the young soldier is positively discouraged from fraternizing with the Army. The majority of recruits are politically unsophisticated and often drawn from underprivileged, backward areas of Central Asia. As such they can be relied upon to have little sympathy for the grumblings of the comparatively affluent Western Soviet citizen whom they will willingly suppress if so ordered.

Internal troops can be distinguished by the dull brick-red tabs on their lapels, far darker than the crimson of conventional motor rifle troops, and by the letters 'BB' worn by sergeants and below on their maroon shoulder boards. Suitable candidates attend one of three MVD military schools for four years, after which they are awarded a higher degree and commissioned. Thereafter the best are sent to a Higher Political Military College and the very best to MOD Staff College.

The main task of the MVD is to maintain an internal security force capable of nipping political agitation in the bud and of suppressing public disorder. The use of minimum force has never been considered a prerequisite; nor is resentment and unpopularity regarded as important. Recent pro-Islamic demonstrations in the southern state of Uzbechistan were crushed brutally by MVD troops deliberately drawn from areas unsympathetic to Muslim fundamentalism. Not only does the employment of the MVD in this way allow the Army to distance itself from riot control, and thus to retain its grass-roots popularity, but it also serves to assure the general populace that near at hand there exists a force ready and more than willing to use brutality if need be to maintain the Party line.

The secondary and more sinister role of the MVD is to guard and administer the huge and highly secretive system of an estimated 1,100 labour camps still in existence deep within the Soviet wastelands. Punishment, not rehabilitation, is the aim of these camps, known collectively as the Gulag. Although they have undoubtedly decreased in number and ruthlessness since the days of Stalin, they are nevertheless far more brutal than anything within the Western penal system.

In addition, MVD troops are tasked with guarding vulnerable targets such as industrial plants, railway stations, bridges, airports and food stocks. The Soviets have never lost their fundamental xenophobia and, although in part the guards are positioned to prevent the very real risk of pilfering, they are far more concerned with sabotage by foreign agents working alone or with internal dissidents. Superficially this seems paranoid, taking into account the fact that many of the key points are literally thousands of miles from the nearest hostile border. However, it must not be forgotten that such guarding was essential in the Great Patriotic War.

The Interior Army also serves as a counterbalance to the Soviet Army in the event of unrest. Although the Army is now considered to be politically reliable and the possibility of insurrection remote, the MVD retains control of ammunition stockpiles in the larger camps. Although never designed to be deployed in battle, MVD troops would act as mechanized infantry in an emergency. It is more likely, however, that in time of war they would maintain rear area security and assist the KGB Border Guards in ensuring the safe passage of military supplies to the front.

Despite the ominous role of the MVD, the Soviets make no attempt to shield it from foreigners. The Dzerzhinskiy Special Operations Motor Rifle Division, based in Moscow, plays an important role in all parades when it deploys openly in groups of up to battalion level.

The MVD troops occupy a privileged position, distinct from the armed forces, under the Ministry of State Security. This lieutenant is having a day off, accompanied by his daughter.

NAVAL SPETSNAZ

Scuba equipment will be specially adapted to minimise the escape of tell-tale air bubbles

Naval Spetsnaz equipment is secretive and probably personalised

Frogmen will probably carry sufficient air to enable them to remain submerged for two to three hours

Divers engaged in beach reconnaissance will carry survey and other equipment

Naval Spetsnaz wear uniforms identical to the naval infantry division which they support. In this instance, a member of the Black Sea Fleet has possibly posed for propaganda purposes.

Naval Spetsnaz is the smallest and most secretive of all Soviet special forces. Although its members work closely with Naval Infantry personnel, often wearing their uniform as a mode of disguise, it is in fact totally independent.

The Soviet Union first realised the potential of the mini-submarine as early as the mid-1930s. After several years of research, the M-400 midget submarine, capable of spending many hours silently on the sea-bed yet able to move at great speed when surfaced, entered service in 1939. Despite its tremendous potential there is little evidence to suggest that the M-400 saw much action in the subsequent Great Patriotic War. However, its scope was not forgotten and there are suggestions that there are now several dozen mini-submarines attached to each Naval Spetsnaz brigade.

At present there are now four operational brigades, one attached to each of the Northern, Baltic, Black Sea and Pacific Fleets. Each brigade consists of an anti-VIP Headquarters Company manned exclusively by regular servicemen, a midget submarine group, three combat-swimmer battalions, a parachute battalion, a signals company and support units staffed mainly by conscripts. As Naval Spetsnaz is nominally a part of the Navy, its conscripts serve for three years.

With the exception of midget submarine crews, who often wear the uniforms of conventional submariners, Naval Spetsnaz members usually wear standard Naval Infantry uniform and are therefore exceedingly difficult to identify. Unlike 'military' Spetsnaz, who omit the 'Guards' insignia badge when disguising themselves as airborne soldiers, Naval Spetsnaz troops have no such scruples and will go to great pains to ensure absolute anonymity. Their barracks are always within the harbour area and closely guarded, so much so that their presence is often unknown to conventional soldiers.

Potential recruits are assessed and vetted whilst still at school. All will be politically reliable and many will be members of Komsomol. A high proportion will have parachuted under the auspices of DOSAFF, although surprisingly some may never have seen the sea.

The failure rate during basic training, which is uncompromisingly harsh and physical, is unknown but must be presumed to be high.

Naval Spetsnaz regard much of their training as 'active-service' with many of their exercises carried out against the hulls of unsuspecting merchant ships. In time of war their tasks would be as diversified as they would be dangerous. Not only would they be tasked with the destruction of enemy shipping at anchor, but also their bridges, docks and port installations. Others would assist in the clearing of beaches, illumination of sentries and neutralization of key installations prior to a beach assault by conventional Naval Infantry forces.

It is highly likely that specialists from the Headquarters Company would be landed covertly before the actual declaration of war to assassinate well-protected civilian and military dignitaries.

It has even been suggested recently that manned Argus-class and unmanned Zvuk-class submarines, designed primarily for scientific research, have in fact been used by Naval Spetsnaz to ascertain the positions of NATO underwater communications cables with a view to destroying or tapping-in to these should the need ever arise.

Scandinavia is regularly visited by Naval Spetsnaz and it is highly likely that the vast majority of territorial incursions complained of recently by the Swedes were carried out by Spetsnaz forces operating from their base at Kronstadt, near Leningrad. It would appear from imprints left on the sea-bed that two types of mini-submarine were used, often in conjunction with a mother ship.

The role of Naval Spetsnaz is crucial today and can only grow as the Soviet Navy expands its 'blue-water' policy. It is likely that its activities will continue to be shrouded in secrecy despite the occasional suspected sighting of frogmen undertaking 'active-service' training.

SOVIET NAVAL INFANTRY

The black beret with the red triangular flash is peculiar to the Naval Infantry

The blue and white hooped tee-shirt is issued to all special forces

The AKMS assault rifle is one of several personal weapons carried

Additional ammunition and equipment are carried in loose-fitting canvas satchels

One-piece light-camouflage suits are now being issued to all Naval Infantry units

The Naval Infantry is the smallest and oldest of the Soviet Union's *élite* forces, tracing its roots back to Peter the Great. During the Great Patriotic War it reached a peak of 350,000 personnel but was hampered by the inactivity of the fleet and was rarely used for its true purpose. It played no part in Stalin's post-war expansionist policies and was disbanded in 1947.

When it was reformed in 1961, the Naval Infantry was given the twin tasks of protecting the huge new naval bases then being built and of providing the dedicated infantry required for any future amphibious landings.

Naval Infantry is divided between the four fleets. One regiment each is stationed with the Northern Fleet at Pechenga, with the Baltic Fleet at Baltysk and with the Black Sea Fleet at Sevastopol. A small division is now with the Pacific Fleet at Vladivostok.

Conscription is undertaken by conventional means via the Military Districts, there being no evidence to suggest that Naval Infantrymen are specially chosen despite the high proportion of Slavs within the ranks. In line with conventional naval policy, conscription is for three years, a full year longer than for the Army.

Training is exacting and by Soviet standards specialized. Many recruits attend parachute courses, the best eventually qualifying for the Fleet Commando Platoon. Others qualify as frogmen and join the regimental engineer company, the reconnaissance company or are taught beach-obstacle clearance. The very best may even transfer to Naval Spetsnaz.

Amphibious assault exercises are often carried out with the support of dedicated motor rifle troops based near the Naval Infantry units and trained specifically to undertake large-scale second-echelon beach landings. The 63rd Guards Naval Infantry Regiment, attached to the Northern Fleet, can for instance call for support from two full divisions based between Murmansk and the Norwegian border.

Exercises in the Baltic are often carried out with the support of such elite Warsaw Pact marine units as the East German 'Ernst Moritz' Arndt Regiment and the Polish 7th Sea Assault Division.

Large-scale landings have recently been made possible by the introduction of new classes of assault landing ships. Not only are these capable of transporting the largest MBTs, but many carry helicopters ideal for the execution of small-scale commando raids against key installations before a major assault.

As might be expected, the uniform of the Soviet Naval Infantryman is a combination of army and navy with a few unique embellishments. As an elite force, camouflage coveralls, similar to those worn by airborne troops, are often issued. However, conventional combat dress of black suit with calf-length black leather boots is still common. A black leather belt, with the appropriate fleet badge on the buckle, is worn although this will often be partially obscured by the attachment of conventional pattern buff-coloured webbing.

A horizontal blue and white tee-shirt, the mark

of the elite soldier, is worn with all patterns of dress. A round cloth badge with an embroidered anchor is sewn onto the left sleeve above the elbow. A 'Guards' badge is worn, together with the usual collection of award badges above the right breast. In operations, a black steel helmet is worn, adorned with a five-pointed red star on the centre and stencilled anchor to its left. Traditionally the marines remove this as soon as possible in favour of the more popular and individualistic black beret. Surprisingly, for an otherwise disciplined force, the marines are seemingly allowed to wear the beret at any convenient angle or shape. Officers wear a large enamelled naval

badge in the centre of the beret and others rank a small red star. All ranks wear a red triangular badge with a gold anchor indicating the reward of the 'Red Banner' to the fleet. This badge may be worn on either side of the main badge dependent on local whims.

Soviet Naval Infantry are trained primarily in speed and aggression. Unlike the US Marines, they are neither equipped nor trained to operate far inland, concentrating instead on the securing of a bridgehead. Their support weaponry, much of which was outdated until recently, is now of the highest standard, as are the ships which carry them. There can be no doubt that the one division and three regiments of the Naval Infantry form a crucial part of Soviet tactical thought and would play an important role in any future conflict.

The characteristic blue and white striped shirt and the naval infantry badge on the left arm are clearly visible. The stencilled anchor on the side of the helmet can hardly be seen. The symbols on the shoulder boards indicate that they are serving with the Black Sea Fleet.

THE SOVIET MILITARY WOMAN

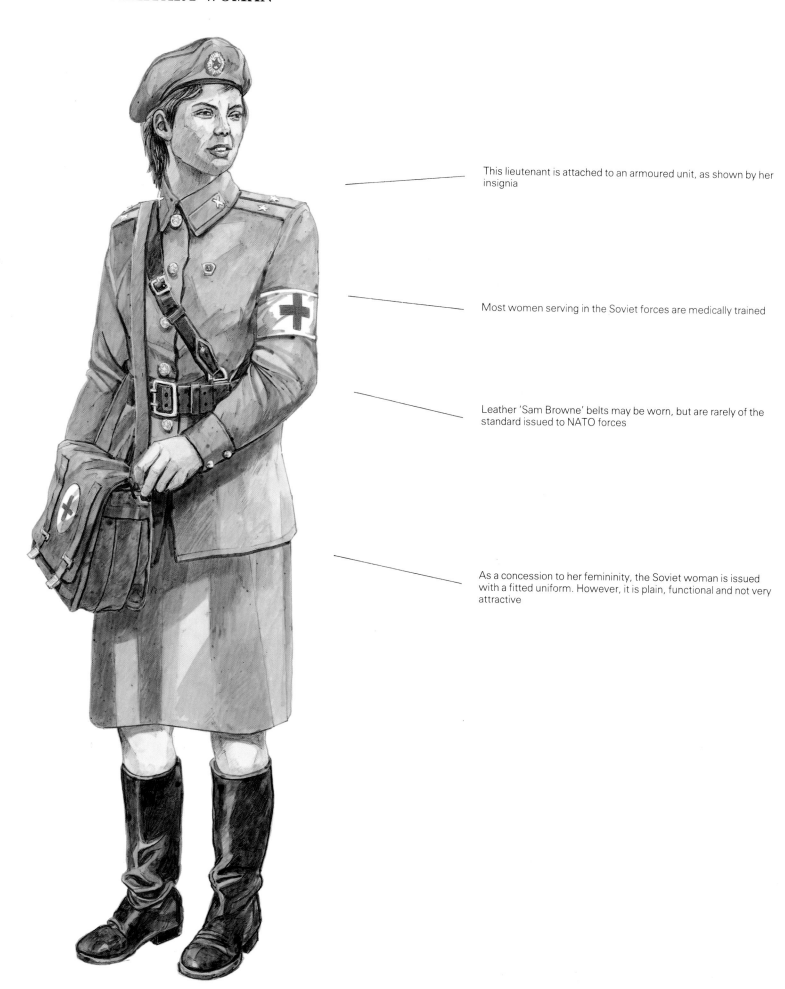

This lieutenant is attached to an armoured unit, as shown by her insignia

Most women serving in the Soviet forces are medically trained

Leather 'Sam Browne' belts may be worn, but are rarely of the standard issued to NATO forces

As a concession to her femininity, the Soviet woman is issued with a fitted uniform. However, it is plain, functional and not very attractive

Women serve as volunteers in most of the services but are never conscripted. Despite the fact that some 800,000 women served in the Soviet Armed Forces in the Great Patriotic War, many as tank commanders and crew, mortar operators and snipers, and 86 were awarded the Hero of the Soviet Union (the equivalent of the Congressional Medal of Honour or Victoria Cross) modern Soviet society is far too conservative to tolerate a return to this position save in the instance of a grave national emergency.

Under the terms of existing legislation passed in 1967, healthy women between the ages of 19 and 40 with medical or other specialist skills may enroll in the reserve and take part in periodic exercises when called upon.

Women who volunteer for the army or navy, whether as soldiers or NCOs, must be aged between 19 and 30, have reached a standard of education at least the equivalent of the United States eighth-grade, be single, healthy and childless. They may volunteer for two, four or six years and continue thereafter to re-enlist until the age of 50, dependent on establishment vacancies set by the Ministry of Defence, often without any recourse to local needs. They have the same rights, obligations and wear a similar uniform as extended service male soldiers, although the walking-out dress is tailored, if somewhat severely, and the tunic designed to button right over left. Civilian clothes may be worn off duty. In line with current British thinking, and unlike their United States' equivalents, they will not be called

upon to operate in the front line, although undoubtedly many would wish to. Upon retirement, women serve in the reserves until the age of 40 or until earlier pregnancy.

Numerous academic posts are filled by women officers although little public credit is awarded them. Many higher military schools and academies rely heavily on female lecturers, particularly in the fields of modern languages and mathematics, whilst the majority of military (as well as civilian) doctors are female. After retirement, officers remain in the reserve until the age of 50, although their liability is reduced to a single two-month period and a series of ten-day training camps.

A small number of women who attain very high physical standards during their membership of DOSAFF will find themselves singled out for special training. Valentina Nikolayeva-Tereshkova, the only Soviet woman to have gone into space, was a colonel in the Air Forces, whilst Valentina Zakoretskaya, who set a world record by making 6,000 parachute jumps, was trained by a paramilitary sports society sponsored by DOSAFF. An unusually large percentage of regular Spetsnaz soldiers are women, many of them Olympic champions.

Although the estimated 10,000 women in the Soviet Army play a far lower profile role than the United States WAAFs or British WRAC, there is no doubt that their numbers could be increased significantly in time of crisis.

A substantial proportion of the staff of this Soviet field hospital will be women, both doctors and nurses. However, they would normally be unlikely to drive the LUAZ casualty evacuation vehicle shown in the background. With its low profile and amphibious capability, it can operate very close to the front line.

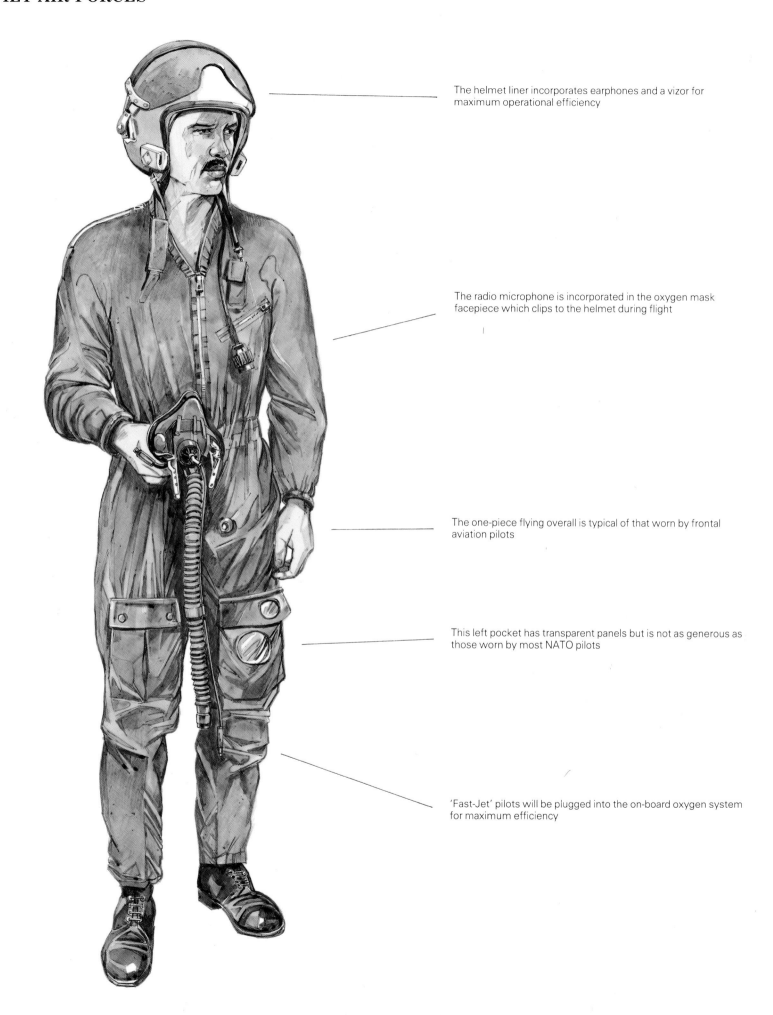

The helmet liner incorporates earphones and a vizor for maximum operational efficiency

The radio microphone is incorporated in the oxygen mask facepiece which clips to the helmet during flight

The one-piece flying overall is typical of that worn by frontal aviation pilots

This left pocket has transparent panels but is not as generous as those worn by most NATO pilots

'Fast-Jet' pilots will be plugged into the on-board oxygen system for maximum efficiency

Despite the obvious importance of their role, the Soviet Air Forces ('Voyenno Vozdushnize Sily': VVS) are only the third most senior of the Soviet Armed Forces. 454,000 officers and men, of whom 330,000 are conscripts called up for three years at the age of 18, serve within the VVS. The Forces themselves are divided into three mutually exclusive parts; Frontal, Long Range and Transport Aviation. Naval Aviation, which controls some of the fastest and most modern bombers, is totally independent.

The VVS is presently undergoing so fundamental a restructuring that it is difficult to offer too precise a breakdown. Suffice it to say not only has the recent introduction of aircraft of the standard of the Mig-29 Fulcrum and Mig-31 Foxhound, both with look-down shoot-down capabilities, enhanced firepower and speeds in excess of Mach 2, destroyed once and for all NATO superiority in the air, but Soviet combat pilots are now actively encouraged to display a level of brashness and exhibitionism once considered the sole prerogative of the West. Squadron insignia, in some instances based on United States cartoon characters, are now appearing on the tail fins of Soviet fighters. More fundamentally, individual pilots, particularly those engaged in reconnaissance, are demonstrating a verve and skill once thought beyond them.

The 4,920 aircraft within the VVS are divided into 16 Air Armies, each of which would be subordinated to a Military Front in time of war. The organization of an Air Army, which is strictly regulated, consists of a combination of three fighter divisions, two fighter bomber divisions, one bomber division, two regiments of light transport aircraft and one regiment each of fighter and bomber reconnaissance. Each sub-division is itself as rigidly divided. A fighter division, for instance, consists of three regiments of 40 aircraft and a command flight of four aircraft (124 in all) whilst a regiment consists of three squadrons of 12 aircraft and a command flight of four.

With the notable exception of the 16th Air Army stationed in East Germany, few are maintained at anything approaching full strength. Reserves from Aeroflot, with its 2,000 transport aircraft, and the Warsaw Pact Airforces, which retain a nominal peacetime independence, would bolster the numbers to full mobilization strength. All Aeroflot aircrew hold reserve commissions; its aircraft are already divided into squadrons, regiments and divisions and its head holds the rank of Marshal of the Air Force and Deputy Commander in Chief. As if to emphasize the preparedness of this, the largest civilian airline in the world, its entire helicopter fleet is painted light green, as it would be if attached to an operational army.

Despite recent stories in the Western press suggesting a breakdown in discipline (there were even suggestions that groundcrew were resorting to the theft of brake fluid for the distillation of illegal alcohol), service in the Air Forces appears to be popular with the ordinary conscript. Pay is better, conditions more comfortable and the food more palatable.

Although the best technical brains are reserved for the Strategic Rocket Force, the Air Forces can nevertheless draw from a large pool of well-educated and partially-trained potential conscripts. Many pilots, navigators and mechanics will have shown a high degree of aptitude during their initial training with DOSAFF-sponsored glider and flying clubs.

It is clear that the role and importance of the Soviet Air Forces are increasing considerably. Aircraft, weapons and radar are all improving and will soon be second to none in the world. Aircrew are given very favourable coverage in the press and all airmen are becoming nationally respected. There can be no doubt that the part played by the VVS in Soviet military thought is becoming far more significant and will continue to expand in the conceivable future.

Top: The flight commander discusses the finer points of air tactics with these YAK-28 Firebar crews.

Above: The wide variations of climate in the USSR demand a variety of uniforms. Note the absence of the fur-lined overjacket seen in the top photograph.

POLISH AIRBORNE TROOPS

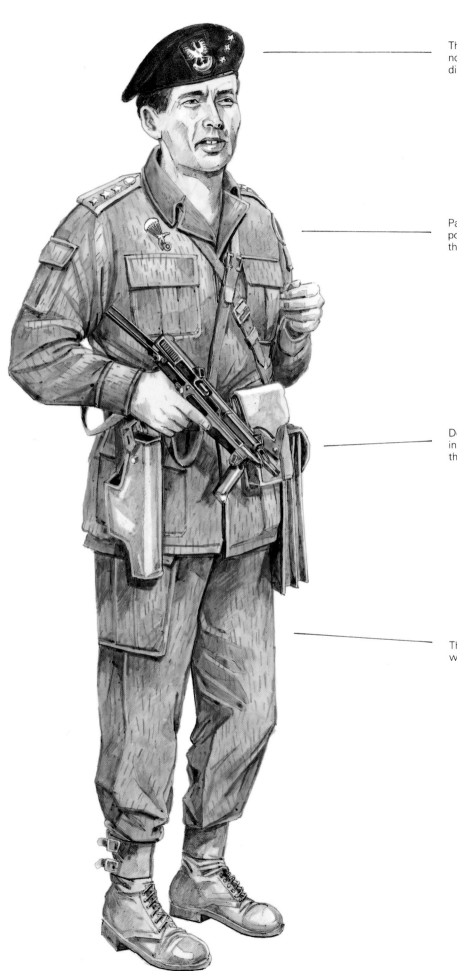

The Polish Eagle has been adopted since the Napoleonic era, but now without the Imperial Crown. Officer's insignia is also displayed on the beret

Parachutist's insignia is worn proudly above the right breast pocket. The divisional badge of the Airborne Division is worn on the left shoulder

Designed with troops such as the airborne forces and AFV crews in mind, the PM-63 9 mm machine pistol measures only 13" with the butt folded and weighs just 1.6 kg (3lb 9oz)

The 'rain' pattern DPM camouflage uniform is similar to that worn by the East German Army

Although the 6th Pomeranian Airborne Division is lightly equipped by Warsaw Pact standards it does nevertheless possess a limited number of BMP-1 A.P.C.s here seen fording a river. The highly vulnerable extra fuel tanks fitted to the rear doors can be clearly seen.

The 6th Pomeranian Airborne Division was created in 1957 and now forms the largest non-Soviet airborne unit in the Warsaw Pact. Although The Polish People's Army (Ludowe Wojsko Polskie) was itself only formed in 1941, and was not fully modernized until 1956, its airborne traditions are among the oldest in the world. The Bydgoszez Military Parachute Centre was formed as long ago as 1938, the 1st Polish Independent Parachute Brigade courageously jumped to virtual annihilation in support of British Airborne Forces at Arnhem in 1944, whilst small groups attached to the Red Army dropped behind enemy lines to aid the Communist-inspired Polish resistance from 1943.

Despite their elite status and privileged position within the military hierarchy, many airborne soldiers are deeply patriotic and very resentful of the Soviet Union. The government of the day was markedly shaken by the reluctance of its elite troops either to suppress the Krakow riots in 1967 or to take part in the invasion of Czechoslovakia in the following year (although units did take part in the capture of Pardubice Airfield) and it is heavily rumoured that many airborne senior officers were replaced soon afterwards. Since then the 6th Air Assault Division has played no part in internal security and is even regarded by some as a potential counter to any threat by extremist hard-liners to topple the relatively moderate government of General Jaruzelski.

Despite its excellent performance in all Warsaw Pact joint exercises, the Soviets are extremely worried by the obvious lack of political motivation shown by members of the 6th Pomeranian Air Assault Brigade and do not trust it to fight to its full potential in any future anti-NATO confrontation. For this reason its size and equipment are kept to a minimum. With a strength of only 4,000 men, it is less than two-thirds the size of its Soviet equivalents, having none of the latter's dedicated specialist support. APCs such as the OT-64 SKOT and BMP-1 with which it is supplied in small numbers are not designed to be air-dropped and are therefore of limited value.

The highly secretive 4101st Paratroop Battalion, reportedly trained in rear area sabotage and reconnaissance and answerable directly to the counter-intelligence network, exists within the Division.

In line with the rest of the Polish Army, paratroopers are conscripted at the age of 19. Having served for two years they are released, but must return to the colours for a further year, or two years if NCOs or officers, before their 35th birthday. Not only is this disruptive to the individual paratrooper's family life but it is of limited value to the Army unless the individual has kept himself extremely fit.

Prior to formal military service many airborne volunteers will have learned to parachute with one of the numerous civilian sky-diving clubs and most will have served in either the 'National Defence League' or 'Voluntary Labour Service'. Jump training consists of 15 'combat' jumps per year, not counting training jumps, and must be undertaken by all troops including support services, cooks and bandsmen.

With the exception of the 4101st Battalion all airborne soldiers usually wear a distinctive red beret. The silver cap badge is large and ornate, resembling closely that worn by Polish troops in the Napoleonic era. Badges of rank are worn on the shoulder straps and beret to the left of the cap badge. A badge depicting an open parachute surmounted by an eagle in flight is worn above the right breast pocket of the field service dress. A divisional patch of similar design and red background is worn on the upper left shoulder.

7th POLISH NAVAL ASSAULT DIVISION

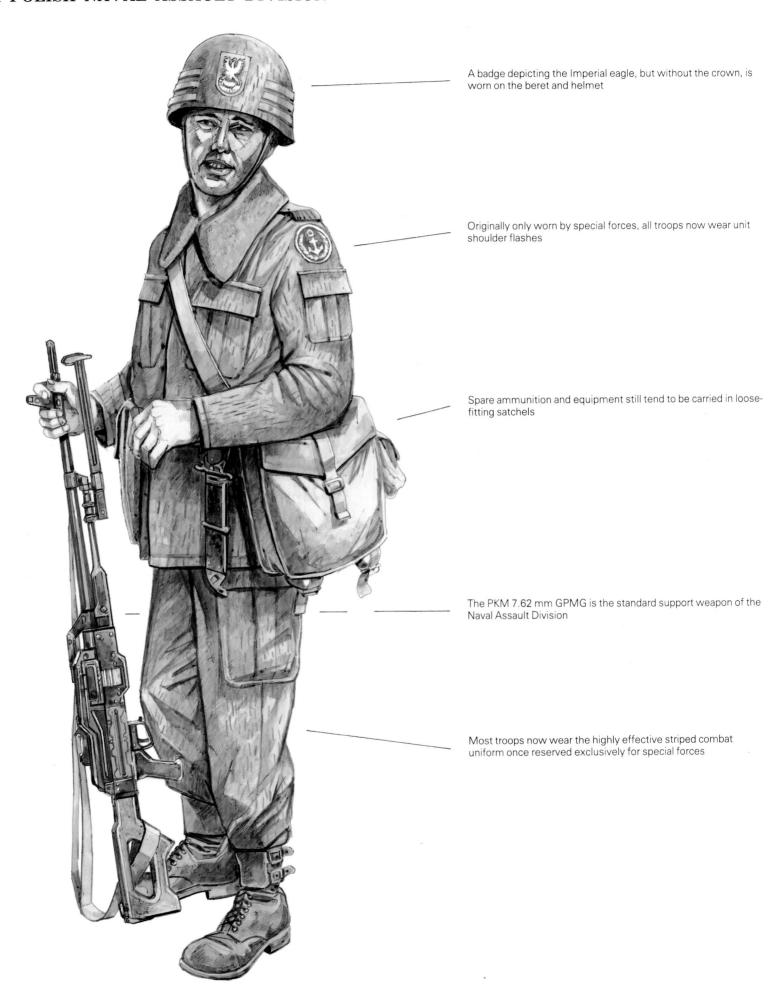

A badge depicting the Imperial eagle, but without the crown, is worn on the beret and helmet

Originally only worn by special forces, all troops now wear unit shoulder flashes

Spare ammunition and equipment still tend to be carried in loose-fitting satchels

The PKM 7.62 mm GPMG is the standard support weapon of the Naval Assault Division

Most troops now wear the highly effective striped combat uniform once reserved exclusively for special forces

Despite its rather misleading title, the 7th Naval Assault Division ('Luzcyka Dywizya Desant-nowa-Morska': 7LDDM) is not under naval jurisdiction but is in fact a regular army unit. Formed in 1967 from the amalgamation of the 23rd Mechanized Division and 3rd Marine Regiment, 7LDDM is now based in the thriving sea port of Gdansk, where it comes under the nominal jurisdiction of the Pomeranian Military District based in Bydgoszcz. Although referred to internally by the euphemism 'Jadnostka Obrona Wybrzeza', or Coastal Defence Unit, the role of the Division is almost exclusively offensive.

In time of war the principle role of the Naval Division would be to assist Soviet and East German troops in the rapid neutralization of Denmark and Southern Norway, to enable the Soviet Baltic Double Red Banner Fleet free access to the Atlantic. An initial attack would almost certainly be launched jointly by the Poles in conjunction with the Soviet 36th Guards Naval Infantry Regiment based at Tallin and Baltiysk, supported by second echelon troops drawn from the 1st Guards Motor Rifle Division at Kaliningrad and the 29th Motor Rifle Regiment based on the East German island of Rugen.

The Soviets learned many lessons from the 110 tactical and four operational beach landings undertaken by them in the Great Patriotic War, not the least being the paramount importance of fire support during the assault and the necessity for speed once ashore. Conventional motor rifle troops conscripted into second echelon beach assault units cannot hope to attain these skills sufficiently without endless practice, and it is therefore likely that the 7 LDDM spends far more of its time exercising with such Soviet and East German troops than it does training with its fellow Poles.

Despite being so near to the volatile Gdansk shipyards, themselves the birthplace of Solidarity, the Division has demonstrated a marked lack of interest in domestic politics. Whether this is due to the considerable amount of time spent in the close proximity of the politically 'reliable' East Germans and Soviets, or whether it has more to do with the fact that its role precludes it from acting in the suppression of street unrest, must remain a question for discussion. What is clear, however, is that the members of the Division, unlike their elite brethren in the 6th Pomeranian Air Assault Division, are held in high esteem by the Soviets and trusted implicitly.

Although a division by Warsaw Pact standards, 7LDDM is only in fact about one-third the size of a US Marine Division, having about 5,500 troops, and is indeed designated a 'brigade' by the International Institute of Strategic Studies. Despite the importance of its role, in line with the Polish Army in general much of its equipment is outdated. Unlike Soviet Naval Infantry, who are issued with main battle tanks together with the new BMP-2, the Poles must rely for firepower on the ineffective 76mm gun of the ageing PT-76 amphibious light tank. Soviet BRDM-2 light armoured cars are employed in ground and chemical reconnaissance whilst the troops them-

selves are carried in elderly TOPAZ 2 APCs.

The uniform worn by the 7th LDDM is essentially similar to that worn by all Polish soldiers, save that a light blue beret – somewhat lighter than that worn by Soviet airborne troops – is worn whenever possible. The shapelessness of the beret is accentuated by the large silver Imperial eagle (minus the crown) worn at its centre and by the silver badge of rank positioned to its left. Until recently only elite forces within the Polish Army wore shoulder insignia, but these are now on general issue to differentiate the various arms of the service. The Naval Assault Division retains the round pale blue flash containing an anchor surrounded by wreaths, worn on both shoulders as its insignia.

Polish T-55 tanks wade ashore from Polnochny Class landing ships using snorkel tubes. Careful beach reconnaissance is essential before such operations.

EAST GERMAN FRONTIER TROOPS

Unusually, the East German Forces wear steel helmets as part of their parade uniform

As might be expected of the East Germans, their uniform is better fitting and of a higher quality than any other within the Warsaw Pact

The shining black leather belt is only worn with parade or walking out dress

Despite East Germany's stated hatred of its Nazi past, the boots show a remarkable resemblance to those worn by the wartime Wehrmacht

Contrary to a popularly held misconception, the border between East and West Germany is controlled by East German Frontier Troops, and not by elite units of the Soviet Army. Although subordinated to the Ministry of Defence, the Frontier Troops have their own headquarters in the small town of Patz and are totally independent of the Army, although since 1961 they have shared the same training facilities and uniforms.

Responsibility for the day-to-day administration of the frontier, or Inner German Border as it is known within NATO, is divided equally between Frontier Command North based at Stendal and Frontier Command South in Erfurt. Based in Berlin-Karlshorst, Frontier Command Centre has overall control of the 106km-long 'Ring Round Berlin' including the Berlin Wall itself, the scene of so many disastrous failed escape attempts since its construction in 1961.

The current Frontier Force consists of approximately 49,000 conscripts and volunteers, of whom some 32,000 serve on the IGB, 12,000 guard the Berlin area and 3,000 monitor the three-mile territorial sea limit. The residue are divided into two small regiments responsible for patrolling the Polish and Czech borders.

In line with normal East German military policy, recruits for the Frontier Troops enlist either in the spring or autumn. Their first six months are spent in one of several special training units, where they learn not only basic military and preliminary frontier-work skills but also undertake intensive political indoctrination. Simultaneously, they are thoroughly vetted by State Security agents and any with the slightest hint of political unreliability are dismissed. Officers, who constitute about 12 per cent of the entire force, attend the 'Rosa Luxemburg Frontier Officers' College' at Plauen before taking their commission. Approximately 16 per cent of the best recruits attend the Egon Schultz College where they study driving, signals and engineering, as well as 'frontier training', before returning to their units as NCOs.

Upon completion of basic training, soldiers transfer to one of the 12 regiments guarding the border or to one of the six regiments surrounding Berlin. Service on the border is not popular. Accommodation is often sparse and invariably in remote villages, in which the few remaining civilians are subject to curfew and closely watched. Recreational facilities and – more fundamentally – female company are scarce, and spells of duty usually long and tedious.

The area in which the Frontier Troops operate is far from hospitable. A 5km-wide control zone, from which unreliable residents have been forcibly removed, runs the entire length of the border. Such civilians as are tolerated must carry special passes, liable to withdrawal at any time, confirming their right to be there. Meetings and public events within the zone must finish, and outsiders leave, by 10 p.m. Beyond this zone a security strip, about 500 metres wide, can only be entered with special permission under the direct supervision of a guard. Trees have been felled and farmsteads razed to ensure a clear field of fire over the

area. Guard dogs, minefields, acoustic alarms and automatic weapons fire from the sentries await anyone foolish or unlucky enough to be spotted in the security strip without permission.

Although precise rules relating to the use of firearms are long-winded, and on occasions imprecise, every Frontier Guard knows that it is his duty to prevent escapes and that failure on his part will be severely punished. All guards are excellent shots, with the result that failure to hit a fleeing target is construed as deliberate. Despite their political reliability, whenever possible guard rosters are arranged in such a way as to ensure that individuals do not work together on consecutive nights, to prevent the possibility of a planned escape. Two-man motor cycle teams constantly patrol the metalled strip running a few metres inside the fence. They invariably contain a single and a family man, on the basis that the latter will be less likely to make an impromptu escape attempt, knowing that he will be leaving his family behind. Furthermore, he will almost certainly shoot the escaping single man, knowing that failure to do so will result in a charge of dereliction of duty and a resultant prison sentence.

With the exception of the dedicated communist fanatic who regards the maintenance of the State as paramount, most East Germans dislike frontier service. Apart from the ever-present possibility of having to shoot one of his countrymen, the guard cannot discuss the border installations, which are secret, with his friends, from whom he often feels isolated. Training is rigorous, discipline harsh and concessions few. Yet there can be no doubt that the East German Frontier Force is efficient and will remain so for as long as there is a need for its existence.

The Reichstag looms over the Berlin Wall and watch-tower while simple crosses serve as silent memorials to failed escapers.

Seen from the Western side of the Brandenburg Gate, two East German Border Guards patrol the Unter den Linden. This is the only gap in the notorious Berlin Wall.

THE ROMANIAN INFANTRYMAN

The fur hat is of standard Soviet design and pulls down over the ears in very bad weather

The Romanian variant of the AKM has a foregrip, unlike its more common Soviet counterpart

The greatcoat, although warm, is of an old design and must prove an encumbrance on the move

The Romanians are among the few soldiers in Europe still to wear leather anklets

Due to complex political geographical reasons beyond her control, Romania fought first for and then against Nazi Germany in World War Two with drastic consequences to herself. Soviet occupation troops stationed in the country from 1944 suppressed ruthlessly any attempt by the population to restore the power of the monarchy, deporting over 250,000 alleged POWs to the Gulags never to be seen again. The puppet Communist Party formally seized power in 1947 and at once declared the existence of the Romanian Peoples' Republic. Unusually, although the anticipated Army purges followed, these did not include the mass arrest of officers who had served prior to the Communist takeover, many of whom were actually restored in their former positions.

Soviet troops were withdrawn in 1958 in recognition of the stalwart support shown by the Government during the Hungarian rising. A new constitution was adopted in 1965, at which time the country was renamed the Romanian Socialist Republic. There then began a slow but steady move away from the Soviet Union towards the present day policy of armed neutrality.

Since coming to power in 1967, Nicolae Ceausescu, the head of the Communist Party and President for life, has hardened this attitude to the point where Romanian troops no longer take part in multi-national exercises nor are foreign units allowed access across her borders.

The armed forces gained considerably from the Warsaw Pact invasion of Czechoslovakia in 1968. Ceausescu was well aware that the army would provide his only line of defence against what many saw as an impending Soviet attack, with the result that immediate steps were taken to integrate the military into Romanian society. Long defunct ranks, pensions and privileges were restored to the officers, whilst the civilian population was encouraged to regard the ordinary soldier as a national guardian. Significantly, the position of political officer was scrapped, responsibility for the soldiers' political as well as military well-being passing to the commanding officers, the vast majority of whom were in any case members of the Communist Party.

Unfortunately, national independence brought with it political despotism and near economic ruin. Huge steel plants constructed at tremendous sacrifice to the economy in the 1970s now lie derelict, a victim of world recession. Industry is outdated, labour-intensive and totally incapable of competing on the open market against more automated factories in the West. The United States, which once offered Romania 'most favoured nation' status, now threatens an embargo unless Ceausescu improves his human rights record, which many see as the worst in Europe. Meanwhile, Soviet heavy industry under Gorbachev is now virtually self-sufficient and, as such, is no longer reliant on Romania for the importation of inferior raw materials.

The Romanian Army (Armata Romina) is particularly susceptible to the current economic and political crisis. Wholly incapable of purchasing expensive Western equipment, it can no longer automatically look to the Soviets for the supply of

slightly out of date weaponry in exchange for economic concessions. With the exception of one battalion of T-72s, all tanks in service are at least 30 years old and are severely hampered by a lack of spare parts. The vast majority of the 90,000 conscripts who comprise 75 per cent of the army serve as infantrymen in one of the eight motor rifle divisions. Due to the acute lack of equipment, only one division is at full strength whilst four completely lack any form of mechanized support, relying heavily on civilian lorries for mobility.

Life for the Romanian infantryman is less onerous than for many of his Eastern Bloc colleagues. Prior to enlistment at the age of 18, he will possibly have served in either 'The Union of Communist Youth' or 'The Voluntary Sports Union for the National Defence of the Fatherland', but as both organizations are virtually bankrupt neither has anything approaching the influence enjoyed by DOSAFF within the Soviet Union. Since 1964, conscription itself has been limited to 16 months, the shortest period within the Eastern Bloc. Much of this time may in fact be spent away from the Army, helping either with the harvest or in the docks in a vain effort to combat the national economic plight. After his period with the colours, the infantryman will join the 500,000 members of the reserve, in which he will serve for five years. Due to the sheer cost of mounting exercises, however, it is unlikely that he will be called upon to take part in more than three short training sessions during this period.

It is a matter of great surprise to many Western analysts that the Romanian conscript has remained so placid during the recent food riots. No one can say with any degree of accuracy what will happen when the Ceausescu régime falls. What is clear, however, is that the role of the Army and of the conscript infantrymen will never be the same.

The Romanian armed forces make a substantial contribution to Nation Day parades and similar occasions.

SWISS PARACHUTE GRENADIERS

The SIG StuG 57 7.5mm assault rifle is slowly being replaced by a 5/56mm developmentus navy sealsus

The distinctive uniform seems gaudy against a white background but in fact offers excellent protection in a built-up environment

All troops are excellent map readers and will carry charts in their cavernous pockets

Rubber-soled high-boots with gaiters provide an excellent weather-proof seal, whatever the conditions

Switzerland's land-locked situation coupled with its long tradition of neutrality has left it with unique military problems. As Norway, Denmark and Holland learned to their cost in World War Two, neutrality in itself is not enough to protect a small country against its more powerful neighbours if the latter regard invasion as strategically necessary.

Despite having no natural enemies, Switzerland with its commanding position in Southern Europe might be considered a legitimate target in any future war and for this reason has always maintained a highly effective Army.

The Army and Air Corps, which are incorporated into a single force concept, consist of 1,500 regular servicemen supported by 18,500 recruits called up in each February and July to undertake 17 weeks basic training. Thereafter the recruits transfer to the Reserve and are liable to report for three weeks refresher training between the ages of 20 and 32, for a further fortnight between the ages of 33 and 42 and for a final 7 days' training over a two-year period between the ages of 43 and 50.

Reserves keep their weapons at home to facilitate mobilization in an emergency, as a direct result of which a staggering 625,000 soldiers, including 45,000 officers, 110,000 NCOs and 3,000 women auxiliaries can be called to arms within 48 hours of a crisis.

However dedicated the Reserves, they are only able to fight within their own parameters. To combat this problem the Parachute-Grenadiers, capable of operating with minimum resupply in the most inhospitable of terrains, were formed in 1968.

All Parachute-Grenadiers are parachute trained and jump regularly under all conditions, often into forested or mountainous areas. Applicants are vetted carefully before formal selection for the Panzer-Grenadiers. All take aptitude tests and interviews at the age of 17 to ensure that they have the strength of character and self-reliance required. A year later, successful candidates attend a two-week parachute training course under non-tactical conditions. Those who succeed in making the requisite 10 static-line and 40 free-fall descents, all at a maximum altitude of 2,000 metres (6,560 feet), receive a civilian qualification before passing on to the recruit school for a further five months' intensive training.

Parachuting is regarded as of such paramount importance that five weeks of the course are dedicated to military jumping during which a further 80 descents are made, by day and night, from all altitudes and under all conditions, with and without weapons and heavy equipment. Both static-line jumping from as low as 100 metres (328 feet) and high altitude jumping in tight formations will be honed to perfection.

Night and close-quarter combat, survival behind enemy lines, covert reconnaissance, navigation under all conditions and the acquisition and use of enemy weapons are all taught to a high degree.

In August 1980 it was decided to create 17 Company, Para-Grenadiers, as an elite within an elite. Unique among the Swiss Army, 17 Company has no dedicated combat role although its members are capable of fighting under any conditions. Fully trained in the concept of Long Range Reconnaissance Patrolling (LRRPs), its members usually operate in teams of three to five under Air Corps command.

Training for 17 Company is so exacting that, of the 300 potential entrants short-listed annually at the aptitude stage, less than 30 are selected for training of whom only 12 to 15 can hope to prove successful.

The SIG MG710 GPMG can be fitted with a tripod and dial sight

As ever, parachute training is exhaustive. All students are taught to calculate glide paths, drop release and opening points for use in HAHO (High Altitude High Opening) operations to enable them to guide themselves through the maze of power cables criss-crossing the Swiss mountains before landing precisely on a small landing zone perhaps perched precariously close to a sheer drop.

Communications skills using sophisticated long range radios, advance medical training and covert intelligence gathering are all mastered in conjunction with the more conventional skills expected of the Regiment as a whole.

Recruits finish the course in a valley near Centovalli, close to the Italian border, in which they spend a week in caves and snow holes living exclusively from the land whilst undertaking difficult and, to others, dangerous feats of cross-country navigation.

The SIG assault rifle can be readily fitted with a night-sight.

The Swiss camouflage uniform blends in with a variety of backgrounds.

IRISH DEFENCE FORCES

A lighter Israeli helmet is replacing the heavy British steel model

Standard '58-issue' webbing is issued throughout the army

NCO chevrons are worn on both sleeves, red on a yellow background. They are easily recognizable from a distance

Although the Steyr AUG 5.56 mm assault rifle is being introduced, most troops are still issued with the 7.62 mm FN FAL rifle

Comfortable dark brown high boots are the norm

The Republic of Ireland has consistently retained a policy of neutrality throughout her existence. Despite considerable pressure, both internally and externally, she denied Britain the use of strategic naval bases in World War Two and subsequently declined an offer to join NATO, on the basis that to do so would have conflicted with her national aspiration to sovereignty over the entire island.

Today Ireland has neither the financial resources nor the political inclination to play a part in European politics and patently regards her Armed Forces solely as a means of securing her borders.

Until recently, Ireland was willing, if only due to geographical expediency, to rely on Britain for her international defence, restricting her own contribution to the provision of a battalion for United Nations service, but the growth in para-military forces over the past two decades has forced a fundamental reappraisal. The Army was forced to expand rapidly to counter the para-military threat and now boasts an establishment of 15,500 men. However, a combination of the better terms of service in the neighbouring British Army, always willing to enlist Irishmen, and a partial recruitment embargo forced on the Government by the acute economic crisis, has reduced the active strength to less than 14,000 – only 75 per cent of the required level.

The Army consists of 11 infantry battalions, excluding the ad hoc force currently serving under United Nations colours in Cyprus and the Lebanon, two independent infantry companies, a small (Rangers) special forces unit, a light tank and four armoured reconnaissance squadrons, three field and one air defence artillery regiment and limited combat support.

Administratively, the country is divided into four territorial commands each controlling a single infantry brigade of two battalions, an armoured reconnaissance squadron and artillery regiment. The border is patrolled by three further infantry battalions and the two independent companies, all of whom rely on the already stretched Western and Eastern Commands for support.

The 50- to 100-strong Ranger Company, kept on constant alert as a quick reaction force, is presently located outside Dublin at the Curragh, a huge rambling complex built by the British in the last century. Ominously, however, suggestions have recently been made that the Curragh be scrapped as a cost-cutting exercise.

The 14,000-strong volunteer Army Reserves, or 'Forsa Cosuinta Aituil' (FCA), are formed into 18 battalions of divergent sizes and with differing roles. Volunteers, who usually train one day per weekend and for one week each summer, are grossly ill-equipped (many still have World War Two bolt-action Lee Enfield rifles), unpopular with their regular counterparts and would be of little tangible effect in combat.

Weaponry is generally old, although the infantry is at present re-equipping with the Austrian Steyr AUG 5.56mm assault rifle, releasing the ageing 7.62mm FN FAL rifles in current service for distribution among the Reserves.

Armour consists of 14 British-made Scorpion light tanks, 100 assorted French APCs and 10 domestically-produced Timoneys. With the exception of two batteries of 105mm light-guns, the artillery is limited to 48 modernized 25-pounders, which first saw service in the 1940s, and an air defence which relies totally on line-of-sight anti-aircraft guns.

Since 1962 all ranks have worn a distinctive light green, open-necked, single-breasted jacket similar in design to the British 'No 2' Dress. Officers and sergeant majors, other than those in the cavalry who wear a 'Glengarry', wear a light green peaked cap, whilst other ranks wear a black beret with cap badge over the left eye. Acting corporals and above wear horizontal red zig-zag bars on a yellow backing on the upper arms of service dress and jackets but on the right arm only when in shirt sleeve order. British standard '58' webbing is issued, although the heavy steel helmet is now being replaced by a lighter Israeli model.

A unit of the Irish Defence Forces displays some of its somewhat antiquated support weaponry in barracks. From left to right, the French 90mm recoilless gun, the Swedish Carl-Gustav, the British 3in mortar and Belgian FN GPMG demonstrate the broad purchasing policy of the Irish Government.

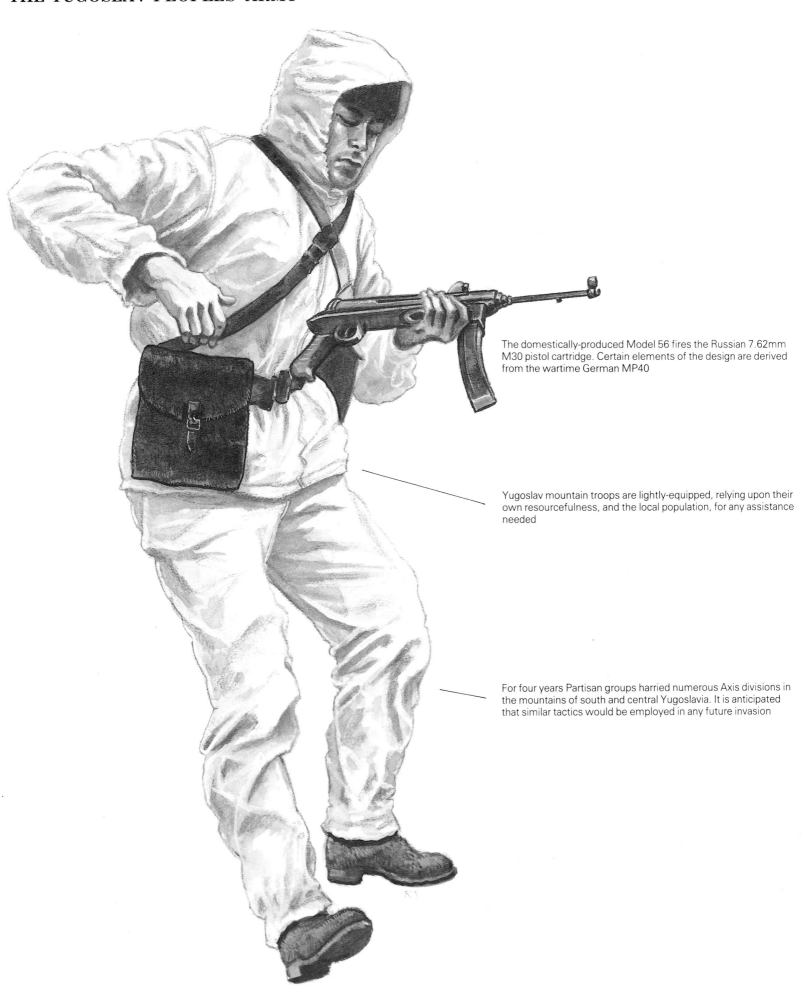

The domestically-produced Model 56 fires the Russian 7.62mm M30 pistol cartridge. Certain elements of the design are derived from the wartime German MP40

Yugoslav mountain troops are lightly-equipped, relying upon their own resourcefulness, and the local population, for any assistance needed

For four years Partisan groups harried numerous Axis divisions in the mountains of south and central Yugoslavia. It is anticipated that similar tactics would be employed in any future invasion

Whereas Yugoslavia is justifiably proud of the fact that it was the only country in Europe to liberate itself from Nazi oppression without the large-scale assistance of a third party, it is equally aware of the devastating losses sustained by its people in that War.

However divided its constituent states may be, and it should not be forgotten that the country itself has been in existence for only 70 years, all Yugoslavs are united in the certainty that, whatever the cost, their country must never be invaded again.

Despite its wartime guerrilla origins, prior to 1968 the Yugoslav Army relied upon large numbers of ill-equipped but highly motivated conscripts to defend its major cities. At that time the basic enemies were seen as Bulgaria to the east and Albania to the south, although neither was considered powerful enough to wage an independent war without Soviet intervention, which was considered unlikely in the face of almost certain NATO opposition.

The invasion of Czechoslovakia in 1968 changed the *status quo* overnight. Protected by a cloud of almost total secrecy and in absolute radio silence, the Soviet Union, with the full support of her Warsaw Pact allies, seized Prague Airport, neutralized the Government and moved large numbers of mechanized and armoured troops into the Czech hinterland. NATO was left shaken, numbed and impotent. President Tito realized immediately that he could not hope to defend his Northern lowlands against a concerted Soviet attack, particularly if Romanian resistance were to crumble, and therefore concentrated on the creation of a force capable of fighting a war of attrition in the more hostile mountains. The lessons of Partisan warfare were resurrected.

The resultant Territorial Defence Force (TDV) fulfilled that role admirably and remains a keystone of Yugoslav defence policy today. In essence, the TDV was a force of locally recruited farmers and factory workers, trained to engage the enemy in a series of localized firefights. It did not hope to win formal battles but rather to wear down the foe, at the same time destroying his morale and ultimately his will to fight.

Despite the huge size of the TDV (at present it can mobilize over one million men in a few days), the more formalized Yugoslav Peoples' Army remains the cornerstone of national defence.

The Army itself consists of 213,000 officers and men, including 123,000 conscripts who serve for a period of 12 months. Despite Government boasts that this number could be swelled to a staggering two million trained personnel in an emergency, it is clear that the country has neither the equipment nor logistics to handle such vast numbers. With the notable exception of some 200 modified T-72 main battle tanks, the eight independent tank brigades which constitute the entire armoured force are equipped with a hotchpotch of elderly Soviet T-55s and United States M-47s. Equally as drastic, the 12 infantry divisions and nine infantry brigades have only a few hundred ageing APCs between them, with the result that the majority of infantrymen must rely on unpro-

tected lorries for mobility. For economic and political reasons, the Soviet Union is now unwilling to supply arms at a discount, whilst the perilous state of the domestic economy precludes open-market purchasing in the West. Although Yugoslavia has a fledgling arms industry, it has neither the capital nor the technology to do more than produce poor copies of existing equipment.

Once it is accepted that the YPA would be able to do no more than slow a determined enemy advance, the crucial role of the TDV becomes apparent. Ominously, however, the once-certain premise that every Yugoslav would fight willingly for his country is now flawed. Although he would certainly fight an aggressor without reservation, his underlying motives are now being called into question by many political analysts. It is quite possible that Serbian, Croatian and Montenegran nationalists, who form a large part of the TDV, would see Yugoslavia's weakness as their opportunity and would attempt to fill any resulting void with a new powerful confederacy, with much of their lost power and privileges returned to the constituent states.

The Yugoslav soldier is as proud and ferocious as any in the world. Although he would certainly fight for his country against an external aggressor, it must remain a matter of conjecture how far his views on the restructuring of post-war Yugoslavia differ from those of the Government.

Volunteers of the TDV can compensate for the variety and age of their weapons with their local knowledge and patriotism in defence of their homeland.

Men and women, young and old, willingly give up their time to the Territorial Defence Force.

ALBANIAN PEOPLES' ARMY

The national coat of arms, representing a double-headed eagle and five-pointed star, is incorporated into the hat badge

The principal duty of the army, other than the suppression of internal dissent, is the constant monitoring of the frontiers

The standard uniform is based largely on the Soviet one of the 1950s, although badges of rank were scrapped in 1961 when Albania began its short flirtation with the Chinese

The original AK-47 remains the standard personal weapon of the Albanian Army

Few armies in the world have suffered so greatly from the extremes of doctrinaire politics as the Albanians. The country itself, with its population of little more than three million, has always been vulnerable to attack by its larger and more powerful neighbours. Its four major cities, all positioned on the long coastal plain, are linked by the only major road system and would fall easy prey to any seaborne landing.

On coming to power in 1944, the Albanian Party of Labour (APL) aggravated the problem by its xenophobic, paranoid and extremely provocative foreign policy. Such alliances as were made – with Yugoslavia (1944 to 1948), the Soviet Union (1948 to 1961) and China (1961 to 1977) – all ended in extreme acrimony due to the total unwillingness of the regime to compromise even slightly its Stalinist beliefs.

For years before the event, world opinion was divided as to the possible fate of Albania after the death of Enver Hoxha, the Secretary General of the APL from 1941 and President for life from 1944. Hoxha ruled his country with an absolute and often bloody hand, relying on his dreaded secret police, the Sigurimi, to suppress the slightest hint of dissent. It is even reported that in 1981 he personally shot dead Mehmet Shehu, his Defence Minister and friend of 40 years, for advocating reform.

At the time of Hoxha's death in 1985, Albania was badly isolated. Although his successor, Ramiz Alia, has taken steps to mend political fences with neighbouring Greece and Yugoslavia, his attitude towards the rest of the world remains uncertain.

These problems have particularly badly affected the Albanian Peoples' Army (APA) which is now more incapable than ever of defending itself. It can no longer rely on Communist allies to donate surplus armaments, nor does it have the hard currency required to buy replacement guns and ammunition on the open market. Much of its equipment is of World War Two vintage and must be regarded at the very least as unreliable, if now actually unoperational.

Under Hoxha, the structure of the APA changed drastically with each new political treaty. Always large in comparison to the population, it grew drastically in 1967–68 to encompass the Chinese concept of 'Peoples' War' national defence, involving virtually every able-bodied man. Literally thousands of pillboxes were constructed throughout the country to enable the general population to wage a war of attrition against the invader. Despite the obvious impracticalities of fighting so static a war against a vastly better-equipped and more mobile enemy, the concept of the 'Peoples' War' has never been fully abandoned and even today, although construction of the pillboxes has ceased, an unnecessarily large force of 150,000 men is kept in reserve.

The Army of 31,500 men, including 20,000 conscripts who serve for two years before transferring to the reserve, would be totally incapable of defeating any enemy whether he approached by land or sea. Although the armoured brigade and two armoured battalions have a notional 190 tanks under command, most of these are ancient Soviet T-34s and T-54s of which it is strongly suggested that no more than 100 are operational. The four infantry brigades have reportedly no more than 13 BRDM-1 reconnaissance vehicles and 80 assorted personnel carriers between them, relying heavily on civilian wheeled transport for mobility.

Inevitably, the APA uniform is an amalgamation of Soviet and Chinese design. Initially, Soviet badges of rank were adopted, only to be abandoned with the coming of the Chinese influence. All ranks wear the national coat of arms representing a double-headed eagle and five-pointed red star above the emblem '24 Maj 1944' on their uniforms, but little else of national significance.

It is entirely possible that under the new regime the power of the APA will grow as that of the Sigurimi diminishes. New uniforms and tactics will be the inevitable result although the Army will never be able to regard itself as a truly credible force until it abandons once and for all the principles of the 'Peoples' War' in favour of basic rearmament.

Obsolescent T-54 tanks represent the mainstay of the Albanian armoured forces.

AUSTRALIAN SAS REGIMENT

The famous SAS sand beret and badge are worn in barracks but discarded in the field

Troops may expect to operate for up to three months in the field. Under such circumstances, 'parade' haircuts are not the order of the day

In common with many other special forces, the Australian SAS choose the weapon most suited to the individual operation. In this instance he is carrying the domestic version of the British L1 A1 7.62mm SLR, produced at Lithgow Arsenal

The basic design of the uniform, including its DPM camouflage, has been borrowed from the British

When 1st Australian SAS Company was raised at Campbell Barracks, Swarbourne near Perth, Western Australia, in July 1957 it became Australia's only special forces group. It was quickly assimilated into the Royal Australian Regiment, the principal regular infantry element of the Army, but regained its independence on 4th September 1964 when it was expanded and reconstituted as the Australian Special Air Services Regiment. Growth continued until by 1966 the Regiment could boast three 'Sabre' squadrons, a headquarters, base squadron and elements of 151 Signals Squadron.

In 1965 1 SAS Squadron was deployed to Brunei in support of a larger British force countering Indonesian infiltration, being replaced in the following year by 2 SAS operating in the Kuching area on the Sarawak coast. Although the British SAS headquarters was in the vicinity, and the latter regularly led ambush parties across the Indonesian border, Australian involvement in cross-border raids has never been officially admitted.

Simultaneously, the Regiment was committed to the Vietnam War, one 'Sabre' Squadron at a time serving in the Phuoc Tuy province southeast of Saigon. Between 1966 and the Australian withdrawal in 1971, the Squadrons not only worked in unison with the New Zealanders, providing long range reconnaissance intelligence and springing ambushes deep into Vietcong territory, but also operated as a 'fire brigade' reserve offering the infantry fire support and expertise in the conventional ground battle.

Despite not having been deployed operationally since Vietnam, the Australian SAS continues to play an important role in its country's defence. Indeed, in an Army which, due to financial constraints, has otherwise been reduced to a single recce regiment, a single armoured regiment and six infantry battalions, its continued existence is in itself a clear demonstration of the esteem in which the Regiment is held by the Canberra Government.

In the field of conventional warfare the SAS can draw on experiences ranging from LRRP patrolling in Vietnam to anti-terrorist counterpenetration in Malaya. Its members have regularly enjoyed transfer postings with the British and New Zealand SAS, the US Special Forces, and the SBS and Arctic and Mountain Warfare Cadre of the Royal Marines.

A counter-terrorist capability was developed in 1979 which during the last 10 years has grown to meet the increasing threat of terrorist infiltration along the country's massive and largely unpopulated coastline. As Australia has only a small navy, with nothing equating to the US Navy Seals or British SBS, the Regiment is also tasked with protecting the increasing number of offshore oil rigs.

As with the British SAS, the Australians draw their recruits from serving soldiers and not from the general public. Selection is based on a series of timed navigation marches which take place in the arid and featureless bush country of North West Australia. During training, not only are the soldiers' physical and mental reserves tested to the full by the conventional rigours of hunger, exhaustion and thirst, but they must also face the added dangers of highly venomous snakes and salt water crocodiles which have the unenviable reputation of being among the most vicious in the world.

Successful candidates learn parachuting, tracking, patrolling, navigation and survival before receiving their coveted badge and must even then undertake continuation training in signals, demolition and foreign weapons before being accepted as a fully-fledged member of a Troop.

All ranks wear standard Australian Army uniform, although many spurn conventional headgear in favour of bush hats or camouflage nets worn round the forehead. The traditional winged dagger SAS cap badge is worn on a sandberet when not operational. British SAS-type straight-topped para-wings are worn on the right upper sleeve.

Under normal circumstances the American M-16 A1 rifle, M-60 machine-gun and M-68 fragmentation grenade are carried, although increasingly these are being replaced by the German Heckler & Koch sub-machine-gun and Israeli Galil SAR rifle which many soldiers find lighter and more convenient.

Special Air Service Regiment (SASR) free-fall parachutists exit from a Royal Australian Air Force Iroquois helicopter. The ability to deploy into action with the minimum of delay is crucial to this elite force.

AUSTRALIAN OPERATIONAL DEPLOYMENT FORCE

A broad-brimmed hat is essential to protect the head from the harsh Australian sun

The heavy-barrel FN 7.62mm calibre compensates for the relatively short combat range of the M16 5.56mm standard personal weapon

To date, the ODF has yet to be issued with the latest combat suit and its members still wear the traditional plain khaki outfit

Conventional boots are replaced by light but sturdy shoes, more suitable to the semi-desert environment of Northern Australia

Australia is well aware that, however high the standards of her Army, it would be far too small to defend her huge land mass against a conventional invader.

Prior to 1982, invasion had always been considered impossible due to Australia's sheer geographical isolation, but the British invasion of the Falklands in the winter of that year destroyed such complacency at a stroke. The regular army, which traditionally had looked to the north for its threat, had now to be deployed nationwide and was soon stretched to breaking point. Defence of the north, with its millions of acres of scrubland, desert and – in the case of the far north – near-tropical rain forest, became a nightmare. Although the SAS Regiment, by the use of stealth and hit-and-run guerrilla tactics, could hope to harry an enemy once he had landed and attempted to move inland, it could not hope to monitor the thousands of kilometres of sparsely-populated coastline. Furthermore, drugs and wildlife smuggling and the importation of illegal immigrants were becoming a problem.

The answer was found in the creation of a quick reaction brigade, designated the Operational Deployment Force (ODF), which was stationed in Townsville on the southern tip of the Great Barrier Reef in Queensland. The brigade, which is kept at constant short notice to deploy, has the ability to mount a full company deployment without prior warning within seven days and to be fully operational in less than a month.

To operate efficiently, the ODF must rely on intelligence gathered from all conventional government and military sources in general and from the Regional Force Surveillance Units (RFSUs) in particular. At present the three RFSUs are responsible for surveillance in the northern halves of Queensland and Western Australia and throughout the Northern Territories.

Each unit is manned by army reservists with small regular components to deal with daily administration and training, and as such is similar in many respects to a British Territorial Army battalion.

RFSU members are chosen for their expertise in the field and their intimate knowledge of local areas rather than for their potential as conventional soldiers. Most are born and bred in the country and learned survival as a matter of course well before joining the Reserves. Many are bushmen trained at their father's knee to read the ground and sense immediately anything unusual or potentially dangerous.

Bushmen and Aboriginals tend to share a mutual respect rarely found in the cities and it has therefore been possible to recruit Aboriginals and Torres Strait Islanders, among the best trackers in the world, and to cross aboriginal areas without causing resentment.

The tasks of the RFSUs are to gather information, survey activity within their areas of operations (AOs) and to assist the military when deployed into their areas. They are specifically not intended to fight for information nor do they operate closely with the SAS. Long-range reconnaissance patrols which can last for five to six weeks under extreme conditions are undertaken in specially modified Toyota Land Cruisers fitted with additional fuel tanks, internal water tanks and raised exhausts to facilitate deep water crossing. Communications are by F1 HF radios. Vehicles are generally used in pairs with three-man crews.

The first RFSU to be formed was the North West Mobile Force, or NORFORCE, based in Darwin with outstations at Alice Springs, Gove and Kununnura. Although some initial confusion arose as to its exact role when NORFORCE was formed from the 7th Independent Rifle Company, problems were soon resolved. Subsequently, the 5th Independent Rifle Company in Western Australia was transformed into the Pilbara Regiment with bases at Port Hedland, Karratha, Tom Price and Newman, and the 51st Independent Rifle Company redesignated the 51st Far North Queensland regiment with bases at Cairns, Innisfail, Thursday Island and along the Queensland coast. To date, only NORFORCE is up to strength with 300 men, but the other RFSUs are growing steadily and will soon be fully complemented.

Although as units of the Field Force the RFSUs operate independently in time of peace, they would regroup in an emergency. Soldiers are issued with standard Australian Army uniform including the slouch hat and are armed with the American M-16 A1 rifle. However, in the best traditions of the Australian fighting forces, dress regulations and overt discipline relax markedly when operational.

The ODF is considered a reconnaissance unit and would not usually be expected to fight for information. If needs be, it can call upon the firepower of the regular army, in this instance the para-trained 3rd Battalion, The Royal Australian Regiment, for support.

NEW ZEALAND SAS SQUADRON

The British-style jungle hat and camouflage neck scarf have both proved popular operationally

'Belt Order' escape kit rather than formal webbing is the norm

The New Zealand SAS will normally carry US weaponry. In this instance the M16 with M203 grenade launcher has been issued. A spare bandolier of ammunition, draped around the waist, is carried for additional firepower

Resilient high boots are issued for most occasions and are ideal for parachuting, or operations in the jungle or desert

The New Zealand Special Air Service Squadron was formed in 1954 specifically to fight alongside the British and Rhodesian SAS in Malaya. As with C Squadron, Rhodesian SAS, volunteers were taken straight from civilian life, but so rigorous were the standards demanded that of the 800 original applicants only 138 were accepted for continuation training. By the time the Squadron moved to RAF Changi, Singapore, for parachute and jungle training in November 1955, 49 of these potential entrants had left and had been replaced by 40 regular officers and NCOs.

The Maoris, who formed one-third of the operational contingent, prove to be not only excellent trackers but also first rate ambassadors, succeeding in winning the 'hearts and minds' of the uncommitted jungle aborigines where others before them had failed. During their two years in Malaya the sabre troops spent no less than 17 months in the jungle, killing 26 terrorists including two area leaders for the loss of one scout killed in an ambush. Despite its success the Squadron was disbanded upon its return to New Zealand in December 1957.

Under the auspices of Lieutenant-Colonel Rennie, its ex-commanding officer and now Director of Infantry and Training, the SAS was reformed in 1959. Subsequently, in 1962, a small Squadron was sent to Korat in Thailand where it operated with United States Special Forces in support of the South East Asia Treaty Organization (SEATO).

Although the action lasted only five months, strong ties were made with the Americans, so much so that the name was changed to 1 Ranger Squadron, NZSAS.

During the Indonesian Confrontation of 1965–66, four detachments served in Borneo with the British and Australian SAS, and in a few instances with the SBS, gaining an excellent reputation for deep reconnaissance and jungle craft. 4 Troop NZSAS served in Vietnam between November 1968 and its withdrawal in 1971, during which time an officer and 25 men provided five-man long-range reconnaissance and ambush patrols under the command of an Australian SAS Squadron based at Nai Dat.

During the last 20 years the Squadron has participated in exercises in Brunei, Malaysia, the Philippines, Singapore, Fiji and Australia, and has hosted allied special forces training concentrations at home. Redesignated 1 NZSAS since April 1978, the Unit is now stationed near Auckland and consists of five Troops, a headquarters and small training establishment.

Training and selection remain akin to that of the larger British SAS, with a few refinements including a swim with boots, full pack and rifle. New Zealand has no SBS, with the result that considerable emphasis is given to maritime infiltration. Although capable of conventional operation (NZSAS contains some of the finest free-fall experts in the world), the Squadron is principally committed to counter-terrorist missions.

All ranks wear standard New Zealand Army uniform. Unusually they wear the standard para-red beret rather than the sand-beret more commonly associated with the SAS, although they do wear the standard winged-dagger cap badge and insignia and have adopted the universally respected motto 'Who Dares, Wins.'

THE ISRAELI PARATROOPER

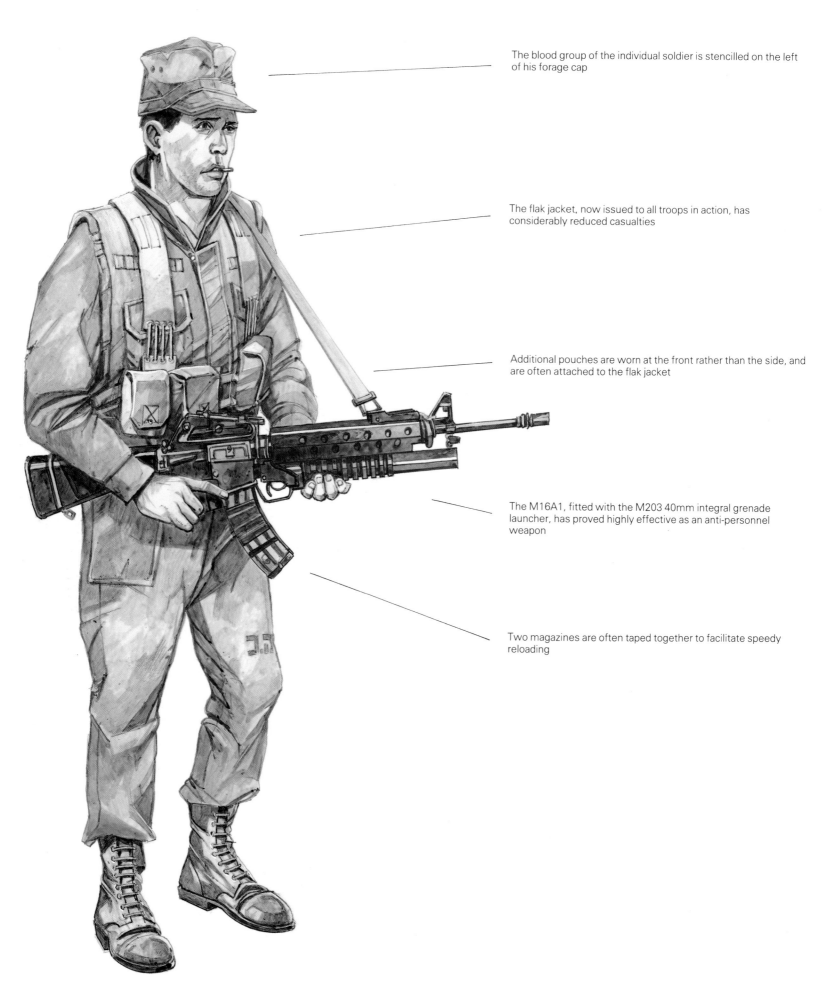

The blood group of the individual soldier is stencilled on the left of his forage cap

The flak jacket, now issued to all troops in action, has considerably reduced casualties

Additional pouches are worn at the front rather than the side, and are often attached to the flak jacket

The M16A1, fitted with the M203 40mm integral grenade launcher, has proved highly effective as an anti-personnel weapon

Two magazines are often taped together to facilitate speedy reloading

No soldier in the world has seen so much concentrated action or played so crucial a part in the survival of his country as the Israeli paratrooper. The paratroops were originally formed on 26th May 1948 during the War of Independence and at that time consisted of a loose collection of British-trained soldiers, resistance fighters, Holocaust survivors and the occasional mercenary. During its first few years, the force grew steadily in size as its reputation for carrying out successful reprisal raids against Arab groups spread, until in 1955 it was expanded into the 202nd Brigade.

After more years of reprisal raids, the paratroopers were involved in the Six Day War of 1967, when they spearheaded the capture of Gaza and the Suez Canal and were instrumental in the recapturing of the Old City of Jerusalem.

After the war, further increasingly daring raids were undertaken, including that against the PLO Headquarters in Jordan in 1968, the capture of a complete Soviet radar installation in 1969 and the rescue of hijacked hostages in Lod Airport in 1972. During the Yom Kippur War, paratroops were involved in desperate fighting to stem the brilliantly executed Egyptian attack before going onto the offensive. In 1976 they gained world-wide respect when, against enormous odds, they executed the raid on Entebbe and rescued all but one hostage from the grips not only of Arab terrorists but also the unstable President Idi Amin, whom ironically they had taught to parachute many years earlier.

Today the Israeli Defence Forces (Zahal) maintain three regular paratroop brigades, the 202nd, 890th and Na'ha'l (Pioneer Fighting Youth) 50th, as well as three reserve brigades.

All fit Israeli men are liable to undertake three years national service (4 years for officers) followed by regular periods in the reserve until the age of 54. Many volunteer for the parachute brigades and ancillary para-trained infantry units, but only a minority are accepted. Initial selection lasts for just over a day, during which time the recruit must prove himself physically, intellectually and mentally. Those selected undertake six-months basic training during which they may volunteer for specialist reconnaissance units for which they must undergo even longer and more arduous training.

The first phase of basic training lasts for 14 weeks and is geared to physical fitness, when the recruit is taken to the limits of his physical and mental endurance. During weapons training he familiarizes himself not only with Israeli and Western weapons but also with a whole series of small-arms which he is likely to capture from an Arab enemy. Most of the training is under field conditions and much of it consists of long, harsh, forced marches. There are, however, indications that these are being reduced in intensity due to the high incidence of stress fractures among new recruits.

At the end of the first phase the successful candidate is awarded his unit tag and joins a training platoon where he is assigned such specific duties as machine-gunner, radio operator or mortarman, which he spends two months master-

ing. The final phase of training is spent at the Tel Nof Jump School where, having undertaken five successful static line jumps, the recruit is awarded his coveted wings (worn on a blue background) and red beret. With basic training over, the paratrooper is posted to an operational unit where he continues his advanced training.

During any period of his training the recruit may ask to be considered for transfer to a sayeret or reconnaissance unit, all of which are para-trained yet independent of the brigades. Formed originally as quick reaction border guards, a number of sayeret now exist. They include the highly secretive Sayeret Matkal which is under the direct control of the Defence Minister, the Sayeret Haduzin which consists of Druze Muslims, and the Sayeret Golani, made up entirely of regular soldiers.

For many years Israeli paratroops were armed with the 9mm Uzi sub-machine-gun but this is now being replaced with the more versatile 5.56mm Galil assault rifle. Conventional paratroops wear normal Israeli Army uniform and helmet, although wherever possible the latter is replaced by the red beret. The silver parachutist's badge is worn on the left breast above the campaign medals. Free fall/HALO wings are awarded, as are master parachutist's wings for those who have completed 50 jumps. Uniquely, the soldier's blood group is written on his olive green fatigue cap and not engraved onto the dog tag which he wears around his neck.

Sayeret personnel wear standard fatigues, heavily supplemented where possible by privately acquired articles of United States uniform.

Few elite soldiers in the world appear as scruffy as the Israeli paratroops when operational (many neither shave nor wear any form of headgear) but few can be as highly motivated. The men of the Israeli Parachute Brigades have saved their country from extinction before and, if need be, would do so again.

The Ramta RBY is a fast, lightly-armoured recce vehicle specially designed to meet local conditions. It combines good cross-country performance with a low silhouette and moderate firepower provided by the 7.62mm GPMG and TOW missile launcher. Some 400 are in service with the Israeli Armed Forces.

ISRAELI ARMOURED CORPS

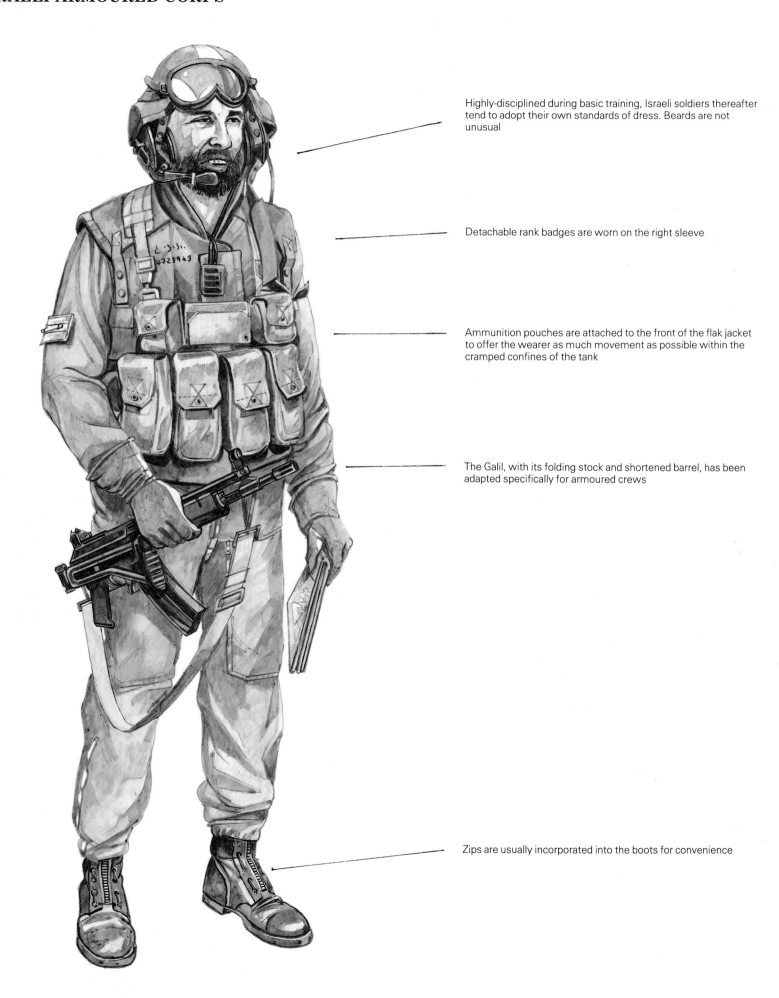

Highly-disciplined during basic training, Israeli soldiers thereafter tend to adopt their own standards of dress. Beards are not unusual

Detachable rank badges are worn on the right sleeve

Ammunition pouches are attached to the front of the flak jacket to offer the wearer as much movement as possible within the cramped confines of the tank

The Galil, with its folding stock and shortened barrel, has been adapted specifically for armoured crews

Zips are usually incorporated into the boots for convenience

The Israeli attitude towards armoured warfare changed drastically as a result of the 1973 Yom Kippur War. Prior to that, her forces had operated a limited war of attrition against sporadic terrorist groups and as a result had failed completely to realize the destructive potential of the new generation of anti-tank missiles then entering Arab service.

The traditional use of small independent groups of tanks, infantry and artillery proved ineffective against Soviet-produced Sagger man-portable anti-tank missiles and RPG-7 rocket-propelled grenade launchers, the former of which could destroy Israeli tanks beyond the range of the latter's guns.

Immediately after the War the whole structure of the IDF was altered and a 'combined arms' concept introduced. Armoured forces no longer operated in open areas independent of the infantry, simply relying on air-superiority (itself brought into question in the War) for support. The infantry were re-equipped, mechanized and trained to act as a protective screen for the armour moving ahead of it to destroy enemy anti-tank emplacements whenever possible.

Operation 'Litani', mounted in 1978 to crush PLO activity in Southern Lebanon, although not wholly successful, in itself nevertheless proved the effectiveness of the combined arms concept and gave the Israeli military leadership invaluable experience in mounting large-scale operations. The lessons learned then remain effective today and form the cornerstone of modern Israeli armoured warfare strategy.

The modern Armoured Corps consists of 3,900 tanks ranging from some 400 old Soviet T-55s and T-62s captured from the Arabs to 500 domestically-produced Merkavas. The latter have a forward-mounted engine to give the crew added protection against anti-tank missiles and a small compartment in the rear which can be used either for the carriage of extra ammunition or a half-section of fully equipped infantry. The 11 armoured divisions, many of which are at reduced cadre or mobilization strength, each comprise three brigades of three tank and one mechanized infantry battalions.

Although many members of the Corps volunteer, the majority are conscripts enlisted at the age of 18, or later in the case of immigrants taking Israeli nationality. Basic training, which itself consists of rigorous physical exercise and the use of combat assault weapons such as the Glilon and Galil automatic rifles, lasts for two months. At the culmination of training, those lacking the dash and élan required of all armoured crewmen are assigned administrative roles within the Corps.

A small minority who show a particular aptitude are sent on a specialist medical course, during which they are taught to handle tank-related injuries before returning to the Corps. The majority of recruits are sent to the IDF armoured school for one month where they learn the skills of driver, signaller/loader or gunner. Despite the acute lack of manpower, the diversity of operational equipment makes it impossible to teach the recruit more than one skill at this stage.

Once attached to an individual brigade, soldiers undergo 'in-house' crew, platoon and company training before being awarded their Armoured Corps tunic pin, worn above the left breast as an indication of their status as a qualified tank crewman.

Upon the completion of training a select few are sent to tank commander course from which they will emerge as sergeants. Thereafter the very best will opt to take commissions and return to their units as platoon commanders. Unusually, the IDF does not operate military academies. All officers must serve in the ranks for at least one year prior to attending the course and, if successful, will tend to remain with the same unit throughout their career, getting to know intimately the conscripts and reservists under their command.

Tank crewmen do not wear the standard uniform. Nomex coveralls are issued and worn beneath a Kevlar flak jacket where practical. Conventional webbing has been abandoned in favour of a less cumbersome set with the pouches to the front. Small dog tags are attached to each zip-up boot on the morbid basis that identification may otherwise be difficult in the event of a tank explosion. A new light-weight helmet, giving protection to the neck as well as head, has recently been issued.

Despite the complexity of modern tank fire control systems, Israeli reservists must be as proficient as their conscript counterparts.

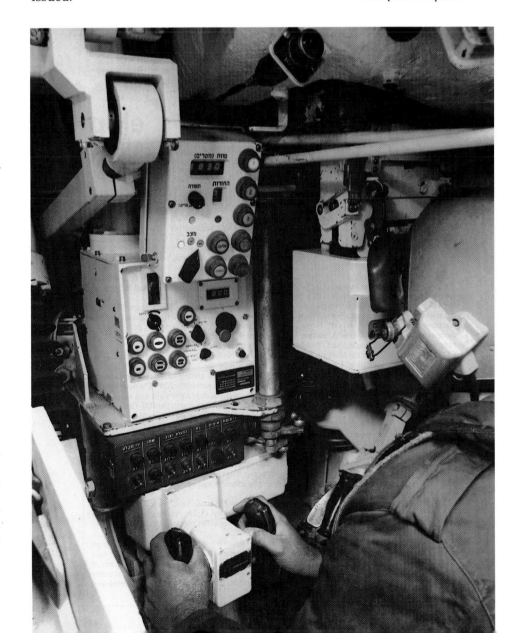

THE GOLANI INFANTRY BRIGADE

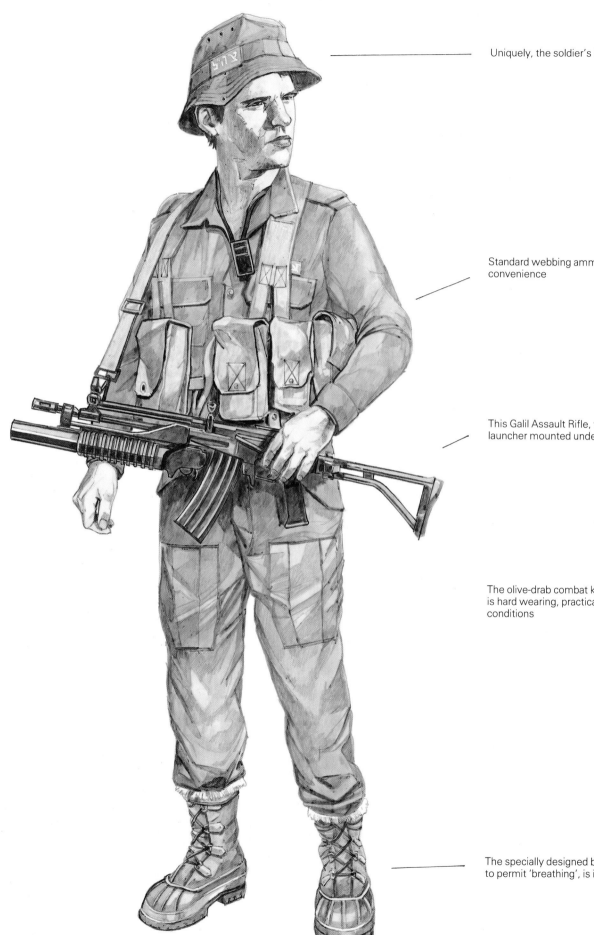

Uniquely, the soldier's blood group is marked on the hat band

Standard webbing ammunition pouches are often modified for convenience

This Galil Assault Rifle, with folding butt and a 40 mm grenade launcher mounted underneath the barrel, is peculiar to the IDF

The olive-drab combat kit worn by the majority of Israeli soldiers is hard wearing, practical and suited to all but the coldest of conditions

The specially designed boot, with rubber sole and canvas upper to permit 'breathing', is ideally suited to arid conditions

Of the 12 infantry brigades comprising the bulk of the Israeli Defence Forces, only the Golani Brigade has regular army status. Unlike the reserve brigades, which have trained in close co-operation with the armoured and artillery wings since the Yom Kippur War of 1973, the Golani Brigade has retained its independence. As such it is ideally suited to undertake crucial, if small-scale, quick-reaction duties and consequently since its formation it has almost certainly seen more action than any other unit within the IDF.

Despite its regular army status, the Golani Brigade contains a high percentage of conscripts undertaking their three years of national service (four years in the case of officers). In its infancy the brigade suffered markedly from the social, economic and political divergence of its conscripts, many of whom were recent immigrants from countries as far afield as the Soviet Union, United States and Germany. More recently, however, a series of hard fought battles and terrorist actions has successfully instilled into the Unit a pride and tradition strong enough to overcome internal differences.

Basic training, which is similar in structure if less intensive than that undertaken by the paratroops, lasts for 18 weeks. Discipline, which relaxes markedly once the soldier joins his operational unit, is harsh and punishment severe.

Training itself is divided into two parts, an initial phase in which the recruit concentrates on individual combat and weapon training and a final phase in which he masters his field craft. Although all soldiers are expected to be physically fit (training culminates in a 100km march) the Golani Brigade is in fact highly mechanized and much time is therefore dedicated to training with the United States' M113 APC.

Prior to entry into the brigade as a full combatant, and promotion to the rank of 'rifleman 5th class', the recruit passes out in a highly emotive ceremony held at the foot of Mount Hermon, itself captured from the Syrians by members of the brigade in October 1973. Trained personnel, both male and female, wear a brown beret. Combat personnel wear the Golani tunic pin, fashioned in the shape of a tree superimposed on a horizontal knife with a red background, on the left breast pocket flap.

During his remaining period of service the infantryman may attend medical, radio or vehicle maintenance courses and, if suitable, train as an intelligence operator.

After an initial six-months service the very best infantrymen are invited to apply for transfer to the Sayeret Golani. Arguably the finest reconnaissance unit in the Israeli Army, Sayeret Golani acts as the vanguard in all operations conducted by the brigade and is used extensively in anti-terrorist operations. In 1974 members of Sayeret Golani stormed a school on the Lebanese border in which nearly 100 pupils were being held by three gunmen. In the ensuing battle the gunmen were killed but, tragically, not until they had murdered 25 children and wounded 70 others. More successfully, a mechanized element took part in the Entebbe raid using their M113

This soldier has an extended magazine holding 50 rounds in place of the more usual 35-round magazine on his Galil rifle. This makes it obligatory to fire from the hip.

APCs to secure the airfield perimeter and destroy Ugandan fighter aircraft, frustrating any attempt at pursuit. Initial selection is uncompromising and failure common. Unsuccessful candidates return to the brigade whilst the more fortunate undergo in-depth physical and psychological tests prior to undertaking further training, including a parachute course at the Tel Nof Jump School.

The Golani Brigade wears a hybrid parade uniform consisting of an olive-coloured general service shirt, paratroop trousers and brown beret. Operationally, soldiers dress for comfort. Although conventional webbing is issued, most troops carry their six pouches attached to the front of their flak jackets with their water bottle attached to the rear. An olive-coloured bush hat, with the blood group stencilled to the side, is worn as standard in all but the coldest of conditions.

Derived largely from the AK-47, the 5.56mm Galil was developed to replace the heavy 7.62 FAL after the 1967 war. Both the standard ARM and SAR (Shortened Assault Rifle) in Israeli service have folding stocks, a useful feature for a highly-mechanized army.

JORDANIAN SPECIAL FORCES

The US Colt M16A1 is standard issue

Much of the equipment is influenced by Western designs. Note the American pattern webbing and helmet

It is common practice to carry a standard fragmentation grenade strapped to the front of the webbing

Despite the fact that King Hussein completed his military education at the Royal Military Academy, Sandhurst, and has always looked to Britain and more recently the United States for support and advice, paratroopers were not introduced into the Jordanian Army until 1963. The initial company-sized formation quickly proved its value and was steadily increased in size until today it constitutes the Jordanian Special Forces Brigade.

The present force of approximately 1,600 men consists of three commando/paratroop battalions organized on the standard Jordanian pattern. Heavily influenced by post-war British experience, each battalion is approximately 500 strong with three companies of three platoons.

The brigade, which has a dual military and internal security role, has acquitted itself bravely in all the Arab-Israeli wars since its formation. It has often found itself pitted against the battle-hardened Israeli paratroopers, invariably with heavy resultant losses to both sides.

Despite the existence of an independent Royal Guards Brigade, King Hussein has often relied upon his Special Forces to crush internal dissent, particularly among the Palestinian refugees. Specialist counter-insurgency elements worked closely with the 4th Mechanized Division to crush Palestinian Liberation Organization (PLO) camps along the Salt-Aman highway in September 1970 whilst simultaneously blocking a Syrian invasion from the north. In 1976 they once again played an important part in the storming of the Inter-Continental Hotel and the subsequent release unharmed of hostages held by PLO extremists.

The Special Forces are so well regarded that in 1983 the United States Government suggested they should be expanded to two-brigade size to spearhead a peace-keeping force in the Gulf area. As soon as it was realized that the scheme would cost $200 million, that it would not be possible to double the size of the brigade overnight and, more ominously, that the newly enhanced Force might be unleashed against its Israeli neighbours in the future, it was conceded that the plan owed more to the current feelings of frustration and impotence in the Pentagon than to hard reality and it was dropped.

Members of the Special Forces are hand-picked Bedouins with tribal links to the Hashemite Royal Family and a proven record of loyalty.

All potential recruits, who undertake a selection process as rigorous as any in the world, are volunteers either from the regular army or from among the conscripts who serve for a period of two years. Training, which both physically and mentally is among the hardest and roughest undertaken by soldiers of any Arab army, includes detailed instruction in guerrilla and anti-guerrilla warfare, long range reconnaissance, patrolling and raiding.

After service with one of the battalions, officers and men may volunteer for service in the highly selective counter-insurgency brigade, itself composed of special security groups or SSGs. Although little is known of the Group, its role is

becoming increasingly important with the growth of Shi'ite fundamentalism and Palestinian unrest.

The three battalions are equipped with American arms including Dragon anti-tank guided missiles, 106mm recoilless, rifles, mortars, M16 rifles and M60 machine-guns. The uniform betrays both British and United States influence, although the latter now predominates in all but parade dress. Parachute wings are worn on the left breast and the Special Forces badge in the form of a white bayonet surmounted by a Hashemite crown and surrounded by yellow wings, the whole backed by a maroon shield, is worn on the right upper sleeve. When non-operational, a maroon beret is worn in the manner of the British Parachute Regiment but with the conventional infantry cap badge.

Top: These Jordanian officers are being instructed in the finer points of the British-designed Bailey Bridge.

Above: Much of the Jordanian Army equipment comes from the USA, including the ubiquitous M113 APC. The M1 Garrand rifles have been superseded by the M16A1.

SULTAN OF OMAN'S LAND FORCES

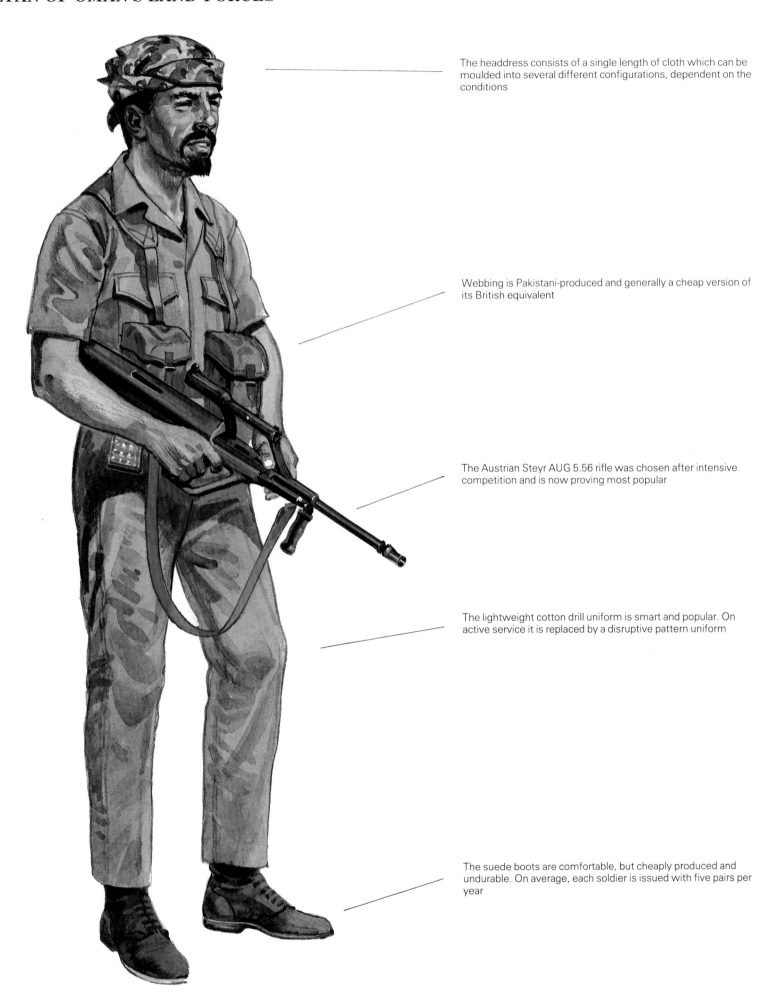

The headdress consists of a single length of cloth which can be moulded into several different configurations, dependent on the conditions

Webbing is Pakistani-produced and generally a cheap version of its British equivalent

The Austrian Steyr AUG 5.56 rifle was chosen after intensive competition and is now proving most popular

The lightweight cotton drill uniform is smart and popular. On active service it is replaced by a disruptive pattern uniform

The suede boots are comfortable, but cheaply produced and undurable. On average, each soldier is issued with five pairs per year

The Sultan of Oman's Land Forces (SOLF) are among the best-equipped and trained in the Southern Gulf. Prior to 1970, when Sultan Qaboos bin Said, a Sandhurst-trained Anglophile, seized power from his father in a bloodless palace coup, the country was an economic and political backwater. Slavery, albeit on a small scale, was still practised, the Dhofaris in the South were waging a protracted and successful civil war and all foreigners, with the exception of a few British military advisers, were banned.

Sultan Qaboos immediately set about enlarging and restructuring his Armed Forces along British lines. Heavily assisted by the British SAS, the Omanis destroyed the final vestiges of the Yemeni-backed and Communist-inspired Dhofari rebellion in 1975.

Within the last 10 years, SOLF has been transformed from primarily an infantry force with very limited artillery, engineering and armoured support, to an Army capable of waging conventional war. Although still predominantly infantry, it has gradually developed into a more balanced organization equipped for motorized warfare in desert conditions. Its artillery, armoured and engineering wings have grown steadily and are continuing to do so.

Sophistication has, however, brought its own problems. Until 1970 few Omanis were well educated and technology was kept out of the Sultanate and away from the population. Omani personnel in their late thirties, who should now be forming the nucleus of the senior officers and NCOs, would therefore have received little or no technical education in their formative years and are now betraying an understandable but worrying lack of sophistication in their dealings with the latest available equipment.

Until recently, SOLF relied heavily on loan service personnel and contract soldiers to command, train and administer the majority of its units. However, a policy of 'Omanianization' has now been introduced, as a result of which many 'advisers' are not having their contracts renewed and are being replaced by nationals. This has led not only to a drop in standards but to a rekindling of tribal rivalries.

A sizeable minority of the 20,000 soldiers serving in SOLF are not true Omanis. Three Baluch infantry battalions raised to fight in the Dhofari War still operate in the South. Until 1958, part of the Baluchistan, now a province of Pakistan, belonged to the Sultanate and it was natural that strong ties should exist. However, due to poor pay, the loss of British loan officers and a growing insularism amongst the Baluch, who speak their own language and maintain their own traditions, relationships are now strained. As a result, Baluchi recruitment has ceased and the battalions, once regarded as the finest anti-insurgency troops in the Gulf, have been stripped of their support weapons and are in effect little more than old-fashioned pure infantry units.

The 2,600-strong Special Forces, who are stationed and operate mainly in the South, are largely of Dhofari stock. Nicknamed 'the Lavender Hill Boys' by the rest of SOLF in response to

their gaudy beret, the SSF are SAS-trained, tough and aloof. They are also in many instances the sons of those who fought so actively against the Sultan in the earlier Dhofari Wars!

Omani officers in all services have to serve for one year in the ranks before attending the Officers' School near Muscat. The soldiers also train centrally under the auspices of the Training Regiment based a few miles north of Muscat. Soldiers are under no contractual obligation to remain in the army and need give only the minimum notice of their intention to leave. Basic training is rudimentary, consisting largely of drill, weapons training and acclimatization to a way of life far more westernized than many will have been used to in their villages.

Uniforms are British in design but usually Pakistani in manufacture. A disruptive pattern combat suit, khaki-coloured suede boots and shapka are worn in the field. Surprisingly, the shapka, or head dress, is made in England. Consisting of a single square of rough cloth, it is folded into a triangle and wound round the upper head in such a way that the apex of the triangle covers the neck, offering it some protection against the sun.

Oman has been careful to purchase the best weapon systems available and as such has a very diversified arsenal. The artillery is supplied with British 105mm light guns and Soviet and Chinese 155mm medium guns, the former acquired from the Egyptians. The infantry is armed with the Austrian Stayr rifle, arguably one of the finest assault weapons in the world.

Oman is presently suffering an economic decline due to the instability of the dollar and the falling price of oil. This is having a definite effect on Army morale, but to what extent has yet to be seen.

The 'Firqua' raised locally in the Jebel are lightly-armed but determined fighters who have worked closely with the Baluch and Regular SOLF to combat incursions from the Yemen.

A Baluch sentry stands guard in the mountains of the southern border area.

IRANIAN REVOLUTIONARY GUARDS

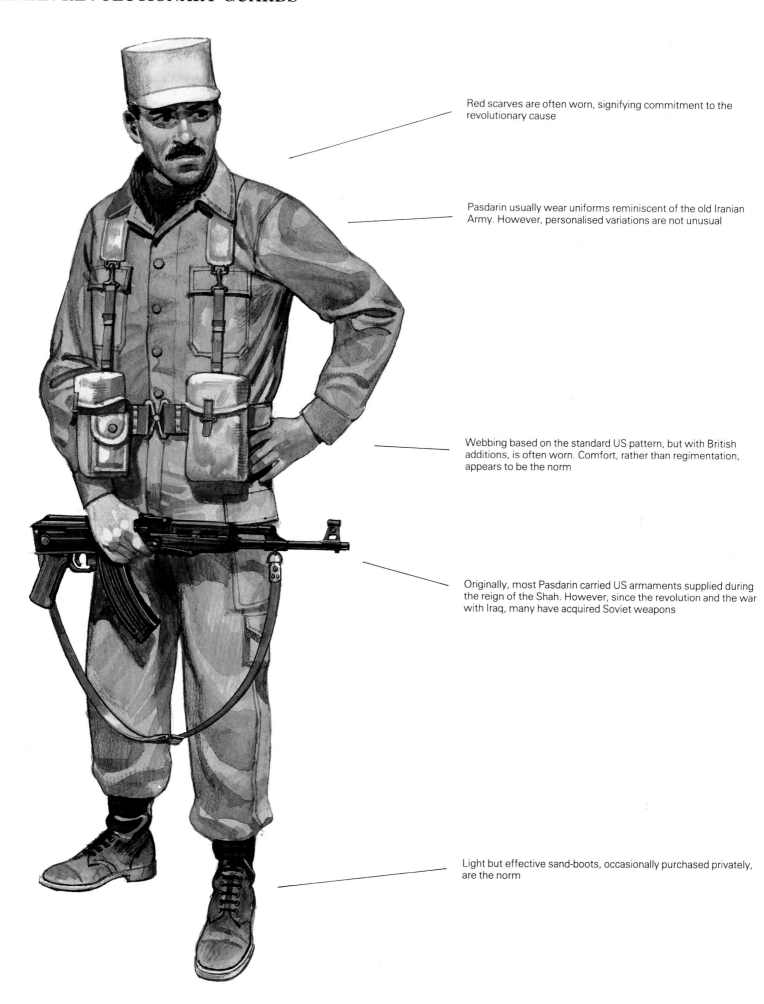

Red scarves are often worn, signifying commitment to the revolutionary cause

Pasdarin usually wear uniforms reminiscent of the old Iranian Army. However, personalised variations are not unusual

Webbing based on the standard US pattern, but with British additions, is often worn. Comfort, rather than regimentation, appears to be the norm

Originally, most Pasdarin carried US armaments supplied during the reign of the Shah. However, since the revolution and the war with Iraq, many have acquired Soviet weapons

Light but effective sand-boots, occasionally purchased privately, are the norm

Iran's Revolutionary Guards, or Pasdarin, now outnumber her regular army both in size and influence. They receive the latest equipment, man the most dangerous areas of the 700-mile front line and invariably sustain losses far greater than any other combatants in the protracted and bloody war with Iraq. To date, an estimated 600,000 Pasdarin have lost their lives and an undisclosed number have been savagely injured.

The exact size of the Iran Revolutionary Guards Corps (IRGC) is difficult to quantify and reports vary drastically. The main forces are divided into eight divisions with numerous independent infantry, armoured, airborne, artillery, engineering and air defence brigades in support. Although armed and equipped by the Army, the Corps remains totally independent. It regards itself as answerable to the Parliamentary Speaker, Hashemi Rafsanjani, and through him directly to Ayatollah Khomeini rather than to the military commanders, many of whom it still regards as having dangerous latent pro-Shah sympathies.

During 1987 the Revolutionary Guards established at least five bases on abandoned oil platforms or tiny islands in the Gulf and later that year wrested control of the huge naval base of Banda Abbas from the regular navy. In April 1987 Hussein Alael, commander of the Guard's naval arm, boasted that he controlled the north of the Gulf with coast-to-ship missile batteries and heavy artillery and threatened to bring Iraq and her allies to their knees through economic blockade. Although this was a clear exaggeration, it has nevertheless since taken the might of six neutral navies to keep the sea lanes of the Gulf open and at least partially safe from the attention of marauding Iranian Revolutionary Guard speedboats.

New battalions of Pasdarin, each consisting of about 150 men, are formed when reinforcements are required for a new offensive and are given only the most rudimentary training before being committed straight to the front.

'People's Liberation Volunteers' (Basij) consisting of lightly armed youths are formed into battalions of 300 to 350 men and operate under the control of the Pasdarin. Iraqi propaganda references to attacks made against their positions by children bearing arms allude to the Basij, many of whom are in their young teens yet have proved to be among the most fanatical in vicious hand-to-hand fighting.

Over one million women have currently volunteered for the Basij and some 90 training centres, staffed by 1,000 women, exist throughout Iran, although to date there are no intentions of committing them to battle.

The power base of the Pasdarin lies emphatically in the desperately poor and underprivileged villages and hamlets of the countryside, which account for over 70 per cent of the population. It is not unusual for one in ten of the entire population of a village or small town to be engaged with the Pasdarin or Basij at any one time.

Although casualties are glorified rather than hidden, to the extent that pictures of war wounded, their limbs shattered by shrapnel, occupy

places of honour in public buildings, the policy of relying on human-wave attacks which have inevitably led to shocking losses is now being questioned at every level. Reports now circulating from the remote East of the country suggest that villages are becoming increasingly unwilling to allow their young men to volunteer for second or subsequent tours at the front, while elements of the Hizbolla youth movement, once the scourge of Tehran are now actively advocating reconciliation.

Although the Pasdarin are at last creating a viable command structure they are still in many respects irregulars. They have no specific uniform, wearing whatever they can beg, buy or borrow and are armed with a wide variety of both NATO and Warsaw Pact weapons.

The variability of Revolutionary Guard 'uniform' is apparent in these photographs of the crew of the Iranian minelayer *Ajr*. The lifejackets, protective headgear and plastic handcuffs are by courtesy of the US Navy.

THE IRAQI ARMY

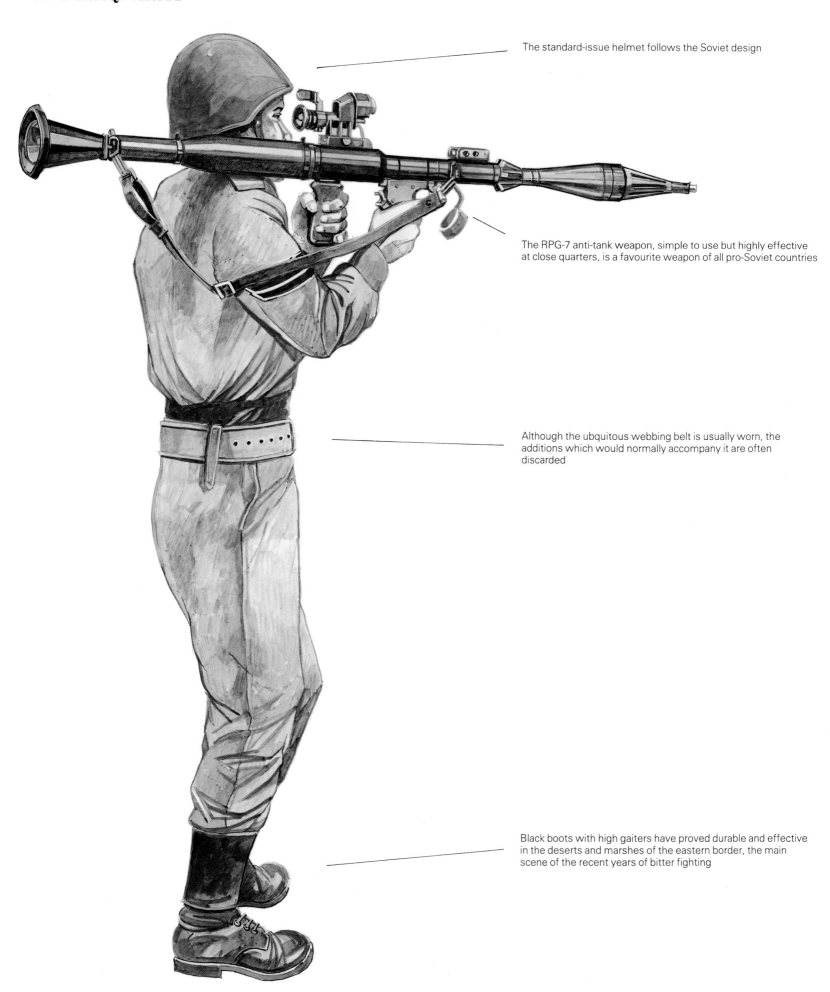

The standard-issue helmet follows the Soviet design

The RPG-7 anti-tank weapon, simple to use but highly effective at close quarters, is a favourite weapon of all pro-Soviet countries

Although the ubiquitous webbing belt is usually worn, the additions which would normally accompany it are often discarded

Black boots with high gaiters have proved durable and effective in the deserts and marshes of the eastern border, the main scene of the recent years of bitter fighting

The SCUD-B missile is capable of delivering a high explosive or chemical warhead considerable distances. Its wheeled transporter/erector/launcher vehicle is highly mobile and can be rapidly redeployed to avoid revealing future intentions to the enemy.

The Iraqi Army, although superficially stronger than its regular Iranian adversary, has little in the way of uncommitted reserves. At present the 800,000 men under arms include an estimated 230,000 active reserves, nine reserve brigades and fifteen voluntary infantry brigades all on active duty. Conscription is normally for a period of 21 to 24 months, although this has been extended somewhat unilaterally during various stages of the War.

Iraq far exceeds Iran in the field of technology and equipment. From figures released by the International Institute of Strategic Studies, it would appear that even as late as mid-1987 Iraq was still capable of fielding no less than 6,000 main battle tanks. Whereas admittedly a few of these were old Soviet T–54s and T–55s, the majority were 115mm Chinese T–59s and Soviet T–62s. A growing number of 122mm T–72s, the latest Soviet export and a match for any Iranian tank, were also held. Over 4,000 armoured fighting vehicles (AFVs), including Soviet BRDM–2s, East German FUG–70s and French MOWAG reconnaissance vehicles, 1,000 Soviet BMPs and numerous BTR 60 and Czech OT–54 armoured personnel carriers (APCs) provided mobility and protection for the infantry.

Support is provided by over 5,500 assorted Soviet, French and United States artillery pieces ranging in calibre from the US 105mm M–56 pack howitzer to the 155mm French AMX–30 GCT. All are well maintained and ammunition does not seem to be a problem. In excess of 200 multi-barrel rocket launchers (MBRLs), including several batteries of the ferocious Soviet 122mm 40–barrel BM–21, capable of clearing a map grid per battery volley, are held as are 30 FROG–7 and 20 SCUD–B surface-to-surface missiles with ranges respectively of 42 miles (67 km) and 62 miles (100 km). An undisclosed number of Soviet SS–12 Scaleboard missiles, capable of destroying much of Teheran from firing positions well behind the front line, are also reportedly held.

The current state of morale among the Iraqi rank and file is difficult to assess. Until recently the infantry was able to remain in comparative safety behind strong, well-defined defensive lines and could rely on the vastly superior Iraqi Air Force to disrupt enemy concentrations whilst destroying his artillery. Radically new Iranian tactics involving the Regular Army, Pasdarin and Air Force, first seen in the battle of Karbala–5 in January 1987, have however now completely revolutionized the battlefield, particularly in the Basra area where the majority of troops are concentrated.

Hand-to-hand combat has now returned to the trenches with a resultant increase in loss of life for the Iraqi defenders. Unlike the Iranians, who seem to revel in the death of relatives and comrades even to the extent of exhibiting photographs of the mutilated remains by the graveside, the Iraqis are more circumspect, it having even been suggested that bodies are now being returned to their home towns and villages in batches so as to minimize the true extent of the losses. That said, Iraq is not a free society and open criticism of the State or of its prosecution of the War is dealt with quickly and ferociously.

Members of the National Liberation Army of Iran (NLA), formed in June 1987 mainly from Mujahideen Khalq guerrillas fighting the Khomeini regime, are armed by and operate closely with the Iraqi Army in the Northern Front. Estimates of the exact numbers of the NLA, currently based in Iraq and fighting as part of their Army, vary greatly from a few hundred to 15,000, although indications suggest that the latter figure is more accurate.

There can be no doubt that the Iraqi Army has a stock of chemical weapons which it has used and would not hesitate to use again if circumstances demanded, whatever the effect on world-wide opinion.

The Iraqi soldier is tough and resilient. Although his weapons and vehicles are good, his personal kit and equipment often appear lacking in quality and quantity, with little conformity among the ranks.

LEBANESE IRREGULAR FORCES

The colourful headgear is often red to depict religious commitment to the Muslim faith

Most Irregulars carry Soviet-design weapons, in this instance the popular AK-47

The Palestinian flag, depicted on the webbing, is a personal introduction

Uniforms vary considerably both in style and standard. In this instance the red, green and black disruptive pattern offers excellent cover for street fighting operations

Lebanon, once the financial jewel in the Arab crown, is today beset by a vicious civil war fuelled by a combination of centuries of religious bigotry, political extremism and a drastic change in the balance of power since the influx of huge numbers of Palestinians from Jordan in 1970. President al-Assad, who has always regarded Lebanon as morally a part of 'Greater Syria', has gone to great lengths to wrest control of the Palestinian Movement from Yasser Arafat, the Palestine Liberation Organization (PLO) chairman whom he detests, and from the host of smaller, often Marxist-orientated groups, such as the Democratic Front for the Liberation of Palestine (DFLP) and the Palestine Liberation Front (PLF). In so doing, he has driven an already suspicious Israel to the brink of war.

Syria's principle agent in Lebanon, the Amal Militia, gained world-wide notoriety in October 1986 when, with the aid of the Hezbollah with whom they then had a tenuous alliance, they laid siege to the massive Palestinian refugee camps at Bordj al Barrajneh, Sabra and Chatila. Although in December Amal offered to lift the sieges in exchange for the Palestinian evacuation of several hilltop strongholds around Tyre, an agreement was not reached. By the time the sieges were eventually raised by Syrian troops in February 1987, thousands of refugees, including hundreds of woman and children, had died from starvation, disease and the lack of medical attention despite the valiant attempts of a small courageous team of doctors and nurses.

The main belligerents in the War are the Maronite Christian factions, numbering 5,000 regular and 30,000 reservists under the broad control of Samir Geagea and based north of Beirut; the Druze Militia, based in the Chouf Mountains with about 4,000 men and 20,000 res-

ervists led by Walid Jumblatt; and the Lebanese National Resistance (LNR), a loose alliance of primarily Shia Muslim factions, including the pro-Syrian Amal Militia led by Nabih Berri with about 5,500 regulars and 15,000 reservists.

The Hezbollah, or 'Party of God', and LNR splinter group, has grown steadily in the slums of southern Beirut and in the poor hamlets and hill villages along the barren wadis to the east of the ancient sea port of Tyre, where Moslem fundamentalism has its strongest roots. In late 1987, in retaliation for the kidnapping and humiliation of several of her soldiers, Syria rounded up and summarily shot 23 Hezbollahi as a warning against further unrest but nevertheless still refrains from ordering her Army into their strongholds.

Recently the Hezbollah and Amal have come into open conflict over the question of hostage-taking, regarded as politically acceptable by the former but denigrated by the latter. Furthermore, unlike its associates in the LNR, the Hezbollah favours a Palestinian presence in the south, taking advantage of the Amal-Palestinian conflict to establish a revolutionary Shia presence near the Israeli border.

The power and influence of the PLO within Lebanon has waned considerably within the last two years, although cross-border attacks are still launched periodically against targets of opportunity in Northern Israel.

With the exception of the Christian Militia, who occasionally receive shipments of arms and equipment from Israel, most Irregulars carry Soviet weapons, notably the AK–47 Kalashnikov assault-rifle. Few wear formal uniform and in the case of the reserves it is often difficult to tell them apart from the civilians in whose areas they operate.

The 'AK' or 'Kalashnikov' has become almost synonymous with the words 'freedom-figher'.

NORTH KOREAN SPECIAL PURPOSE FORCES

Unlike their Chinese mentors, who have yet to reintroduce them, the North Koreans wear badges of rank on both shoulders

Special forces are issued with a variety of weapons, both Soviet and Western in design. In this instance an AK-47 is in use, probably of Chinese origin

Uniforms are generally of a high quality and very durable, a necessity in the harsh winter climate

Good quality thick boots are necessary for soldiers who may be asked to operate under vastly differing conditions at very little notice

North Korea boasts one of the largest and best equipped special forces in the world. Designed specifically to disorganize, confuse and weaken South Korean defences before a major attack, to carry out reconnaissance and sabotage missions in peacetime and to assassinate key political and military figures when expedient, the Special Purpose Forces as they are known, were formed soon after the Korean War and now number some 80,000 personnel; over 10 per cent of the entire Army.

The cream of the Special Forces are formed into four reconnaissance brigades deployed one apiece with the four corps bordering the demilitarized zone. Each brigade has a strength of approximately 4,200 and is organized into a headquarters, support services, signal company and 10 recce battalions, themselves divided into squads of 10 men. Experience has shown that operations against the South are invariably carried out by teams of at least two but rarely more than six individuals.

Assassination or abduction, which is undertaken by specific elements within the brigade, is carried out in liaison with the highly secretive Central Committee's Research Department, thought to have been responsible for the bombing of the Korean Airlines aircraft in the winter of 1987. Officially the Special Purpose Forces are all male, but in reality an undisclosed number of women are attached from the Political Security Department to add credibility to units operating covertly on hostile territory.

Reconnaissance bridges are responsible for intelligence gathering throughout the peninsula. Long-range patrols are usually inserted by sea or air although occasionally infiltration tunnels are dug beneath the demilitarized zone. Selection and training are rigorous. Although not renowned for their initiative or independence of thought, all Korean soldiers are nevertheless highly motivated and well disciplined. Conscripts are drafted between the ages of 17 and 21, continuing in service until the age of 27. Due to the extremes of climate, wherever possible field training is limited to the summer months.

At the end of an initial one-month basic training course, recruits are posted to an operational unit where training continues in platoon and company drills. Those joining Special Forces units concentrate particularly on subjects such as infiltration, unarmed combat, demolition and intelligence-gathering, which will be of particular use to them in the years to come.

In time of war, diversionary troops drawn from the reconnaissance brigades would disguise themselves in South Korean or United States uniforms and undertake a variety of disruptive operations to confuse and undermine the morale of the enemy. Convoys would be rerouted into ambushes, headquarters and communications centres overrun and landing zones secured for subsequent heliborne and airborne landings.

Equipment scales are flexible, international and light. Most troops carry a dagger or bayonet, a silenced version of either the Browning 9mm or Soviet Tokarev 7.62mm automatic pistol and

either an AK–47 or M16 rifle. Soviet man-portable rocket launchers such as the RPG-7 or AT–3 Sagger are carried if required. During training, reconnaissance troops wear standard North Korean uniforms but during operations often change into the mottled-green summer uniform or all-white winter garments of the South Korean Army.

North Korea has for many years provided military assistance to foreign governments, revolutionary organizations and revolutionary groups. Members of the Special Forces currently operate an estimated 30 guerrilla warfare facilities which between them have trained in excess of 5,000 foreign revolutionaries in the last 25 years. 'Advisers' drawn from the reconnaissance brigades currently operate in 35 countries throughout South America, Asia and Africa and are presently playing a large part in the Angolan civil war.

Although more discreet than the Libyans, there can be no doubt that the North Koreans are actively supporting their political allies on a worldwide scale.

These North Koreans, part of the peace negotiations team at Panmunjom, are wearing Soviet-style parade uniforms. In this instance, the rank insignia are worn on the collar.

SOUTH KOREAN SPECIAL FORCES

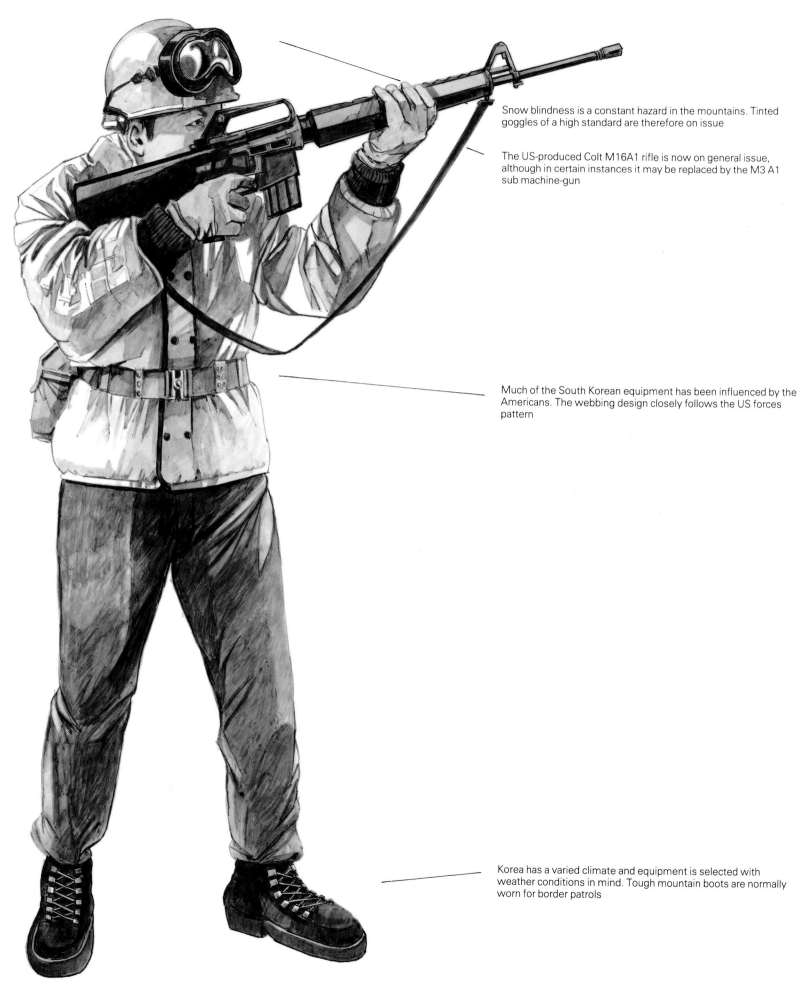

Snow blindness is a constant hazard in the mountains. Tinted goggles of a high standard are therefore on issue

The US-produced Colt M16A1 rifle is now on general issue, although in certain instances it may be replaced by the M3 A1 sub machine-gun

Much of the South Korean equipment has been influenced by the Americans. The webbing design closely follows the US forces pattern

Korea has a varied climate and equipment is selected with weather conditions in mind. Tough mountain boots are normally worn for border patrols

The South Korean people will never forget the ease with which the forces of the Communist North destroyed her unprepared armies in the days following the invasion of 25th June 1950. Although the combined might of the United Nations restored the status quo and forced the invader back across his borders, Koreans are fully aware that an armistice and not a peace treaty was signed in July 1953 and many regard themselves as at least technically still at war. The huge North Korean Army remains massed on the border and on the alert.

To combat this threat, the United States maintains a huge military presence in the South. The 8th Army, comprising the 2nd Infantry Division, 19th Support Command, numerous support units and a complete wing of the US Air Force would be more than adequate to 'hold the line' pending the arrival of reinforcements in the unlikely event of the North ever launching another full scale attack.

Should an attack ever occur, it would undoubtedly be spearheaded by the 80,000 North Korean Special Purpose Forces, elements of which are trained in underwater demolition, VIP assassination and long range reconnaissance. To combat these, the Republic of Korea has formed seven Special Forces brigades organized in the manner of US Special Forces Groups, with whom they have a close affinity, but without the latter's distinction between Special Force and Ranger roles.

The South Korean Units are attached to individual corps, within which battalions may be deployed on an Assault Commando (Ranger) role or in the anti-terrorist/reconnaissance (US Special Forces) role.

The best elements are given advance training in HALO (High Altitude, Low Opening) and sea-landing techniques to enable them to parachute behind enemy lines and in demolition, escape, evasion and resistance to interrogation to enable them to cause maximum damage whilst there. Others specialize in counter-guerrilla warfare and would be tasked with the tracking down and capture of Northern deep-reconnaissance units which would almost certainly attempt to infiltrate prior to the commencement of hostilities.

Despite strenuous protestations of innocence, the North regularly attempts to infiltrate its elite troops into the South, either by boat or aircraft or via a series of deep tunnels dug beneath the demilitarized zone, with the result that the South Korean Special Forces are kept at a constant state of battle-readiness.

Potential recruits undergo initial physical and psychological tests borrowed from the US Special Forces. Suitable candidates are then trained in fieldcraft and weapons handling to the highest level, attend a parachute course, become experts in day and night navigation and survival and are expected to qualify to Black Belt level in Tae Kwon Do (Korean karate) or a similar martial art which they practise for up to five hours a day when non-operational. The lethal potential of soldiers highly trained in a combination of

Standard military parachuting is regarded as a basic skill among the South Korean Special Forces. These soldiers are about to start an exercise by jumping in with full kit.

fieldcraft and martial arts was ably demonstrated by a section of South Korean Special Forces serving in Vietman who, on coming unexpectedly across an entire company of North Vietnamese, used their unarmed combat skills to dispatch them in absolute silence.

The survival course undertaken by all recruits contains a unique element: the killing with a karate chop, skinning and eating raw of a highly venomous snake!

Special Forces are almost totally reliant on the United States for weapons and equipment. The elderly US M3A1 0.45 sub-machine-gun, M16A1 rifle and M60 medium machine-gun are issued as standard at present although moves are afoot to replace these with locally-produced armaments more suited to the harsh Korean environment.

Normal uniform is a camouflage combat suit worn with a black beret and silver SF badge when non-operational. Pocket patches in the form of a lion for the special warfare branch, eagle for the 3rd Brigade, dragon for the 5th, Pegasus for the 7th, winged cat on a parachute for the 9th, lightning bolt for the 11th and panther for the 13th are worn when to do so would not compromise security.

THE VIETNAMESE PEOPLE'S ARMY

The pith helmet, originally worn by the British in India, was adopted by the Vietnamese during the war of independence against the French and has been retained

Limited webbing only is worn, the soldiers preferring to live off the land

The Kalashnikov AK-47 provided in large numbers by the Chinese was the principal weapon used against the Americans. China is now no friend of Vietnam but the weapons are still being supplied by the Soviets

Vietnamese soldiers will normally wear boots. However, many still prefer the traditional sandal when in the jungle

The 1,100,000 members of the 'Self Defence Force' of the People's Republic of Vietnam in reality constitute the third largest army in the world. Only the Soviet Union and China with their massive populations have more men under arms. Although superficially the epithet 'Self Defence Force' seems strange when applied to an army which currently has 10 per cent of its entire resources tied up in the subjugation of neighbouring Kampuchia, it was not always inaccurate. From its formation on 22nd December 1944, the People's Liberation Army (PLA), the forerunner of the People's Army of Vietnam (PAVN), fought a series of defensive and guerrilla actions first against the Japanese and later against the French, only going onto the offensive in 1954 when General Giap took the opportunity to strike a devastating blow against the demoralized and divided French Army at Dien Bien Phu. However, from the partition of Vietnam later that year until the final massive defeat of the South in 1975, the policy of the PLA was one of unmitigated aggression.

Ironically her very success in battle, combined with her resultant expansionist policies towards Laos and Kampuchia, made Vietnam an enemy of China, which until then had rendered her considerable assistance. In 1979 China mounted a limited invasion of Vietnam which, although not pressed home, forced the latter to seek crucial Soviet assistance. Despite continued Soviet aid, given in exchange for permanent access to the naval bases of Cam Ranh Bay and Kampong and the air base at Da-Nang, the Vietnamese still find it necessary to station over half of their huge forces on their northern borders as protection against future Chinese aggression.

The Vietnamese people, although friendly to those whom they trust, are nevertheless ferociously and unremittingly warlike, lending themselves perfectly to large-scale guerrilla and irregular combat. Over 4.5 million men, or around eight per cent of the population, serve in the regular forces, paramilitary forces, or as Ministry of the Interior internal security troops.

Although the PAVN is large, it is still totally dependent on the Soviet Union for its equipment, much of which is now obsolete. None of the 58 infantry divisions is fully mobilized and are therefore totally incapable of fighting in a nuclear environment. Whereas immediately after the United States' withdrawal the Vietnamese Army was able to boast considerable stocks of captured equipment including over 800 M113 APCs and even a few M60 tanks, the vast majority of these are now considered to be unoperational due to a lack of spare parts.

The PAVN plays an important social and economic role within the country. Not only do her paramilitary forces keep internal order (Vietnam has nothing directly equating to the MVD) but her surprisingly large force of engineers spend far more of their time engaged in economically productive civilian construction than they do on military exercises.

In short, the bulk of the Army is lightly armed, under equipped and totally lacking in mobility or

firepower. Fortunately for Vietnam, its Chinese potential adversaries are no better off.

Little is known about the Special Operations Force save that it contains an airborne brigade. It is likely that the 'Death Volunteers', renowned as the most ferocious of the Liberation Army's shock troops, have been incorporated into the special forces. Formed in 1951 to carry out the most dangerous, often suicidal, tasks, this small band of political ideologists would be given the best equipment available, but no extra training, and would be expected to lead 'forlorn-hope' charges, to act as rearguards and even to sacrifice themselves as human bombs if the situation required.

It is difficult for the West to comprehend the Oriental acceptance of death. However, so long as the Vietnamese Army boasts men willing to regard death as a duty and even a privilege it will, despite its obvious lack of equipment, remain a force to be reckoned with.

Although the modern Vietnamese Army draws basically upon the North for its uniform and traditions, it has not wasted the large amount of equipment captured from the South. Certain units will therefore be seen wearing US-style helmets and webbing.

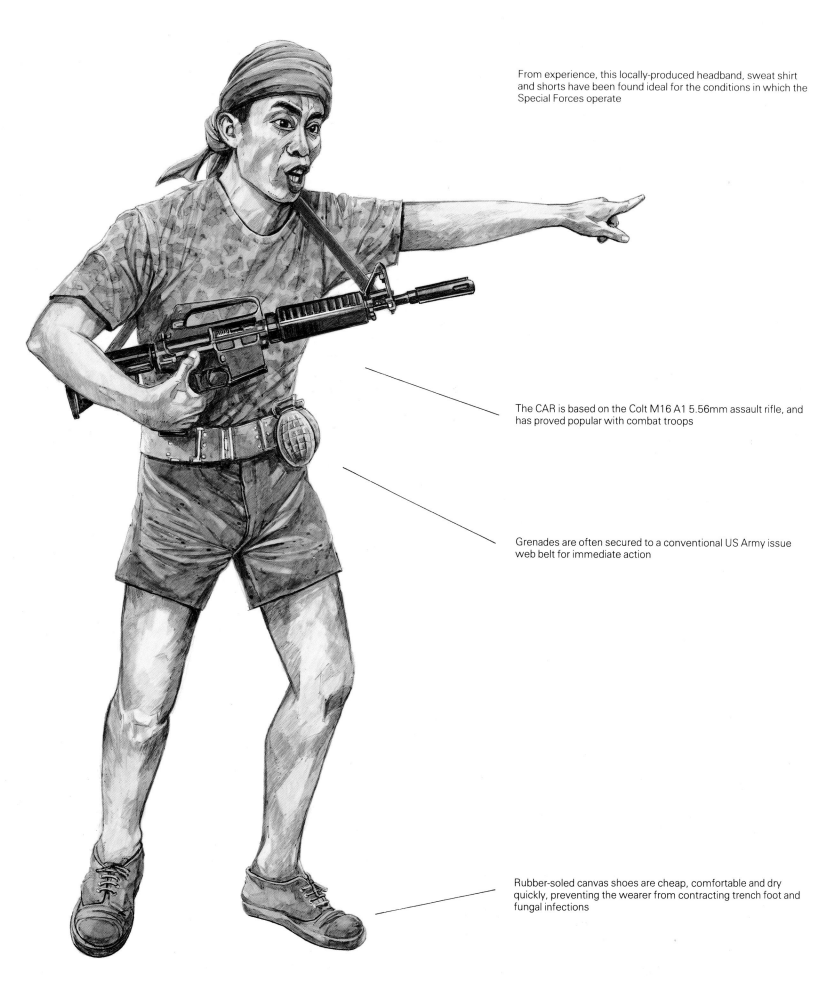

From experience, this locally-produced headband, sweat shirt and shorts have been found ideal for the conditions in which the Special Forces operate

The CAR is based on the Colt M16 A1 5.56mm assault rifle, and has proved popular with combat troops

Grenades are often secured to a conventional US Army issue web belt for immediate action

Rubber-soled canvas shoes are cheap, comfortable and dry quickly, preventing the wearer from contracting trench foot and fungal infections

Taiwanese elite forces maintain a constant guard against incursions from the Chinese mainland.

When Chiang Kai-shek and the remnants of his Chinese Nationalist Army fled mainland China in December 1949 they stated publicly that they would return. Today, some 40 years later, despite the overwhelming might of their adversary, their internal financial problems and virtual abandonment by the United States, this remains their dream. Fortunately for them, the People's Republic of China is less aggressive. Although it made unsuccessful attempts to invade the offshore islands of Quemoy and Matsu in 1955 and 1957, China now seems willing to co-exist with a policy of armed diplomacy on the basis that to do otherwise would alienate the West, to whom she is looking increasingly for industrial 'know-how' and commercial outlets.

The 425,000-strong Taiwanese Army is efficient, highly motivated and well trained. Conscripts serve for two years, after which they pass to the reserves with whom they serve to the age of 30. The Civil War veterans who formed the nucleus of the original Army received a tremendous boost when in 1953 50,000 Chinese and North Korean POWs taken prisoner by the United Nations forces in the Korean War refused to return home and in most cases volunteered for a new life in Taiwan. Although these veterans have now retired from active military service they remain a compelling propaganda force and a constant reminder of the short-falls of life on the mainland.

The 18 infantry divisions and six mechanized brigades are based principally on the main island of Taiwan, some 160km (100 miles) from the Chinese shore. However 55,000 men are stationed on Quemoy and a further 18,000 on Matsu, both of which are within shelling range of the mainland.

A Special Forces Headquarters exists consisting of four Groups structured independently of the conventional armed forces. Two small para-brigades act in an assault-commando role, combat swimmers specialize in sabotage and long-range amphibious reconnaissance commandos in intelligence-gathering, often on the mainland. There is an exceptional amount of overlap in the training and deployment of these forces. All elite troops are para-trained, whilst combat-swimmers are also schooled in small boat operations more usually associated with recce-commandos.

Perhaps inevitably, there is a growing relationship between the politically isolated countries of Israel, South Africa, Taiwan and Singapore. Although superficially they may not offer each other total political support, there are strong suggestions that at a military level 'know-how' and equipment are changing hands, that Taiwanese Special Forces have undertaken short term attachments with Israeli and South African forces and that elite troops from Singapore have attended training courses in Taiwan.

Recce-commandos and combat swimmers based on Quemoy regularly test mainland defences by landing intelligence-gathering agents. Conversely it is said that communist Special Forces occasionally land in Taiwan as part of their training, returning with souvenirs as proof of their success.

Until recently, Taiwanese forces wore uniforms almost exclusively acquired from the United States. However, this may now change as the rift grows between the two once-firm allies. Operationally, Special Forces wear a very light, locally-produced camouflage uniform which often includes shorts and canvas training shoes. Taiwan now produces its own Type 65 5.56mm rifle and sub-machine-gun, though many units are still equipped with the US M16A1 rifle.

THAILAND SPECIAL FORCES

Black cloth low-visibility insignia are worn on the upper sleeve

The ubiquitous MI6 A1 is the basis of Thailand Special Forces firepower

A camouflaged two-piece combat uniform is favoured, specially designed for jungle conditions

High rubber-soled jungle boots are well suited to the role of the Special Forces

Thailand epitomizes the political problems and confusions of South East Asia. Malayan Communist insurgents have operated from bases within Southern Thailand for decades and now pose a very real internal threat, the neighbouring left-wing government of Burma is becoming increasingly hostile and Royal Thai Army forces now find themselves facing heavily-equipped and well-trained Vietnamese units along the Kampuchian border.

The Royal Thai Army (RTA) consists of 166,000 officers and men, approximately half of whom are conscripts serving for two years prior to transfer to the reserves. The majority of troops serve in one of the seven infantry divisions, including the Royal Guard, although small numbers serve with the wholly inadequate armoured and artillery units.

The two Special Forces divisions which form the elite of the RTA can trace their history back to the formation of the 1st Ranger Battalion (Airborne) in the 1950s. This organization grew steadily in size and importance until reorganized and redesignated the 1st Special Forces Group (Airborne) in 1963. Since then it has expanded considerably, both numerically and in scope, until recently its constituent groups have been upgraded to regimental status.

In the tradition of the American Green Berets, these regiments are primarily concerned with anti-guerrilla warfare, often behind enemy lines, intelligence gathering, psychological operations and civilian support. They also, however, learned the importance of the 'hearts and minds' strategy used so successfully by the British in Burma and Malaya and spend much of their time training and equipping friendly village defence units in the expectation that these will not only be able to control their immediate localities but also provide invaluable current information on guerrilla activity.

In July 1982 the four Special Forces regiments combined with a psychological operations battalion, a long range reconnaissance patrol company and the Special Warfare Centre to form the three special forces regiments of the 1st Special Forces Division, with its headquarters at Fort Narai in Lophuri province. The 2nd SF Division was formed a year later, although its third regiment was only added recently, and both now constitute the Special Warfare Command subordinated direct to Thai Army Headquarters.

The RTA Special Forces, which include an independent psychological operations (Psy Ops) battalion, a long-range recce company and several specialized 'A' teams, are considered among the best in Asia.

Volunteers wishing to join the 3,000-strong elite must complete Ranger and Airborne training before being considered for selection. Training is both tough and realistic, demanding the highest degree of motivation. General training is undertaken at the RTA Special Warfare Centre at Lophuri, during which great emphasis is placed on physical fitness, endurance marches, survival, camouflage and jungle navigation. The specialized skills of jungle

survival, escape and evasion are taught at a survival school and all recruits are expected to master Thai boxing, a particularly lethal form of the martial arts involving the simultaneous use of feet and arms.

Thai Special Forces use US equipment and weapons in the main but are taught to use a selection of foreign weapons which they might expect to capture from communist insurgents. Soldiers wear a two-piece camouflage uniform with low visibility black-embroidered rank and qualification badges. However, occasionally when operational this may be replaced by an SAS-type all-black outfit of combat suit, boots and knitted balaclava. A camouflaged floppy jungle-hat is worn on exercise, but immediately upon returning to base all ranks revert to a red beret with gold woven national army cap-badge.

Communications skills are an important part of special forces training. Intelligence-gathering patrols must be able to relay their information in good time.

Much Thai equipment comes from the USA. This soldier has a Colt M16 rifle and, unusually, is wearing the American pattern steel helmet in place of a jungle hat. The low-visibility rank badge can be seen clearly only at this close range.

193

CHINESE PEOPLE'S LIBERATION ARMY

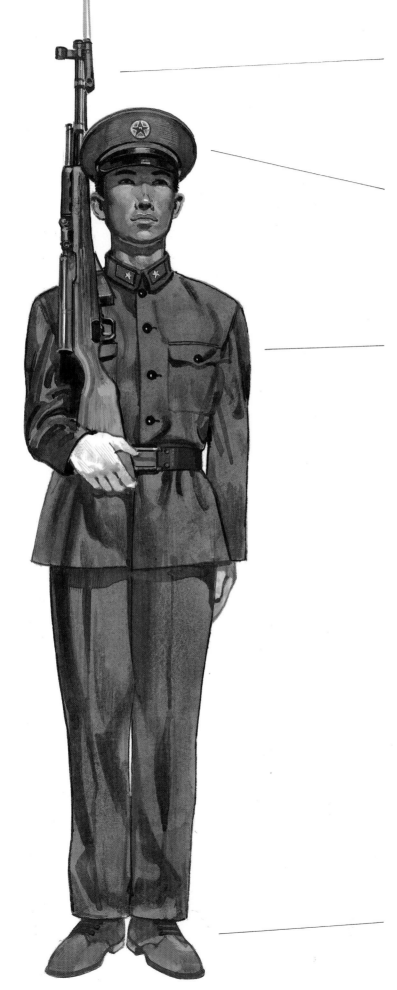

The Type-56 semi-automatic rifle, a Chinese version of the Soviet SKS, is clearly identifiable by the permanently-attached bayonet

A new service-dress peaked cap, with red five-star badge on a circular background, is now being issued to all forces. The colour will vary according to the unit

Smart new Western-style uniforms have been issued for parade dress. Badges of rank have not yet been reintroduced

High quality brown boots, which do not show the dust of the average parade ground, ably complement the revolutionary new uniform

The Chinese Army is at present undergoing tremendous changes both in personnel and equipment. The traditional reliance upon sheer numbers, epitomized by the Korean War, has been replaced by a yearning for up-to-date technology, much of it Western. The exact size of the modern Army remains a matter for conjecture. As long ago as 1982, attempts were made to reduce it by two million men but were met by stiff resistance from factions entrenched within the Armed Forces and were eventually scrapped. If, as has been suggested, the Armed Forces have in fact recently been reduced by 'over 700,000', and even taking into account the fact that a further 300,000 railway construction troops have been taken out of the military ambit and transferred to the civilian authorities, the Armed Forces remain a staggering 3.2 million strong, of whom 2.4 million are ground forces. Demobilization, particularly among senior officers some of whom are veterans of the Long March, is continuing. Official reports suggest that 100,000 officers retired in 1987 alone and there are indications that this trend has been continuing.

The Army contains some 1,075,000 conscripts called up on a selective basis to serve for three years. Administratively the country is divided into seven Military regions divided into 29 Military Districts based on the Provincial Regions, an independent Military District and three Garrison Commands.

A comprehensive reorganization of the ground forces within the Military Districts has been taking place. The term 'Group Army', traditionally used to denote the largest tangible command was changed to 'Group Corps' a few years ago, presumably in an attempt to ape the Western concept, but has recently been altered yet again to 'Integrated Corps'. Each of the 28 'Corps', consisting of approximately 46,300 men, commands up to four divisions with associated support.

The 'Regional Forces', based on the 29 regions, have been renamed the 'People's Armed Police' but remain under military control. Its 1,850,000 members, who are divided into 1,029 battalions, take responsibility for border security (in which they mirror the KGB Border Guards) and for limited internal policing, although additionally in time of war they would almost certainly be used as a buffer force against an invasion, giving the regular forces time to deploy. In this they would be aided by the 4.3 million men and women of the Basic Militia, all of whom have had, or will have, military service, are aged between 18 and 28 and undertake 30–40 days a year training with the Forces. To a limited degree help will also come from the six million members of the Ordinary Militia, who receive basic training often limited to local air defence and generally are unarmed.

Training at all levels has improved immeasurably. Until recently, many of the PLA's officers would have graduated from the Military Academy at Shrijiazhuang, to the south of Peking, but since 1986 future leaders have been trained at the National Defence University of the People's Liberation Army, incorporating under

one roof the Military, Political and Logistics Academies. Courses run from six months to three years, the latter resulting in the award of a degree.

Until recently many younger officers, frustrated at having to wait for promotion until the retirement of their often patently incompetent elders, were resigning in large numbers, preferring to trust their future to the newly opening free-enterprise markets. This is now changing. Western-style ranks are slowly appearing among the officers (the chief lecturer at the National Defence Academy is designated a 'colonel') but the old-school still fears elitism and it may be a number of years before a full rank structure is re-introduced.

The infantry soldier remains one of the best in the world. Highly motivated, extremely fit and capable of covering long distances on foot and with minimum resupply, he is at his most effective at close quarters. Many units are now becoming mechanized, which can only improve their potential.

After the 'Cultural Revolution', the Chinese armed forces adopted a drab uniform and abolished ranks. The new, more colourful, uniforms for the Navy, Army and Air Force engender much more *esprit de corps* in their wearers.

The patrolling of China's vast borders is an onerous task. These horsemen are well equipped with quilted jackets and fur hats. The mixture of old and new equipment is emphasized by the 1896 Mauser pistol carried by the soldier on the left.

INDIAN PARACHUTE REGIMENT

The cap badge, with its winged dagger, bears more than a passing resemblance to that of the British SAS. The maroon beret worn proudly by all paratroopers was inherited from the British

A variant of the Belgian FN 7.62 mm FAL is normally carried

The 'Dennison' smock and green denim trousers are standard issue for most operations

The rubber DMS boots and puttees are ideal for all operational conditions

Indian parachute units are among the oldest in the world. The 50th Indian Parachute Brigade consisting of the 152nd (Indian), the 151st (British) and 153rd (Gurkha) battalions was formed in October 1941. In 1944 it was decided to form a division (44th Indian Parachute Division) and at the same time to authorize the formation of an independent Indian Parachute Regiment.

As a result of Partition in 1947, the parachute units were split between India and the newly constituted Pakistan. The 50th Brigade remained with India, seeing action in the Kashmir campaign of 1947–49.

During the Indo-Pakistan border conflicts of 1965, special para-commando units were formed from existing Army commandos and in July 1966 were merged with the residue of the commandos to form the 9th Parachute Battalion. In the following year the 9th Battalion gave birth to its sister unit, the 10th Battalion. Both units, redesignated Commandos in 1969, are fully para-trained but operate as special forces independently of the Brigade.

The Indian Army today has one para-commando brigade (the 50th)) with seven attached and two independent battalions. It has its own supporting arms and services including artillery, engineering and signals, and is capable of operating in any climate from the snowy wastes of the Himalayas to the sun-baked plains of the South.

All Indian paratroops and para-commandos are volunteers. Some enlist direct from civilian life whilst others transfer from other regular army units. Potential recruits undergo a 30-day selection course during which they are tested physically and mentally and many are rejected. Those who are successful are sent to the Paratroopers' Training School at Agra where they undertake five descents, including a night jump, prior to the award of the coveted wings and maroon beret. Para-commandos undertake further more specialized training prior to joining 9 and 10 Commandos. Although formal details of this training remain a secret, it is known that Indian commandos have in the past trained the Iraqi special forces now engaged in the war with Iran.

Paratroopers carry either a locally-produced variant of the British L2A3 9mm Sterling sub-machine-gun or a variant of the Belgian FN 7.62mm FAL automatic rifle made under licence in Ishapore. Section support is supplied by the popular and successful British L4A4 light machine-gun, effectively a 7.62mm conversion of the Second World War 0.303in Bren gun. Reports are circulating that small numbers of the L34A1 silenced version of the Sterling are on issue to the para-commandos, but these have yet to be verified.

A light-weight short-barrelled 5.56mm assault rifle for issue to airborne troops is currently under development at the Armament Research and Development Establishment at Pune but no timetable for its introduction has as yet been announced.

Troops wear green denim trousers, a 'Dennison' smock, rubber DMS boots and puttees when operational. The maroon beret, borrowed directly from the British Parachute Regiment, has been the headgear since the Regiment's inception in 1945. The badge, which was changed in 1950, represents a fully opened parachute on two symbolic wings with an upright bayonet. Para-commandos wear the conventional maroon beret but with a cap badge depicting a winged dagger above a scroll, bearing more than a passing resemblance to that of the SAS.

India is the largest operator of the Vickers Main Battle Tank. First introduced into Indian service in 1965, India has since built approximately 500 tanks locally under the designation of 'Vijayanta'.

THE PAKISTAN ARMY

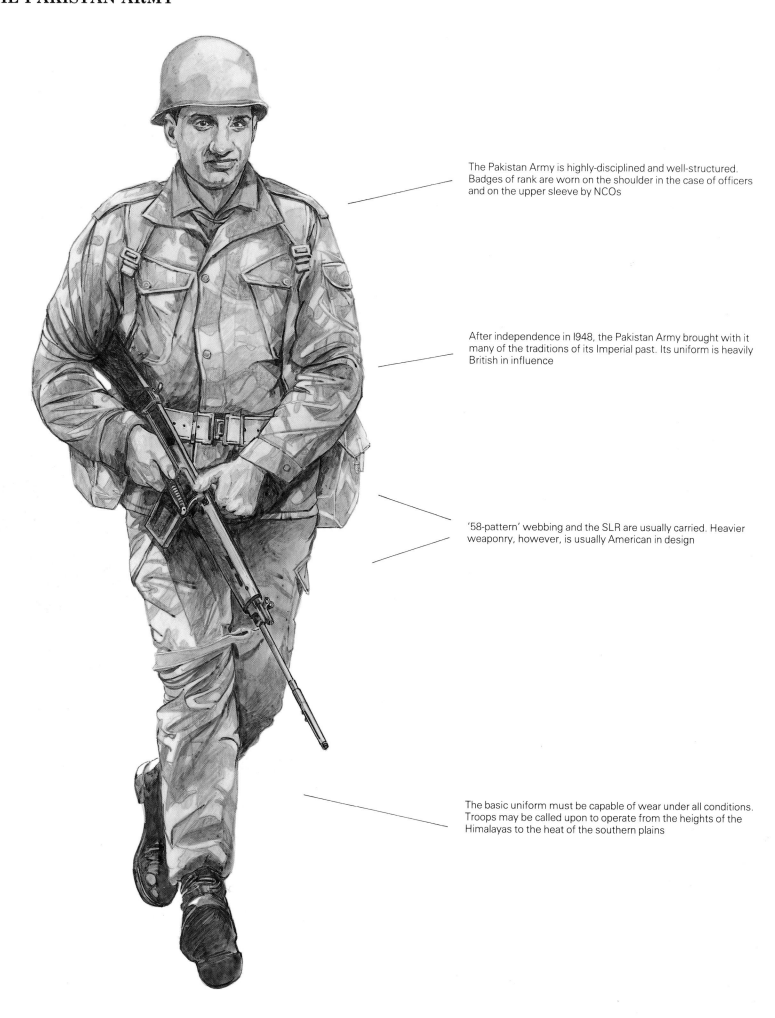

The Pakistan Army is highly-disciplined and well-structured. Badges of rank are worn on the shoulder in the case of officers and on the upper sleeve by NCOs

After independence in 1948, the Pakistan Army brought with it many of the traditions of its Imperial past. Its uniform is heavily British in influence

'58-pattern' webbing and the SLR are usually carried. Heavier weaponry, however, is usually American in design

The basic uniform must be capable of wear under all conditions. Troops may be called upon to operate from the heights of the Himalayas to the heat of the southern plains

Despite its size, the Pakistan Army is dwarfed by its Indian and Soviet neighbours. With the coming of partition in 1947, the old Indian Army was divided in the ratio of three-to-one in India's favour, all Muslim soldiers going to Pakistan. The eight infantry regiments allocated to Pakistan were so depleted that it was necessary to amalgamate them into three, the Punjab Regiment, the Frontier Force Regiment and Baluch Regiment, to which the Azad Kashmir Regiment was later added.

The original eight cavalry regiments remained unchanged, continuing to bear such uniquely British titles as the 5th Horse (Probyn's) and 6th Lancers (Watson's), although four new Lancer regiments have since been formed.

The old British traditions of drill and mess life were retained both by India and Pakistan. Regimental depots were set up to enable recruits to be trained locally, prior to joining their battalions in the field.

Reports of the size of the Pakistani Army vary greatly. The authoritative International Institute of Strategic Studies suggests that the regular army consists of some 450,000 volunteers supported by 500,000 reserves liable to call-up for eight years after service or to the age of 45 for soldiers and 50 in the case of officers if earlier, but other reports suggest a far lower figure.

Soldiers, or sepoys, usually enlist for an initial period of seven years, but the military is held in high esteem socially and many ultimately re-enlist, serving for a full military career.

Officer training is not unlike that which until relatively recently was undertaken by British officer-cadets. Candidates for regular (full career) commissions usually have either University Officer Training Corps (OTC) experience or were fortunate enough to have attended one of the cadet schools and as such are drawn from the social elite of the country. All attend an Inter-Service Selection Board, after which successful candidates attend a gruelling 30-month course at the Pakistan Military Academy, Kakul, during which considerable time is dedicated to etiquette and tradition. Career officers can expect to attend a 10-month junior staff course at the Command and Staff College at Quetta, whilst the most successful will ultimately attend the National Defence College at Rawalpindi.

The Army is divided into two armoured and 17 infantry divisions with a further four independent armoured and eight independent infantry brigades. Several national or home guard organizations exist, of which the Mujahid Force, Janbuz Force, National Cadet Corps and Women's Guard are the largest. The 75,000 members of the National Guard are supported by a further 89,000 para-military regulars serving in the Frontier Corps, Pakistan Rangers and Northern Light Infantry. Although the para-militaries receive little training or equipment and are lightly armed, most are North-West Frontier tribesmen to whom arms and fighting are second nature. This does, however, bring with it problems as well as advantages. The hill men are fiercely inde-

pendent and in the case of many Baluchis are actively seeking autonomy, so much so that their potential as anything other than defenders of their own tribal lands must be questionable.

Despite a strenuous policy of 'military self-reliance' and a domestic arms industry capable of producing its own G3 automatic rifle and 7.62mm machine-gun, all heavy equipment is still imported. Of the 1,450 tanks in service, over 1,000 are Chinese-made T–59s, although new US M60s are now being delivered. The 1,000 artillery pieces vary from ancient British 25-pounders to the latest US 155mm M 109A2 self-propelled guns.

Until recently over 10,000 Pakistani soldiers served 'on loan' to Saudi Arbia but, due to Pakistan's refusal to recall the Shia element, which comprises 10 per cent of her Army, the political situation between the two countries deteriorated and the entire force has now been withdrawn. Not only does this severely reduce Pakistan's influence in the Muslim world but it removed a very valuable and much needed source of foreign income. Three battalions of Baluchis serve on contract with the Sultan of Oman's Army but, again, this contingent is being reduced.

Pakistan adopted much of the uniform and many of the traditions of the British after Independence. Despite its age the Bren Gun seen in the foreground is still a formidable weapon. It is however now being replaced by a domestically produced 7.62mm automatic weapon.

THE MUJAHIDEEN

Any comfortable form of headdress which is proof against the summer sun may be worn

A blanket is normally carried. Not only does this provide warmth at night but a degree of protection against aircraft when thrown over the head

Ammunition is invariably carried in loose satchels. Formal webbing is considered too restrictive

Although a certain amount of US weaponry is now in service, most Mujahideen carry captured or stolen Soviet guns, in this instance an AKSU, presumably once the property of a tank crewman

Sandals rather than heavy boots are the norm

The hill fighters of Afghanistan, the Mujahideen, are among the toughest irregular troops in the world. Fiercely independent, they defeated Alexander the Great in 372 BC, destroyed an entire British expeditionary force in the nineteenth century and are at present defying the might of the Soviet Army.

The Mujahideen are in essence an independent collection of six large, and countless small, groups divided along tribal, ethnic and political lines. Although all factions are anti-Soviet, not all are anti-Communist, with the result that every attempt to form a Government in exile since 1979 has ended in failure.

Approximately 12 factions have their headquarters in Peshawar, a lawless frontier city just across the Pakistani border, from the relative safety of which they vie with each other for foreign aid. Recent reports, however, have suggested that much of the equipment and money sent to Peshawar has not subsequently reached the front line guerrillas and late in 1987 a battery of Stinger missiles destined for the Mujahideen actually fell into the hands of the Iranian Revolutionary Guards.

The fighters themselves vary in age from young boys barely capable of lifting their weapons to gnarled veterans of the North-West Frontier campaign. Many are rural farmers driven from their homelands by the bombing and the deliberate 'scorched earth' policy of the Kabul Government. Others are city or small town dwellers forced to flee the ever-present danger of the press gang and enforced service in the Afghan Army. The vast majority of guerrillas fight on a part-time basis, returning to their families, themselves often now living as refugees in Pakistan or Iran, during the winter. It is therefore impossible to assess with any accuracy the strength of the Mujahideen. United States sources estimated their strength in 1981 at between 90,000 and 120,000, whilst in 1984 Afghan sources increased this figure to a staggering 744,000. Although the latter is almost certainly exaggerated, it is nevertheless probably a fair indication of the numbers willing to offer at least passive assistance to the fighters.

The Mujahideen travel light: a blanket serves both as a protection against the freezing night air and as overhead cover against discovery by the gunships constantly prowling above the tracks and valleys. Each man carries his personal weapon, which may be a captured AK–47, World War Two vintage Lee-Enfield or even an ancient but nevertheless deadly accurate Martini-Henri, together with as much ammunition as he can muster. Very little food or water is carried as the guerrillas rely upon the support and traditional Muslim hospitality of the villagers en route to supply basic sustenance. The recent Soviet tactics of forcibly redeploying entire villages away from known guerrilla routes into Government-controlled areas has caused severe logistical problems although, as was ably proved by the siege of Kohst in 1987, the Mujahideen are still capable of mounting large-scale operations.

Western reporters who have travelled with the Mujahideen have marvelled at their sheer stamina and extremely high pain threshold. Guerrillas will walk for days at the same plodding pace, making no allowance for gradients, stopping only for meals and a little sleep until they reach their destination. Injured fighters, often with hideously mutilated limbs, have been known to cross mountain ranges unaided to reach the safety of Pakistan rather than fall into enemy hands.

The greatest enemy of the Mujahideen, other than their sheer disunity, lies in their total lack of tactical understanding. Most prefer to rely on traditional hit-and-run tactics, refusing to stand and fight in conventional battle despite the fact that, when resorted to, the latter tactics have often proved successful. Few understand ammunition conservation, preferring to expend vast quantities of scarce ammunition for the simple exhilaration of firing it off rather than preserving it for another day and a new battle. Although larger weapons are available in the form of captured RPG–7 anti-tank rockets, SA–7 surface-to-air missiles and the much publicised Stingers, few Mujahideen have any real idea how to expoit them to their full potential.

Despite their shortcomings, the guerrillas of Afghanistan have fought magnificently. Estimates of Afghan dead vary from 250,000 to one million. Although most were innocent civilians, a sizeable minority were Mujahideen fighting for the freedom of their country.

The Soviet 81mm mortar, captured in quantity from the Afghan Army, constitutes the main artillery weapon of the Mujahideen. It can be mule or man-packed and is robust and reliable.

The leather webbing is old, and inadequate for the conditions

Most conscripts tend to wear their webbing belt above their standard issue belt

The RPD light machine-gun typifies the ancient equipment issued to the Afghan Army

The uniform is old, ill-fitting and of poor quality - hardly proof against the mountains in which the majority of the troops operate

Despite the well-publicised presence of over 100,000 Soviet troops in Afghanistan, it is the Afghan Army itself which has been involved in the majority of the anti-guerrilla fighting since 1979. It is responsible for the entire War along the Eastern provinces and for garrisoning the most remote and vulnerable outposts. Because the vast majority of the 45,000 soldiers comprising the Army are conscripts, many of whom were press-ganged into service for an indefinite period, morale is low and the incidence of desertion high. Although in theory the Army is capable of fielding three armoured division, 12 infantry divisions and a commando brigade, equipment is scarce (much of it having been sold or surrendered to the Mujahideen) and many of the units are reportedly operating at below 25 per cent strength.

Many Afghan junior officers are illiterate and, although some certainly fight out of political conviction, many are simply drawn by the very high salaries paid to officers and senior NCOs and have little ideological conviction. During the early 1980s, in a vain attempt to stem the growing tide of desertions and in order to bolster the size of the Army, which had fallen to 20,000 in 1980, automatic commissions were offered to volunteers upon completion of two years satisfactory service in the ranks. Whereas this desperate policy might have succeeded had the War ended in the mid-1980s, in reality it has if anything weakened an already shaky command structure.

Theoretically the chain of command runs from the Prime Minister through the Minister of Defence to the three Corps commanders, but real authority in fact lies with the Soviet advisers present at every level.

Relations between the Soviet and Afghan Armies are very low. In the last few years the Mujahideen have treated captured Afghan soldiers well, regarding them as fellow Muslims rather than as enemies. The result has been that on numerous occasions, at the first sign of battle, soldiers have simply surrendered en masse, leaving their Soviet 'allies' to a less savoury fate.

Despite intervention by the Khad (Afghan Secret Police), most Army units are heavily infiltrated by guerrilla supporters and in some cases by activists. Consequently the Soviets are unwilling to share intelligence at any level with them, although this does not prevent the Mujahideen gaining advance notice of most major Communist offensives.

Despite lack of manpower, the Army retains a pretence of conventional divisional organization although divisions are in fact the size of weak brigades. Each contains three three-battalion infantry regiments (one mechanized), an artillery regiment and tank battalion, but may receive reinforcements for a specific mission if required.

At the commencement of the War a number of elite formations existed, but these have now been largely dissipated. The 26th Airborne Battalion mutinied in 1980 whilst the 444th, 37th and 38th Commando Brigades sustained such severe losses in subsequent fighting that today each is no more than an independent battalion.

The majority of Afghan troops are stationed in old hill forts and garrisons, emerging only occasionally to sweep the area or undertake convoy duties, and as such are easy targets for the more mobile Mujahideen. Only older Soviet armaments are issued, SA–7 surface-to-air missiles and RPG–7 anti-tank rockets having been withdrawn after many fell into enemy hands in the early stages of the War. Mechanized units must rely on elderly Soviet BTR–152 APCs and T–55 tanks, a number of which are dug into static defences.

Afghan uniforms are old-fashioned and of extremely poor quality. A soft cap, trousers and blouse of shoddy grey drab are standard issue as both field and service dress. Lengthy old-fashioned greatcoats are issued as winter wear. Webbing belts and pouches are usually worn over another belt to give a confusing and extremely scruffy appearance. There can be no doubt that once the Soviets leave Afghanistan the Afghan Army itself will prove no match for the Mujahideen and, unless a peace initiative has been agreed, will disintegrate virtually overnight.

Afghan conscripts with their T55 tank man a checkpoint near their capital, Kabul.

THE BURMESE ARMY

A standard ubiquitous jungle hat is worn at most times

Webbing, which is cheap and domestically-produced, is loosely based on the British 44-pattern, now long discarded

The Burmese Army is poorly armed and equipped. The immediate post-colonial influence of the British is still apparent, however, and the better units are armed with the SLR

Camouflage is one of the items capable of being produced locally. It is cheap, ill-matching but effective

The Union of Burma is one of the world's most introverted and divided nations. Held together by the British for 150 years and once part of the Indian Empire, it is now in economic chaos. Any pretext of national unity, carefully nurtured by British settlers before the War, was savagely destroyed by the Japanese invasion of 1942. Without foreign help or interference, local tribes and factions established resistance movements throughout their own localities. With the coming of peace in 1945, leaders of most of these groups showed a natural reluctance to relinquish their newly discovered and hard-fought-for powers, with the result that in many cases central power was only re-established at the point of a gun.

When Burma gained her independence and lost the protection of the British Army, the fledgling government found itself facing six major and numerous minor rebel forces. Some 40 years later the situation has not improved.

The Union of Burma Army consists of 170,000 volunteers supported by 73,000 para-military police and militia. The 87 infantry battalions are subordinated to seven light infantry divisional headquarters spread throughout the country. Three of the divisions have three brigades apiece. Equipment is antiquated and often unoperational due to a lack of spare parts. Britain willingly supplied a small number of tanks and armoured cars after independence but became unwilling to replace these as the Burmese Government moved increasingly to the left. At present the only two armoured battalions have less than 20 Comet tanks, first manufactured in 1944, between them. There are no more than 45 Ferret armoured cars and 40 Humber APCs, similar to those brought back by the British for service on the streets of Northern Ireland, available for distribution amongst the rest of the Army. Only the artillery is reasonably provisioned, having obtained some 120 76mm Yugoslavian mountain guns and 75 towed 105mm US guns since independence.

Due to its total lack of airpower, the Government has not been able to prevent the larger enemy forces from establishing permanent powerbases in friendly towns.

The Karen community, for instance, has been allowed to establish the independent 'Republic of Kawthoolei' in the Irrawaddy Delta, to raise a standing army 3,000 to 4,000 strong, to enforce conscription among its own people (young men serve for seven years without pay!) and to exact 'tribute' amounting to five per cent of their goods from passing traders. The static nature of most of the groups, who have rarely exported their battle, preferring to entice the Burmese Army into attacking them, has recently allowed the Government to concentrate its meagre resources against individual factions but this has now changed. The Kashin with 8,000 troops and a power base along the Chinese border have recently linked with the Karen and approximately 10 smaller groups to form the National Democratic Front (NDF) capable of putting 20,000 men into the field. Once-safe Government strongholds are now coming under attack and battalion-sized units are being ambushed. The Union of Burma

Army realises that if it is to stand any hope of success it will now have to pursue a united enemy into its home bases, yet fully appreciates that its soldiers have neither the training nor equipment to do so.

Perhaps inevitably, military frustration is manifesting itself in indiscipline among the junior ranks of the Army with reports spreading of brutality and theft. Although the various dissident groups are unlikely to unite further and consequently will never be strong enough to defeat the Army in open battle, it in turn will never be capable of defeating them without a vast injection of weapons and equipment. As neither of the major power blocs seems willing to supply loans for the purchase of arms, on the basis that it is highly unlikely that the Government would ever be in a position to repay them, the Army will inevitably remain under-equipped and impotent.

The Karen National Liberation Army is well-trained and equipped. It has its own anti-aircraft emplacements and a sizeable stock of modern US weaponry. The Burmese Army would be hard-pressed to defeat the numerous 'liberation armies' challenging its authority.

SOUTH AFRICAN RECONNAISSANCE COMMANDOS

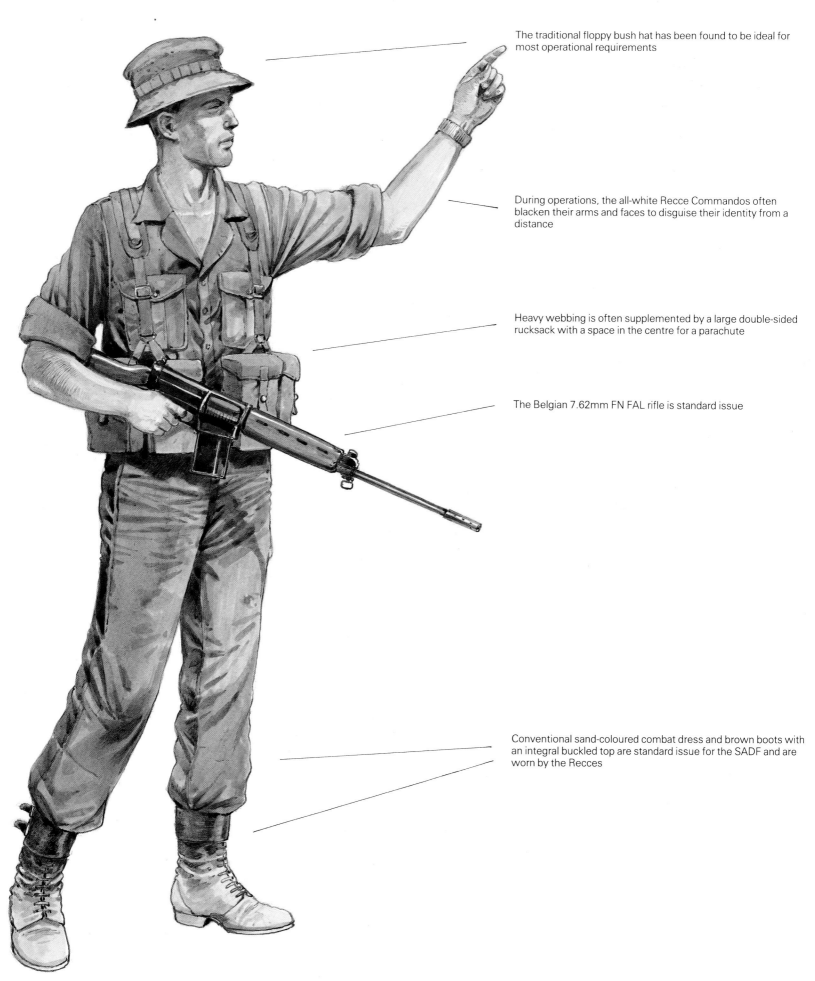

The traditional floppy bush hat has been found to be ideal for most operational requirements

During operations, the all-white Recce Commandos often blacken their arms and faces to disguise their identity from a distance

Heavy webbing is often supplemented by a large double-sided rucksack with a space in the centre for a parachute

The Belgian 7.62mm FN FAL rifle is standard issue

Conventional sand-coloured combat dress and brown boots with an integral buckled top are standard issue for the SADF and are worn by the Recces

South Africa has long recognized the fact that not only is she surrounded by potential enemies but for all intents and purposes she is without a friend in the world. The Boer generals in control of the South African Defence Forces have never feared adversity and over the last 20 years have formed a number of elite units under the auspices of the 1st Special Forces Brigade, based at Bloemfontein in the Orange Free State, to spearhead the defence of their country and its way of life.

Of these, the Reconnaissance Commandos, or 'Recce Commandos', are regarded as the best. The word 'Commando', used increasingly loosely by many armies, is revered in South Africa in memory of the irregular bands who fought the British in the 1898-1902 Boer War. Accordingly, its inclusion in the Unit's title is an honour in itself.

The Commando operates deep inside enemy territory, gaining intelligence, tracking enemy guerrillas and where necessary destroying terrorist concentrations in punitive missions. A similar task was carried out to a high degree of professionalism by the now disbanded Selous Scouts of the old Southern Rhodesian Army and one may be sure that many ex-Scouts, together with former members of C Squadron Rhodesian SAS, are now offering their services to the Commando. Many senior South African officers in the Commando saw service in Rhodesia prior to their country's disengagement in 1975 and all have seen service in Angola.

All ranks in 'recce' are para-trained, qualifying in both static and free fall techniques and many are HALO (High Altitude, Low Opening) trained. Selection and basic training are based on British SAS methods and are designed to test the individual to the maximum of his mental as well as physical capabilities. Selection courses, which are open to serving members of the Navy and Air Force as well as the Army, are held biannually and last for 42 weeks. Prior to acceptance on a selection course, a potential recruit has to prove himself not only physically fit enough to complete a route march of 32 km (20 miles) in six hours carrying a rifle and 32-kg (70 lbs) sandbag but must complete various swims, exercises and runs in a strict time scale. Standards are uncompromising and a single failure will result in the candidate being RTU'd (returned to unit). All candidates are examined medically and psychologically to ensure that they have the right temperament and political motivation to carry out orders without question.

Selection, which takes place under operational conditions, is held in the wilds of Northern Zululand. During one of the final tests the candidate is left alone in the bush for several days with just his rifle and a limited supply of ammunition to protect himself against the wild animals which frequent the area.

After basic training, the eight per cent of candidates accepted undergo continuation training in survival techniques, native languages, tracking, scouting and the use of foreign firearms. Many commandos are barely 20

years old and it is vital that during training they learn sufficient self-reliance to work alone if need be in one of the most hostile and uncompromising war zones in the world.

Standard South African small arms including the 7.62mm FAL rifle and FN MAG light-machine-gun are carried, often supplemented by fighting knives for hand-to-hand combat.

In the field, commandos wear conventional sand-coloured combat dress with brown high-boots and floppy hat. A large double-sided rucksack, with a space in the centre for the fitting of a parachute if necessary, is carried supported by heavy webbing. During operations, members of the all-white 'recce' often blacken their faces and forearms completely to disguise their race until they are close enough to their enemy to give him no chance of escape.

South African Recce Commandos are honed to a peak of fitness. Training is exacting, but never brutal, and designed to push the individual to the limits of his physical and mental endurance. Even so, only eight percent of candidates for selection are successful.

SOUTH AFRICAN DEFENCE FORCES

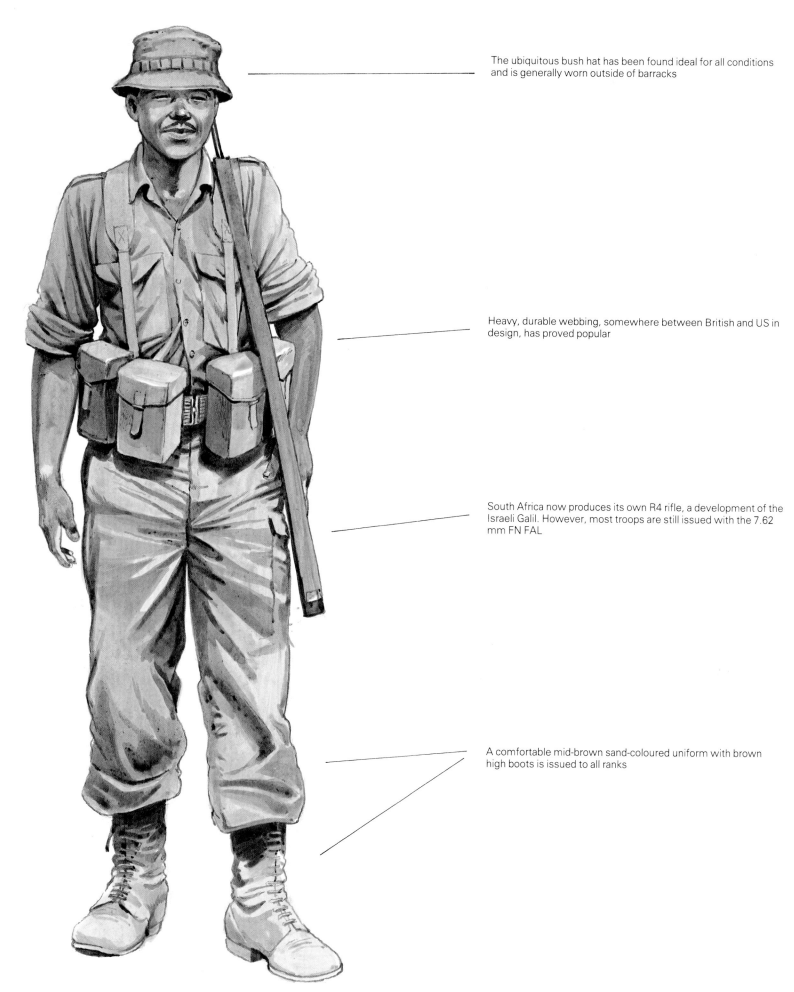

The ubiquitous bush hat has been found ideal for all conditions and is generally worn outside of barracks

Heavy, durable webbing, somewhere between British and US in design, has proved popular

South Africa now produces its own R4 rifle, a development of the Israeli Galil. However, most troops are still issued with the 7.62 mm FN FAL

A comfortable mid-brown sand-coloured uniform with brown high boots is issued to all ranks

South Africa, although formally at peace since 1945, has in reality been fighting a counter-insurgency war for the past two decades. Several members of the Organization of African Unity (OAU), led by Nigeria, have openly discussed the raising of an Army to wage conventional war against South Africa but at the moment there is no indication that the OAU has either the organizational ability or trained troops to carry out such a task. Nevertheless South Africa is forced to maintain large conventional forces to combat such a contingency in the future. The immediate threat comes from insurgents, armed and trained by Cuba and the Eastern bloc, who make regular sorties across the long sparsely-populated border. Specially trained counter-insurgency troops, operating independently of the conventional forces, are maintained to combat this growing problem.

Although the South African Army is now multi-racial, the different races still form their own units and battalions. However, an increasing number of non-whites are being commissioned with a few actually reaching battalion commander status in the Cape (Coloured) Corps. Training is identical for all troops, and officer and NCO cadres are completely integrated.

Operations in Angola are undertaken by specially constituted battalions consisting of a headquarters company manned by regular (Permanent Force) soldiers supported by operational companies drawn on a rotating basis. These companies, which carry out a one-month special training course in Namibia before being declared operational, are drawn from all available resources and may be white national servicemen, black or coloured volunteers or members of the 55,000-strong part-time Citizen Force, called up for their compulsory mobilization period.

All white males, whether or not South African citizens, are called up for 24 months national service. This is followed by a period of 12 years in the Citizen Force, during which time they may spend a maximum of 720 days on full-time duty, but never more than 120 days continuous service in any two years. Thereafter they serve for a further five years in the Citizen Force Reserve, during which they may be called up only by special authority, before transferring to the Commando for home defence duties until the age of 55.

Non-whites may volunteer for two years, after which the best are allowed to join the Permanent Force. Service in the armed forces is popular and all units are heavily over-subscribed, ensuring the maintenance of the highest standards. A number of non-whites serve in the Commandos, as does a growing group of volunteers who give up their spare time above and beyond their legal obligation in order to undertake Internal Security (IS) duties.

Training, especially the initial 12-week basic training period, is demanding and arduous. High standards of drill and discipline inherited from the British have combined with generations of bush experience to produce one of the best and most feared armies in the world.

Recruits are streamed and tested for leadership potential three weeks after induction into the Army. Training lasts for 12 months, including three months border service, and is followed by a second year spent either on the border or internally, with the possibility of a tour of duty in Angola. University students may elect to defer their national service until after graduation, in which instance they will serve as officer cadets although they must still undergo basic training. However, the Armed Forces have their own university offering degrees in Military Science to suitable officers in the four services (uniquely the Medical Service is an independent entity).

The South African Army contains a number of unique battalions. A horse and motor cycle company with six platoons each with mortar, motor cycle and equestrian sections, operates on the border, where it has worked extremely successfully in close cooperation with black and white trackers in follow-up raids against terrorist gangs. A bushman battalion, located at Omega West Caprivi, and the multi-racial 32nd Battalion have both been enlisted from among disaffected Angolans and are proving highly competent and ruthless adversaries, much feared by the SWAPO guerrillas.

Attempts by the United Nations at an arms embargo have proved to be a blessing in disguise. South Africa now produces its own R4 rifle, especially designed for sandy conditions, plus its own APCs and artillery. Its personnel and equipment are battle tested and excellent, and for the conceivable future will prove more than a match for any potential adversary.

Due to an arms embargo, South Africa has been forced to manufacture an increasing number of its small arms locally. Here a corporal-armourer checks the battalion stock of R4 rifles. Unusually, the weapons have been racked with the magazines fitted. The habit of storing ammunition and weapons in the same building would be frowned upon within NATO.

NIGERIAN ARMY

The black or navy blue beret has been retained from the days of Imperial Britain, as has the wearing of the cap badge over the left eye

'58-pattern' webbing is issued, together with twin ammunition pouches, yoke, water bottle and kidney pouches

The 7.62mm self-loading rifle is the standard personal weapon

DMS (or Directly Moulded Sole) boots and traditional gaiters are still issued

Theoretically, Nigeria with her large population, oil reserves and economic potential should be the leading force in black Africa. In reality, however, a series of military coups since Independence, a crippling civil war and the incompetence of the later civilian government has left the country heavily in debt. Furthermore, Nigeria is plagued by internal factionalism compounded by ethnic and religious disunity. The Muslim Hausa of the North, who have traditionally provided the military backbone have little in common with the Christian Ibos of the East or the economically strong Yorubas in the West, with whom they share neither a language nor a culture.

Although in principle the Nigerian Army remains supportive of the federal system, a disproportionate percentage of officers are drawn from the North. As it is the officer corps which has traditionally led the succession of post-Independence coups, the influence of the North within the Armed Forces, and therefore by implication within the country, is out of all proportion to its size.

The 80,000 men constituting the Army are divided into one armoured, two mechanized and one composite division, each with a supporting artillery and engineering brigade and reconnaissance battalion. The vast majority of equipment is of British origin, old and in a poor state of repair; a problem compounded by Nigeria's total lack of either an indigenous arms industry or of heavy repair facilities. The 1st Armoured Division boasts a paper strength of 72 Vickers Mk 2 tanks, 40 Soviet T–55s (purchased during the Civil War, at which time Britain exercised a limited arms embargo) and 50 British Scorpions, but in reality it is unlikely that more than half of these are operational.

Nigerian soldiers are all volunteers. Initial engagement is on a short service basis, although this may be extended if the individual is suitable and circumstances permit. The majority of recruits are strong and willing although many, particularly in the North, are illiterate. The Army does attempt to educate its recruits to a basic level and promotion to sergeant and above requires the passing of a simple academic test. The huge number of dialects spoken by the recruits, particularly those from isolated areas, does however make this task all but impossible. Training areas are spread throughout the country in an attempt to facilitate integration but, due to their higher educational backgrounds, the Ibos and Yorubas tend to qualify for promotion more quickly than their more numerous Hausa colleagues, with resultant resentment from the latter. By black African standards, discipline and efficiency are good, although much of this has been due to the fast-waning British influence and standards are definitely dropping as the number of loan-service British NCOs is reduced.

Although no official figures exist, it may be assumed that the officer corps is approximately 10,000 strong, of whom one-third are undertaking short service commission. Of the residue, one-third hold the rank of major or above – a staggering figure for so small an Army.

Regular officers attend a two-year course at the National Defence Academy, Kaduna, itself based very much on the Royal Military Academy, Sandhurst. Specialist-to-arm training is carried out once the young officer has received his commission and has been posted to his new unit. Suitable applicants subsequently attend the Command and Staff College at Jaji, near Kaduna. During their year at Jaji many officers develop a degree of elitism which on occasions manifests itself into political intrigue, with the result that strenuous measures are taken to ensure that senior officers are kept content. This in itself may account for the extraordinary number of senior officer promotions.

Despite claims to the contrary, usually made in the rarefied atmosphere of the Organizations of African Unity (UAO), the Nigerian Army is in no way capable of fighting a war abroad, particularly against South Africa. It is, however, more than capable of protecting its own national borders, particularly as none of its neighbours is hostile.

The Nigerian Army, the most powerful in black Africa, is plagued by internal factionalism. In 1967 this manifested itself into Civil War when Biafra attempted cessation. Here a Federal Nigerian patrol is seen fighting its way towards Owerri deep in the Biafran heartland.

UNITA ARMED FORCES

Badges of rank, where they exist, are worn on the beret as well as on both shoulder boards

Individual weapons, in this instance a .357 Magnum revolver, are worn in a cavalier manner

Uniforms are extremely personalised. They are nevertheless far smarter than might be expected, an indication of the discipline prevailing within the Force

Jungle boots are strong but, above all, permeable in order to let the feet breathe

The National Union for the Total Liberation of Angola, or UNITA, has been fighting the Popular Liberation Movement of Angola, or MPLA, for the control of Angola since the latter seized power soon after the granting of independence by Portugal in 1975. Although nominally a guerrilla force, UNITA boasts some 26,000 'regular' troops, many of whom have been conscripted for between one and two years service, and 34,000 militia. It has a small arsenal of Soviet T–34 and T–55 tanks captured from the Government forces, together with an assortment of light artillery, mortars, heavy and medium machine-guns and an adequate selection of small arms.

UNITA is intensely nationalistic in its outlook, demanding as a pre-requisite to any peace talks the total withdrawal of all foreign troops, and as such has guarded United Nations and Organizations for African Unity (OAU) support. It is well aware that the ramshackle government forces are demoralized and, militarily, are held together only by the 15 regiments of Cuban 'advisers' (25,000 men supported by 12,500 civilian workers in all!), by the 1,600 highly trained Soviet specialists and the 3,500 East German intelligence, communications and transport operatives.

UNITA receives considerable United States support, including the delivery recently of a number of Stinger hand-held surface-to-air missiles which have proved so effective in Afghan Mujahideen hands. Despite criticism from its black-African neighbours, UNITA continues to receive assistance from the South African Defence Forces, who have provided air power, men, equipment and, more crucially of late, transport when required. South African interest in the civil war would appear to be purely objective, there being no suggestion that it would require more than a secure border with Namibia in return for its assistance should UNITA succeed.

During the early stages of the war against Portugal, UNITA was more politically than militarily active. However, under the command of the extremely astute Jonas Savimbi it has now taken the initiative. In the spring of 1987 its main theatre of operations was moved from its traditional power base in the south-east to the north-eastern provinces of Malanje and Luanda. Although Savimbi retained Jamba in the extreme south-east as his provisional capital, he moved his 'infrastructure', including schools, hospitals and supply dumps, further north to Mavinga to be closer to the fighting.

His regular forces, organized into battalions of 900 to 1,500 men, 'mobile battalions' of 350 to 400 men and 'special forces' of 25 to 45, fight conventional operations on the borders of the liberated areas, attempting constantly to constrict the Government MPLA into a tighter circle. Where possible, regular forces wear conventional uniforms as an indication of their disciplined status.

UNITA guerrillas, or militia, work conventionally behind enemy lines. Groups designated 'independent columns' build up a network of sympathisers, spread propaganda and, if

necessary, resort to intimidation, gradually paving the way for more formally-organized 'compact columns' to move in and actively harry the enemy troop and supply lines.

Training takes place in well-defined and excellently-run camps, usually in the Jamba area. Three months basic training is given, often by Portuguese mercenaries, after which the best recruits are retained to become specialists in demolitions or air defence.

Logistics, potentially a nightmare, is handled efficiently by a 6,000-strong dedicated force. Daily supply columns, comprising a selection of the 80 Toyotas, 200 Mercedes trucks, 110 Unimogs and 50 Soviet Ural trucks captured from the MPLA, leave Jamba for the front line. The monthly fuel consumption, estimated at 50,000 litres of petrol and 600,000 litres of diesel, is reportedly supplied by South Africa.

The RPG-7 anti-tank weapon is popular with all guerilla forces not only for its anti-armour capabilities but also for its potent effect against bunkers and trenches.

The Soviet-designed RPG-7 anti-armour grenade launcher is a popular weapon with freedom fighters and UNITA is no exception. Although there is comparatively little in the way of an armoured threat to them, the RPG-7 is excellent for providing 'fire support'. It is light, easy to use and quickly reloaded. The addition of a bipod (above) and/or an optical sight (below) adds considerably to accuracy and effective range, particularly against static targets such as bunkers and dug-in weapons.

MOZAMBIQUE NATIONAL RESISTANCE MOVEMENT

Renamo forces are not divided into disciplined regiments and as such would not wear conventional cap badges. The beret badge worn here is little more than an adornment

Any convenient camouflage uniform, often supplemented from equipment stolen from Government forces, is worn

Belted ammunition carried like this is prone to damage. Nevertheless, the rebels seem keen to display their potential firepower wherever possible

The Soviet-made PMK is a favourite weapon of the rebels and Government forces alike

Combat high boots are ideal for jungle operations

Mozambique, a former Portuguese colony, has been a battlefield for the past 12 years. Within months of its precipitous independence in 1975, its already poor economy was shattered by the mass exodus of skilled Portuguese workers, often to South Africa, compounded by the ill-conceived policies of nationalization introduced by the new Marxist Government.

In 1977 Rhodesian Central Intelligence created the Mozambique National Resistance, known as Renamo or the MNR, in the hopes that the resultant civil war would reduce the amount of assistance then being given by Mozambique to the Zimbabwean resistance fighters. The fighting which followed was brutal, destructive and Pyrrhic. The agricultural heartlands were devastated and mass starvation followed.

In 1982 South Africa, which shares a long border with Mozambique, embarked upon a campaign to ensure that the latter would never become a threat to her security. Recce Commandos raided the capital, Maputo, destroyed storage tanks and derailed trains in the central Beira corridor (also used by the recently-founded Zimbabwe to export her raw materials), whilst the Defence Forces began to train, arm and transport Renamo guerrillas.

Although South Africa and Mozambique signed a peace pact in 1984, as a result of which Mozambique agreed to ban African National Congress (ANC) fighters from its territory in exchange for South African undertakings to cease aiding Renamo, the treaty was never fully honoured by either side and virtually disintegrated after the death in a plane crash of President Machel in October 1986.

Although the crash was almost certainly due to pilot error, certain reports stating that the Soviet pilot had been drinking, most black African States accused and continue to accuse South Africa of complicity in the crash.

Machel was succeeded by Joaquin Chissano, a less doctrinaire and more internationally accepted figure. Under Chissano's leadership, Mozambique has signed a mutual defence agreement with Malawi, thus freeing her ramshackle and virtually leaderless Army for the fight against Renamo. Chissano is at present assisted by a contingent of over 10,000 Zimbabwean soldiers, 1,500 Cubans, 350 Soviet and 80 North Korean military 'advisers', together with approximately 200 East German security advisers many of whom are drawn from the elite 40th Willi Stanger Parachute Battalion.

Renamo has 20,000 fighters spread throughout the length and breadth of the country, of whom half have received at least rudimentary training. Four 'regular' battalions operate from the jungle, as does a small special forces group of no more than 200 men. Standards vary drastically and, whereas many guerrillas are little more than armed bandits stealing and raping their way across the countryside, others are trained and dedicated idealists. Strangely, the leadership does little to bring under control the unruly elements despite the severe effect they are having on international public opinion.

About half of the Renamo forces are loyal to Alfonso Dhaklama, the self-styled 'President' who still retains ties with South Africa and who no doubt still receives supplies, in the form of Soviet AK–47 assault rifles and RPG–7 anti-tank rockets captured from the ANC, from their intelligence agencies.

Renamo objectives are vague. Although all fighters share anti-Communist sentiments, few have any real idea what they would wish to see in its place and many profess a desire simply to return to decentralization, with the power of the tribal chief and witch doctor re-established as paramount. Unlike the Communist Frelimo, who have their power base in the North, most Renamo activists come from the Matupa area in the South and are supersitious of anyone challenging their centuries-old ancestor-worshipping mores.

Few of Frelimo's 69 combat aircraft are operational, whilst her small arsenal of tanks, artillery and APCs cannot penetrate the jungle in which Renamo usually operates. 'President' Dhaklama will not lay down his arms until Mozambique has free elections and all foreign troops are withdrawn. President Chissano, realizing that the former might well lead to his overthrow, and the latter certainly to his destruction, will not agree to either term, with the result that the war, which to date has claimed over 250,000 lives, will continue for the foreseeable future. In the interim, Cuba is showing an inclination to withdraw its troops from Angola and would almost certainly withdraw from Mozambique at the same time, while Zimbabwe is rapidly tiring of a war she can neither afford nor win. If Renamo can hold out for a few more seasons, and if it is willing to countenance the total economic collapse of the country, victory could well be the outcome.

Renamo receives a regular supply of Soviet-produced arms captured by the South Africans from ANC fighters. Her Engineers have become experts at laying mines to inflict maximum casualties among the enemy.

ILLUSTRATIONS

Keith Howard drew the artworks on pages 20, 22, 24, 30, 32, 34, 36, 40, 44, 46, 50, 52, 54, 56, 58, 60, 66, 68, 76, 78, 84, 86, 88, 92, 98, 100, 102, 112, 114, 116, 118, 120, 122, 124, 126, 130, 134, 136, 138, 140, 142, 144, 148, 154, 168, 170, 172, 174, 186, 190, 192, 196, 198, 200, 202, 210 and 214.

Colin Woolf drew the artworks on pages 10, 12, 14, 16, 18, 26, 28, 42, 62, 74, 80, 82, 90, 94, 96, 104, 106, 108, 160 and 182.

Photographs

Peter Macdonald Associates: pages 4/5, 13, 15 (bottom), 17, 21, 25, 27, 31, 33, 35, 37, 39, 63, 65, 67, 69, 71, 77, 79, 81, 87 (bottom), 89, 93, 95, 97, 99, 161, 163, 187, 191 and 207.

Leslie McDonnell: pages 43 (bottom), 51, 53 (top), 55, 129, 147, 177 and 185.

The Research House: 59, 61, 73, 101, 105, 137, 139, 179, 193 and 205.

Robert Hunt Library: pages 189, 199 and 211.

Guy Taylor: page 41.